WHY CAMUS MATTERS

WHY PHILOSOPHY MATTERS

Series editor: Professor Constantine Sandis, University of Hertfordshire, UK

Why Philosophy Matters focuses on why a particular philosopher, school of thought, or area of philosophical study really matters. Each book will offer a brief overview of the subject before exploring its reception both within and outside the academy and our authors will also defend different provocative outlooks on where the value of philosophy lies (or doesn't, as the case may be). Why Philosophy Matters is accompanied by an ongoing series of free events (talks, debates, workshops) in Bloomsbury. Podcasts of these events will be freely available on the series page.

BOOKS IN THIS SERIES

Why Human Nature Matters, Matteo Mameli
Why Cicero Matters, Vittorio Bufacchi
Why Collingwood Matters, Giuseppina D'Oro
Why Delusions Matter, Lisa Bortolotti
Why Climate Breakdown Matters, Rupert Read
Why Solipsism Matters, Sami Pihlström
Why Medieval Philosophy Matters, Stephen Boulter
Why Iris Murdoch Matters, Gary Browning

WHY CAMUS MATTERS

MATTHEW SHARPE

BLOOMSBURY ACADEMIC
LONDON • NEW YORK • OXFORD • NEW DELHI • SYDNEY

BLOOMSBURY ACADEMIC

Bloomsbury Publishing Plc, 50 Bedford Square, London, WC1B 3DP, UK
Bloomsbury Publishing Inc, 1359 Broadway, New York, NY 10018, USA
Bloomsbury Publishing Ireland, 29 Earlsfort Terrace, Dublin 2, D02 AY28, Ireland

BLOOMSBURY, BLOOMSBURY ACADEMIC and the Diana logo are trademarks of
Bloomsbury Publishing Plc

First published in Great Britain 2026

Copyright © Matthew Sharpe, 2026

Matthew Sharpe has asserted his right under the Copyright, Designs and Patents Act, 1988, to be identified as Author of this work.

Cover image: *The Just Judges* (1432), Hubert van Eyck and Jan van Eyck
Contributor: Zuri Swimmer / Alamy

All rights reserved. No part of this publication may be: i) reproduced or transmitted in any form, electronic or mechanical, including photocopying, recording or by means of any information storage or retrieval system without prior permission in writing from the publishers; or ii) used or reproduced in any way for the training, development or operation of artificial intelligence (AI) technologies, including generative AI technologies. The rights holders expressly reserve this publication from the text and data mining exception as per Article 4(3) of the Digital Single Market Directive (EU) 2019/790.

Bloomsbury Publishing Plc does not have any control over, or responsibility for, any third-party websites referred to or in this book. All internet addresses given in this book were correct at the time of going to press. The author and publisher regret any inconvenience caused if addresses have changed or sites have ceased to exist, but can accept no responsibility for any such changes.

A catalogue record for this book is available from the British Library.

A catalog record for this book is available from the Library of Congress.

ISBN: HB: 978-1-3505-1249-8
PB: 978-1-3505-1248-1
ePDF: 978-1-3505-1250-4
eBook: 978-1-3505-1251-1

Series: Why Philosophy Matters

Typeset by Newgen KnowledgeWorks Pvt. Ltd., Chennai, India
Printed and bound in Great Britain

For product safety related questions contact productsafety@bloomsbury.com.

To find out more about our authors and books visit www.bloomsbury.com and sign up for our newsletters.

To Peter Richard Sharpe, 31/12/1944–23/5/2024
Craig Peter Sharpe, 10/1/1973–21/12/2024
In grief and gratitude.

Listening, indeed, to the cries of joy rising from the town, Rieux remembered that such joy is always imperilled. For he knew what those jubilant crowds did not know but could have learned from books: that the plague bacillus never dies nor disappears; that it can lie dormant for dozens of yearss in furniture and linen chests; that it bides its time patiently in bedrooms, cellars, trunks, and bookshelves; and that perhaps the day would come when, for the misery and instruction of peoples, it would rouse up its rats again and send them forth to die in a happy city.

—CAMUS, *The Plague* (1947).

There is thus a will to live without rejecting anything of life, which is the virtue I honour most in this world. From time to time, at least, it is true that I would like to have exercised it. Since few epochs require as much as ours that one should be equal to the best as much as to the worst, I should like, justly, to elude nothing and to keep faithfully a double memory. Yes, there is beauty and there are the humiliated. Whatever the difficulties of the enterprise, I would like never to be unfaithful either to the one or to the others.

—CAMUS, "Return to Tipasa" (1954).

CONTENTS

Introduction: Why Camus Matters in 2025 1

   0.1 The Author in the Amphitheater 1
   0.2 Camus's Unique Philosophical Voice 6
   0.3 Parameters and Limits 10

1 Beyond Nihilism: Camus's Task 13

   1.1 Interesting Generations 13
   1.2 "Nihilism" Before Camus 18
   1.3 No, Camus Was Not an Existentialist: From the Absurd to Revolt 24
   1.4 If Nihilism Is Murder, What Then? 31

2 Beyond Contempt: Camus, Post-Truth and Democracy 39

   2.1 Post-Truth, Polarization and Hyper-Truth 39
   2.2 Nihilism, Contempt, and Polemic 47
   2.3 From Rebellion, via Solidarity, to Dialogue 54
   2.4 Why Camus Matters, Beyond "Post-Truth" 59

3 Beyond Political Romanticism: Camus and the *Avant Gardes* 65

   3.1 Commodified Dissent: How Revolt Became the Norm 65
   3.2 Post-Structuralism (or "Postmodernism") as Aestheticized Revolt 72
   3.3 Sympathy for the Devil: Camus Against *Avant Gardism* 77
   3.4 Camus's Nietzsche and the Fascism Question 84

4 Beyond Identitarianism: Camus and the Future of the Left 91

   4.1 Post-Equality: What We Missed While We Were Culture-Warrin' 91
   4.2 Why Camus Matters to the Left Today: Balancing Freedom with Justice 97
   4.3 Beyond Messianism: Camus's Critique of Authoritarian Communism 104

4.4 Beyond Libertarianism: Balancing Liberty with Equality 110
4.5 Race, Camus, and Algeria 115

5 Camus Against Fascism 119

5.1 The Spectre of Twenty-First-Century Neofascism 119
5.2 Competing Theories of Fascism 126
    5.2.1 Fascism as Hypertrophy of Administrative Reason and "Modernity" 127
    5.2.2 Fascism as Politicized Irrationalism 130
5.3 Irrational Terror: Camus's Critique of Fascism 133
5.4 After the Fall: Camus and the Psychology of Fascism 139

6 Nature, the Sacred, and Balance 147

6.1 Beyond Criticism or Negation: Camus's Philosophical Originality 147
6.2 Ecological Crises and Our Discontents 150
6.3 Helen's Exile: Science, Nature, and *Mesure* 155
6.4 Jerusalem with Athens: From Exile Toward the Kingdom 163

Conclusion 173

Notes	179
Bibliography	207
Index	219
References to Camus's work by title	223

Introduction: Why Camus Matters in 2025

0.1 The Author in the Amphitheater

When Albert Camus died in a single-vehicle car crash in January 1960, he was only forty-six. He had by that time managed to live several lives, as we say—or more in one life than most of us could encompass in many. Camus is justly celebrated as a great *litterateur*. He was the author of three classic novels, *The Outsider* (*L'Étranger*) of 1942, *The Plague* (*La Peste*) of 1947, and *The Fall* (*La Chute*) of 1956. In 1957, at just forty-four, he was awarded the Nobel Prize for literature. As well as being a novelist, and the author of the short stories collected in *Exile and the Kingdom* (*L'Exil et le royaume*) of 1957, Camus was many other things.[1] Born in 1913 into an impoverished French family in Algiers, Camus worked firstly as a journalist in Algeria, before moving to the French mainland in 1940, the year France would be overrun by the Nazi *blitzkrieg*. Camus then became involved in the resistance, and in 1944, the editor and a leading contributor to the resistance newspaper *Combat*. Like the philosopher in Plato's *Republic* who reluctantly but out of duty comes back down into the city to assist his fellows, Camus the artist who longed for a life given over to creativity became from 1943–4 onwards a political figure. Soon enough, he would be embroiled in the debates about rebuilding France after the shame of the invasion and pro-Nazi Vichy regime. Camus would speak out, and attract fire, about the growing reconnaissance from Russian emigres about the Stalinist terror and Gulags. Finally, as if these literary and political personae were not enough, Camus was also a philosopher or—since he had hesitations about this term—an artist influenced by philosophy, who addresses grave philosophical questions.[2] Alongside *The Outsider* came the philosophical essay, *The Myth of Sisyphus* (*Le mythe de Sisyphe*) of 1942, on the subjects of suicide and absurdity in a world no longer defined by traditional monotheism. After *The Plague*, drawing from public addresses and essays written between 1946 and 1951, Camus wrote *The Rebel* (*L'Homme révolté*). This is his much longer philosophical work addressing the modern age as an age of revolt against theologically sanctioned injustices that has become prone to forms of systematized injustices of its own.[3]

This book does not need to repeat what many others have said, in admiration of Camus the man and the author. In his own lifetime, he was lauded as the conscience of the times. Showing his colors, Camus was always embarrassed by such praise. Receiving the Nobel Prize set off in him a kind of crisis of conscience. Many a lesser person would have exalted in this recognition, not least in our age of social mediatic self-advertisement and taken-for-granted careerism. For Camus as for the ancient Greek philosophers he admired, fame was an illusory good, beneath friendship, love, solidarity, intelligence, courage, moderation, and justice. This is a book about why Camus matters as a thinker and a writer, today. It makes a case that he arguably matters a good deal more than many of his contemporaries, and indeed, than many critical theorists and philosophers whose ideas have been lauded far more highly, and studied far more widely, in universities since his death.

Camus himself never belonged to academia. Prevented by ill health from going forward in his higher studies (he suffered from tuberculosis his whole short life), Camus's intellectual path was not shaped by the trending scholarly debates of his day. It was shaped instead, first, by the ethical, social, existential, and political problems faced by his generation—a generation born into the Great War, raised in the global instability of the 1920s and then the Great Depression, maturing as European and East Asian fascist regimes as well as Stalinism in Russia led the world into a "Second World War," then learning in due course of the extent of Nazi and Stalinist atrocities and the power of the nuclear bomb to destroy centuries-old cities in an instant. The foci of Camus's work were shaped, secondly, by his own liminal identity, as a French *pied noir* in Algeria whose entire family was illiterate. Albert was the first to complete high school, let alone the *Diplôme* by thesis he passed in 1936.[4] He suffered all his life, as we mentioned, with a disease which he knew could carry him off at any time, a kind of permanent *memento mori*. At a decisive age, he came under the tutelage of the philosopher-author, Jean Grenier, who introduced him to ancient Greek, Roman, and Christian thinking. In contrast to the modern syllabi being taught in the prestigious metropolitan universities, Camus's philosophical and existential sensibilities were hence those of the Mediterranean and of poverty, rather than the celebrated Parisian *écoles*, in whose milieu he felt himself an outsider.

Camus did not like the term "committed intellectual" which became fashionable to describe him, as well as his sometime friend, Jean-Paul Sartre, in the years after 1945.[5] He nevertheless accepted that in the age where modern technology had extended the reach of governments and businesses even into people's private lives, that no artist or philosopher could any longer live the *vita contemplativa* (contemplative life). Each was "impressed" into history, and the political realm, whether they wished it or not.[6] As Camus would say in 1957 about the situation of the artist in the age of competing ideologies, compared to their predecessors of earlier periods:

Instead of signing up, indeed, for voluntary service, the artist does his compulsory service. Every artist today is embarked on the contemporary slave galley... The artist, like everyone else, must bend to his oar, without dying if possible—in other words, go on living and creating. To tell the truth, it is not easy, and I can understand why artists regret their former comfort. The change is somewhat cruel. Indeed, history's amphitheatre has always contained the martyr and the lion. The former relied on eternal consolations and the latter on raw historical meat. But until now the artist was on the sidelines. He used to sing purposely, for his own sake, or at best to encourage the martyr and make the lion forget his appetite. But now the artist is in the amphitheatre.[7]

Hence, Camus was a thinker and artist who addressed the problems of his times. He matters for our times, first, insofar as our later- or postmodern world, tragically, faces analogues or successors of many of the threats, risks, problems, and challenges that faced the "insane times" in which Camus lived. What threats and challenges do I mean? They structure the chapters of this book:

- The problem of nihilism and its symptoms: as social scientific studies confirm, especially in the United States, large numbers of people today experience a sense of alienation from their social milieu, anxiety about the future, and a sense that the world, and their own lives, lacks order, meaning, and direction (Chapter 1)

- The problem of "post-truth" and its symptoms: widespread public and even elite skepticism about the possibility of reaching agreements on matters of political and historical fact, and today, even concerning medical and the natural sciences, coupled with the increasing polarization and incivility that is characterizing public discussion in nations around the world (Chapter 2);

- The problems caused by the cultural ascendancy of romanticist values: the division of the Left, after the 1960s, in ways which have integrated marketized values of becoming, difference, individuality, and creativity, and which have seen the gap between the New Left and the

Left's traditional working class constituency widen, as well as the loss of robust visions of better, more equitable societies to challenge the rise of reactionary political movements (3);

- The problem of growing socioeconomic inequality, which has informed or enflamed many of the nihilistic symptoms identified in Chapter 1, at the same time as political debate has largely shifted away from the economic material concerns of most people, into heated "culture wars" about competing claims to identity and representation (Chapter 4);

- The global renormalization and political ascendancy of the Far Right, culminating (as of early 2025) in the United States with the election of a convicted felon under investigation for insurrection as President, on an ethnonationalist "Make America Great Again" platform with undeniable historical echoes of interwar fascism, including promises of mass deportations, threats to imprison opponents as "vermin," attacks on science and free media, and more (Chapter 5);

- The ecological crisis, encompassing climate change, species extinction, resource depletion and the need for human beings to develop a more balanced sense of our place in nonhuman nature, as stewards of environments which are also the material preconditions for our own continuing collective existence (Chapter 6).

The first thesis of this book is that Camus matters for us as a thinker and a human being, whose integrity is acknowledged by people on both Left and Right (which is rare, today). He is an author who directly addressed the problems that we face in the second quarter of the twenty-first century: nihilism, the failure of media (and social media) to inform democratic populations and their decisions, the divisions of the political Left, the rise of fascism on the Right, and human beings' increasing loss of balance with the natural world. Camus is not, as people poetically say, "our contemporary." Camus could not have foreseen the technological changes we are presently experiencing, led by AI and big tech—albeit one can venture informed hypotheses as to what he would think of these changes, and what they portend for the human future. Camus is a thoughtful, courageous, clear-sighted authority from the darkest period of modern European history, whose thinking responded to sociopolitical and cultural challenges which we clearly have not resolved. He was moreover a thinker who always responded to the problems of his times, as we said, not any other "research program." So, by reading his work in response to the challenges which *we* face today, as this book does, we are honoring his own practice, even as we depart from the letters he was able to write, by applying them to our ongoing crises.

0.2 Camus's Unique Philosophical Voice

Camus matters first of all, this book therefore sets out to show, because we can learn from his responses to the problems of his day, antecedents to our own. Camus matters secondly, it argues, because underlying his fictional writing, informing his political journalism and essay writing, is a distinct philosophical perspective in twentieth-century thought. In the first five chapters of this book, we will be focusing on Camus's specific responses to the issues of nihilism, post-truth, political romanticism, economic inequality, and fascism. However, in the context of these responses, our sense of Camus's unique philosophical perspective, and its specific components, will gradually emerge:

- In Chapter 1, we will examine his famous philosophy of the absurd in *The Myth of Sisyphus*, in contrast to better-known accounts of nihilism (and its continuing popular, romantic misreading), and introduce the idea of rebellion, which is central to the later philosophical work, *The Rebel*.

- In Chapter 2, we will see how the primary value, human solidarity, that Camus claims a philosophy of rebellion uncovers informs his arguments for the bases of democratic politics, in prohibitions against principled deceit, enslavement, and murder.

- In Chapter 3, we will examine Camus's criticisms of romanticism, with its "sympathy for the devil" in the face of divine injustice, and his critique of a philosopher whom he admired, Friedrich Nietzsche, uncovering those claims within his thinking which Camus saw as underwriting and giving cultural credence to fascism and German National Socialism.

- In Chapter 4, we will examine Camus's criticisms of Marxism-Leninism, as it played out in Stalin's Russia, and his attempt to defend a form of socialist democracy which would balance fundamental concerns for economic justice with the defense of political liberties.

- In Chapter 5, we will examine Camus's criticism of fascism in power, centrally presented in *The Rebel*, but also of the psychology underwriting fascism's cynical embrace of the idea that human life is a pitiless struggle for domination, dramatized in Camus's character, Jean-Baptiste Clamence, in *The Fall*.

It is in the culminating Chapter 6, which reads Camus as a respondent *avant la lettre* to our ecological crises, that the uniqueness of Camus's thinking, among thinkers of his time, will be explored. Here, we will explore how, unlike the other celebrated thinkers of his generation in metropolitan France, Camus the *pied noir*, educated in Algiers, was not primarily shaped by modern philosophy, in the German, post-Kantian tradition. The young man read and admired Friedrich Nietzsche and Søren Kierkegaard. At some point, he also was given introductions to Edmund Husserl's and Martin Heidegger's thinking, both of which feature in *The Myth of Sisyphus*.[8] Camus's interest in the problems of nihilism and of suicide, his reference to these thinkers, as well as his friendship with Jean-Paul Sartre, Simone de Beauvoir and others in the 1940s, saw him labeled an "existentialist." It was in vain that he denied the label[9] and protested that "the only book of ideas that has ever published, *Le Mythe de Sisyphe,* was directed against the so-called existentialist philosophers."[10] Then as now, popular labels are likely to stick, when they accord with popular prejudgments. But "I am not an existentialist, although of course critics are obliged to make categories," Camus explained himself: "I got my first philosophical impressions from the Greeks, not from nineteenth century Germany."[11]

This somewhat recondite-sounding point has real consequences. As we will expand in Chapter 6, Camus's philosophy is not overdetermined by reflection on how it is that human beings come to make meaning of their experiences: whether this is the product of their consciousness, their will, the language they use, the cultural and historical milieu in which they were raised, or the forms of power to which they have been subjected. For Camus as for the ancient Greek philosophers, the decisive question is how to live, and how we can live well,[12] as the kinds of creatures that we are. As such, his language generally remains non-technical, like that of Greek philosophers and poets. Unlike almost all twentieth-century philosophers, this includes his unironic appeals to the virtues or strengths of character.[13] Camus in particular favors intelligence (roughly what the ancients aimed at with "wisdom," but Camus often uses the "light" terms, "lucidity" or "clear-sightedness"), courage, moderation (French *mesure*) and justice. His work explores human sentiments and sensibilities, and common experiences such as suffering, love, and generosity.

Decisively, as Camus feels that he has developed a perspective "beyond nihilism," he comes to explore the possibility that, "contrary to the postulates of contemporary thought, a human nature does exist, as the Greeks believed."[14] Our human nature is defined by limits, both in terms of what we can legitimately claim to know concerning the ultimate questions of existence, and what we can therefore claim over and against other human beings with whom we disagree on such questions. These limits are surrounded, moreover, by a nonhuman nature which exceeds our full control, which can visit epidemics and disasters on the innocent, and yet which clearly has its own order and beauty that we as human beings can savor. If modern humanity is to re-find order, Camus argued, it will need to re-sanctify a sense of our own limits. We will need to cultivate the *mesure* or moderation to acknowledge that, while excess and infinite growth seem to be possibilities that humans are free to explore, we are not the center of creation. It is neither admirable nor desirable to do as we please; to for instance create supercomputers capable of destroying our means of existence or removing our needs to learn or love—just because we, or a private consortium, can. Instead, we must acknowledge, and should respect and foster, the natural systems (or the order of God's creation, as believers put it) which make our continuing shared existence, and that of our descendants, possible.

It can be protested against our claim that Camus, specifically, matters today, that other twentieth-century thinkers have opposed nihilism, although with perhaps less clarity and directness than Camus (Chapter 1). Others have presented good reasons not to accept the *faux* radical skepticism about claims to truth which, for a period, was the province of the postmodern Left, but has now given license to the disinformation and cynicism of the online Far Right (Chapter 2). Other thinkers have presented models of deliberative democracy which in practical and institutional terms approximate the kinds of political recommendations Camus made between 1944 and his premature death. Other thinkers again—although many most surely did not—forthrightly opposed fascism and Nazism (Chapter 5). I'm more than happy to grant these propositions: they're all true. My claim is that Camus is nevertheless singular among renowned twentieth-century thinkers for proposing to base these positions on a revival of decisive elements of classical and then Christian thought, which he credibly claimed had been ignored in previous modern thinking (Chapter 6). As at once a defender of beauty, not formalism in art; of creativity, but not singularity or idiosyncrasy; of passion, but restrained by limits; of confronting the absurd, but in order to find reasons for living and to overcome "realistic" cynicism; of rebellion in the name of justice, not of revolution as an exciting Event; of unity in difference, rather than difference or Otherness as ends in themselves; of classical values and a sense of natural beauty, tempered by a Christian and modern sense of the ineradicable dignity of all human beings—in all of these ways, Camus stands out in twentieth-century thought:

> There is thus a will to live without rejecting anything of life, which is the virtue I honour most in this world. From time to time, at least, it is true that I should like to have practiced it. Inasmuch as few epochs require as much as ours that one should be equal to the best as to the worst, I should like, indeed, to shirk nothing and to keep faithfully a double memory. Yes, there is beauty and there are the humiliated. Whatever may be the difficulties of the undertaking, I should like never to be unfaithful either to one or to the others.[15]

If Camus's thought in particular matters in 2025, this book therefore wagers that it is because he brings to the problems we face today (the first reason) resources that he derived from his reading of the ancient and biblical sources, Athens and Jerusalem. In doing so, his thinking informs potential solutions which are insightful, humane and balanced, in an age of accelerating ignorance, inhumanity, and imbalance (our second reason).

0.3 Parameters and Limits

No single book on Camus could say everything about his life, literature and thought. He contained multitudes, beneath the graceful flow of the prose. For interested readers, the author has attempted a more systematic theoretical study of Camus's thought in *Camus, Philosophe: To Return to Our Beginnings*.[16] This book has a different purpose, governed by the titular question of why Camus matters for us today, in 2024–5 and the foreseeable future. The core positions of Camus's philosophy can be found in *Why Camus Matters*. Here, they are presented in relation to our own social, cultural and political challenges: the things that matter for us, and in whose light Camus matters still today, perhaps more than for two generations. Many of the interpretive arguments found in my longer book can likewise be found, in condensed forms, here. But there are other elements of Camus's thinking addressed here which that book neglected. My understanding of Camus, especially in relation to Christianity, but also the issue of cynicism, has changed with the times and with repeated readings.

Camus's literary writings matter for reasons that are aesthetic, as well as because of the human subjects that they address. They need to be read directly to be appreciated, ideally in the original French for those able. This book contains rather less examination of the literary works than some readers might have anticipated, and the author initially supposed. There are glimpses of each of Camus's classic literary works and treatments of some key episodes (spoiler alert). *The Misunderstanding* in Chapter 2 and *The Fall* in Chapter 5 are each given brief, dedicated treatments. But the aims and therefore the scope and foci of this book are different from the many fine studies on Camus in literary criticism, which I warmly recommend.[17]

With these parameters clarified, let me say that, if readers find insight or orientation in these pages, their gratitude should be directed to Camus. In a dark time, personally and politically, it has been therapeutic for the author to have been working again on his *oeuvre*. Camus's identification in the 1940s of the central malignity of our civilization as cynicism about all ideals or sense of public service, short of uncritical obedience to strong men and one-sided ideologies, seems to be tragically discerning by 2025. The writing of this book was begun, not altogether by chance, on November 5, 2024, the day that

Donald Trump was reelected US president, despite his criminal convictions, many untried indictments, and having made a mockery of (or actively vilified) almost every norm, convention, and institution that shaped the American Republic since 1776, courted Right-wing extremists, and provoked an insurrection against the ratification of the 2020 election in January 2021, televised in real time around the world. All that has followed in the first year of Mr. Trump's second ascension, as the book has taken shape, attest that whereas his first administration included farse as well as the tragedy of hundreds of thousands of excess deaths due to COVID-19, this second administration needs to be taken deadly seriously as something more akin to a democratic "catastrophe" or going under, in the Greek sense—with international effects that are almost as troubling and uncertain as the domestic. The increasingly dark history of the United States since 2015, this longtime "leader of the free world," makes it clear that the "realism" Camus always opposed, a "realism" that promotes egoism, tribalism, and a scorn for wider human solidarity, has been supercharged by social media and unsustainable social inequality and alienation. It is pushing even nations which were long considered beacons of liberty toward a new period of oligarchic, or more precisely, plutocratic (rule by the very rich) authoritarianism mobilized through forms of "populist" ideologies promoting xenophobia, conspiratorialism, and the celebration of cruelty toward outsiders.

In this time, Camus's role is vital as a figure of intellectual and political resistance to fascism and fanaticism, a philosopher of his times to be read now as a philosopher for ours. Returning to his unique voice, at once so grave yet often so humane, can be a source of orientation and hope as we face newly emboldened forms of active nihilism and illiberalism. It goes without saying that the limitations of this small book, like the opinions relayed on contemporary events, are the author's own.

1

Beyond Nihilism: Camus's Task

1.1 Interesting Generations

Albert Camus's *The Myth of Sisyphus*, written in 1940 and published in 1942, stands alongside Emile Durkheim's *Suicide* as one of the two most famous twentieth-century books written on the distressing phenomenon of suicide: human beings taking their own lives. Durkheim's approach is sociological, objective, or "third personal." He looks at the available data on numbers of suicides. The sociologist attempts to understand the data in light of contemporary social phenomena: notably, the incidence of "anomie," the breakdown of social norms and solidarity, leaving individuals prone to feeling isolated, disconnected, and without purpose.[1] Camus's book, by contrast, is philosophical. Camus is interested in why people, from the inside, "first person," might take their own lives: "the relationship between individual thought and suicide" (MS, 4).[2] There are many possible causes in different cases: the "personal" reasons that newspapers speak of, and in some cases, incurable illnesses. Across most cases,[3] all we can say is that a suicide is a confession in action that life has become "too much" or that the person cannot see a reason to live any longer (MS, 5).

For the younger Camus, the possibility of suicide which we all face, and which we can all take up at any moment, is "the only truly serious philosophical problem" (MS, 3). This is a big call, and one which we can dispute. What Camus clearly means is existential. As he says, "one must answer" this question de facto, over and over, if only by going on living. Other considerations, across the liberal arts—like whether the sun moves around the earth, or whether language shapes thought or thought language, and a thousand others—are less existentially pressing. You can mostly get on fine without raising or answering them.

So, *The Myth of Sisyphus* explicitly distances itself from Durkheim's sociological aim to address people commit suicide in twentieth century societies, and positions suicide as a timeless existential question facing every human being. With that said, *Myth*'s consideration of suicide is also pointedly of its time in European and global history. "The pages that follow deal with an absurd sensitivity that can be found widespread in the age," he opens the book's "Preface" by saying (MS, 2). Later essays will protest that, far from being academic or wholly detached, the work responded to "an idea in the streets of my time."[4] Camus acknowledges from the start his debts to near-contemporary and contemporary thinkers, such as Kierkegaard, Heidegger, Jaspers, Chestov, who had already begun to philosophically chart the "sensibility" at issue in the book—of what Camus famously calls the absurd. In the world of the twentieth century, after the decline of Christian cultural hegemony (the "death of God"), a world that had experienced world wars, revolutions, depressions, and the rise of fascism and Stalinism, many people were asking the ageless question of whether their lives had any meaning. Indeed, many were perplexed as to whether the larger human world could have any sense. A little into *The Myth of Sisyphus*, Camus acknowledges that "never perhaps at any time has the attack on reason been more violent than ours" (MS, 22–3).[5]

Camus's *The Myth of Sisyphus* was completed as Hitler's *blitzkrieg* decimated republican France. At this moment, the Nazi domination of continental Europe seemed fated. The book is a response to what the Chinese call "interesting times." Camus would later reflect in "The Time of Murderers" of 1949:

> The men of my age in France and in Europe were born just before or during the first great war, arrived at adolescence at the moment of the global economic crisis and were twenty years old when Hitler seized power. To complete our education, we were offered the war in Spain, Munich, the war of 1939, the [French] defeat and four years of occupation and clandestine struggle. To top things off, we are [now] promised the conflagration of atomic war. I thus suppose that we are what is called "an interesting generation."[6]

In such a world, Camus's philosophical question in *The Myth of Sisyphus* had become pressing for many Europeans, indeed, for many people around the world caught up in these extraordinary "disruptions," as we say today. "A world that can be explained even with bad reasons is a familiar world. But on the other hand, in a universe suddenly divested of illusions and lights, man feels an alien, a stranger" (MS, 6). Such a person has become what Durkheim called anomic: without a *nomos* or rule of life. If life has no clear meaning, if there seems to be no lasting sense or abiding order to human affairs, beyond the nihilistic reign of fact and force, then does not reason demand that we "absent ourselves from felicity awhile," as Hamlet ironized—and take our exit from the irrational mess? If life has no transcendent or totalizing meaning—at least, any such meaning that we can comprehend—is it still worth living? Camus comments: "It is legitimate to wonder clearly and without false pathos, if a conclusion of this importance requires forsaking as rapidly as possible an incomprehensible condition" (MS, 6).

Camus's reflections, here as elsewhere, sound uncannily prescient amidst the sociopolitical and larger disorders that characterize our own times of economic inequality, political polarization, and democratic decline. In 2017, researchers Anne Case and Angus Deaton published some troubling statistics.

Focusing on the United States, the "leader of the free world," they documented a dramatic rise since 1999 in what they chillingly called "deaths of despair"—that is, deaths by suicide, drug or alcohol poisoning, and liver disease and cirrhosis associated with such forms of "self-medication."[7] What they found is that suicides had not been so common in the United States since 1938, as Camus was meditating on the absurd. Deaths associated with "the demon bottle" were higher than since 1910.[8] By 2022, over two hundred thousand lives were lost to such deaths of despair, many chosen voluntarily[9]—more Americans than were lost in First World War, and over half of those lost in the four years of Second World War, across the European and Pacific theaters.

What is driving this rise in deaths of despair, and in these numbers of people who assess that life or, at least, their own lives, are not worth living?[10] As Camus stresses, we can never be sure exactly of what decisive considerations are formed in the hearts of individual suicides to push them to the final leap. For many, it will be "personal" reasons, broken relationships, unrequited loves, broken families, career misfortunes, mental illnesses, etc. Nevertheless, if following Durkheim, we do contextualize these figures in relationship with other statistics charting social alienation and anomie, we find much food for thought in relation to what Camus identified as the "absurd sensitivity" (MS, 6): the sense that the larger world in which people strive to flourish does not seem to make sense in the ways that people had anticipated, desired, or hoped.

Any assessment of our generations must begin with the evidence concerning how anxiety-ridden the populations of different countries are. In 2019, some 4 percent of people, one in twenty-five, were estimated by a global study to be suffering from anxiety disorders; a datum reflected in the increasing global consumption of psychotropic medicines, led by anti-depressants.[11] The statistics concerning loneliness and social isolation—as we'll see, key concerns of Camus's, dramatized notably in *The Plague* (1947)[12] and recognized by psychologists as reliable predictors of forms of mental ill health[13]—are also not comforting. About one-third of all human beings surveyed globally in 2021 reported "often" being lonely as COVID-19 lockdowns began, with increasing numbers of people living alone.[14] Globally, it seems that the older a person gets, the more likely they are to experience social isolation. According to a 2022 study, around 34 percent of adults in the author's country, Australia, reported being lonely: 21 percent on an episodic basis, 13 percent experiencing more lasting loneliness.[15] In the United States, 43 percent of adults reported that they felt that they lack companionship and/or that their relationships are not meaningful, with some 39 percent reporting not feeling close to anyone.[16]

As for faith in established authorities' ability to improve their lives, led by governments, these figures have plummeted internationally (see Section 2.1). In the United States, trust in the federal government had fell from 73 percent in 1958, in the height of the post-war boom, to just 24 percent by 2021.[17] Similar, although less drastic figures hold in Western Europe since the 1970s. According to a global 2019 survey, the percentage of populations expressing confidence in their governments across the sixty-two developed and developing countries declined from 46 percent, on average, as recently as 2006, to 36 percent by 2019.[18] These results are reflected in studies on impressions amongst youth that the future will be better than the past. Even in such an historically wealthy nation as Australia in 2024,[19] 98 percent of youth reported a pessimistic outlook. Only 53 percent thought themselves likely to achieve financial security. Australia hosts 62 percent of young people who are worried that they will be worse off economically than their parents. Outside of China, in which 41 percent of the population believes that the world is getting better, the global assessment of people of all ages about the future is pretty dour. At the bottom end, only 3 percent of Australians believe things are on the up, 4 percent of the French, and 6 percent of the (traditionally bullish) Americans.[20]

In short, it seems that we again, and our children, are what Camus in 1949 called "interesting generations." Camus's questions, starting with those surrounding suicide in his first philosophical work, *The Myth of Sisyphus*, are not of interest only to historians of ideas.

1.2 "Nihilism" Before Camus

It is clear enough why one image of Camus that has persisted, despite his own protestations, sees him as a "nihilist." His opening question in *The Myth of Sisyphus*, that of suicide, as well as his phlegmatic anti-hero, Meursault, in the contemporary novel *The Outsider* position Camus as a thinker of dark thoughts. Is he not a celebrant of the senselessness of human existence, like a Jean-Paul Sartre, if not an Emil Cioran? Meursault in *The Outsider*, as most readers will know (spoiler alert), kills an Arab man he has never met, ostensibly on behalf of a shifty character with whom he has no real connection. He can provide no better explanation for his murderous violence than "the sun, the sea," in an uncanny echo of his own name.[21] Camus himself in *The Myth of Sisyphus* acknowledges his kinship with "the themes of irrational and religious thought" which have dominated European thought, at least since Nietzsche:

> From Jaspers to Heidegger, from Kierkegaard to Chestov, from the phenomenologists to Scheler, on the logical plane and the moral plane, a whole family of minds related by their nostalgia but opposed by their methods or their aims, have persisted in blocking the royal road of reason and in recovering the direct paths of truth ... Whatever may be or have been their ambitions, all started out from that indescribable universe where contradiction, antinomy, anguish, or impotence reigns. (MS, 23)

Nevertheless, and this can hardly be stressed enough, Camus from the start positions nihilism, and the widespread sense of alienation and despair he found in the streets of his time, as a problem to be overcome. A fundamentally affirmative thinker, nihilism was never for Camus a condition to be embraced as inevitable, unquestionable, glamorous, or desirable. We should never forget that his answer to the question of whether, even if we do adjudge that life has no lasting meaning, we should therefore commit suicide, is a resounding: *no*.

At the end of *The Myth of Sisyphus* (second spoiler), Camus asks us to imagine that even Sisyphus, condemned by the gods to a senseless eternal punishment for his crimes against hospitality, is capable of being happy. As Camus would stress to American audiences in 1955, on the occasion of *The Myth of Sisyphus*'s translation into English:

> Written fifteen years ago, in 1940, amid the French and European disaster, this book declares that even within the limits of nihilism, it is possible to find the means to go beyond nihilism. In all of the books I have written since, I have attempted to pursue this direction. Although *The Myth of Sisyphus* poses mortal problems, it sums itself up for me as a lucid invitation to live and to create, in the very midst of the desert. (MS, v)

Some of the confusion surrounding Camus's place in the history and philosophy of "nihilism" surrounds the vagueness of the loaded term "nihilism," most famously associated with one of Camus's influences, Friedrich Nietzsche. So, it is helpful to try to get some clarity on this disputed term. Then we can better understand Camus's task, which he identified as the attempt to recreate a philosophy and ways of life "beyond nihilism."

The idea that any living humans could ever believe in nothing, *rien*, *nada*, *nihil* (for instance, that s/he was alive and not dead, etc.), or that nothing "had any value," even relatively, is difficult to parse, when taken in anything like a literal sense. If the nihilist proposes that "nothing has any meaning," they are committed to the meaningfulness of that statement. Like the liar, whose lie depends on others holding his lie for truth, absolute nihilism is a self-cancelling chimera. A recent historian of the term, Jon Stewart, has helpfully identified the core sense of the term as "the troubling idea that nothing is ultimately valuable or meaningful, including our own existence. The world itself is meaningless."[22] In this expanded sense, Stewart notes, "nihilism" seems to be perennial. It is not a specifically later-modern thing. Humans have always faced the unsettling realities of their mortality, transience (and the transience even of our memories, once we have passed), and our vulnerability to forms of seemingly senseless suffering through disease, human malignity, and natural disasters. Many have responded with cosmic despair:

> For the fate of humans and the fate of animals is the same; as one dies, so dies the other. They all have the same breath, and humans have no advantage over the animals; for all is vanity. All go to one place; all are from the dust, and all turn to dust again. (Eccl. 3:20)

Likewise, faced with the most difficult features of human life, many have embraced forms of atheism, alongside epistemic and moral relativism—the ideas that there are no objective truths or moral principles, at least that we could know about. Everything we claim to be true or right really is just our own subjective, tribal, or cultural perspective, a regnant view amongst the "postmodernists." Such a seemingly "realist" stance responding to the facts of cultural and individual differences is at least as old in the Western world as the Greek sophists, although there are interesting ancient Indian and Chinese analogues.

The term "nihilism" entered into modern Western debates, historians of ideas agree, in the last decades of the eighteenth century, "as an early modern polemical weapon for symbolically annihilating cultural opponents."[23] It did so to name distinctly *modern, post-* or *anti-theological* philosophical and ethicopolitical stances. At issue is the exact moment at which Camus in *The Rebel* identifies the foundation of our present period, in what he calls forms of "metaphysical rebellion" (Section 3.3). Such rebellion, taking form in the philosophical deism and atheism of enlightenment free thinkers like Voltaire or D'Holbach (Camus also names Father Meslier, and devotes a section to the dissident rebel, de Sade[24]), was predicated on reasoned skepticism concerning the biblical and theological claims at the heart of Christianity, led by the idea of a benevolent, all-knowing, salvific Creator God. However, the term "nihilism" seems firstly to have been used by German thinkers responding to the philosophy of Immanuel Kant. Kant denied that we could have knowledge, not simply of God, but of any "things in themselves" (or "noumena") in the world, outside of our own ideas of them, as opposed to "phenomena" (things as we perceive them). Thinkers like Jenisch[25] or Jacob Hermann Obereit were horrified at the seeming implications of this critical position for the human ability to know the world. They protested:

> If you think away in advance all existence [*Daseyn*], then utterly nothing remains, neither to intuit [*anzuschauen*] and to feel, nor to think, nor to aim after [*bezielen*], or to want and to deal with, and hereby you have made the greatest of all mortal leaps into absolute nothingness [*Salto mortale ins absolute Nichts*], none greater is possible.[26]

In the aftermath of the French revolution, reactionary critics such as Louis-Sébastien Mercier and Joseph De Maistre gave the term "nihilism" a second, more political turn—albeit one inflected by a theological background. They charged the bourgeois revolutionaries with what de Maistre called "riènisme": the Godless aim to undermine everything sacred.[27] As Domenico Losurdo has documented, this polemical use has been echoed by political reactionaries ever since. It functions as a term to provoke fear and outrage at progressive causes, as notably after the 1848 revolutions in the works of figures such as Gioberti, Rosmini, and Donoso Cortès in Spain.[28] Modern progressivism, these figures charged, is not simply politically mistaken. It is metaphysically catastrophic.

The most abiding, third, usage of "nihilism," and the one closest to popular understanding, hails from theological perspectives. Still prominent within Catholic thought, as well as amongst Islamic and American fundamentalism, it identifies "belief in nothing" (at least in anything robust enough to orient human lives) as the baleful, necessary consequence of modern atheism. From a Christian perspective, God is the source of all truth, being, and value. When human beings deny the existence of God, on whichever grounds, they are hence only spiting themselves, as well as indulging in impious pride. Atheists who claim the non-existence of God are pulling out the metaphysical rug from under their own existential feet, which supports everything which makes human life and the created world itself substantial, beautiful, and meaningful. What is left in a world cut loose from its divine moorings is, at best, the competition of rival perspectives on the world: a clash of egoisms of the kind we find celebrated in a radical, self-professing nihilist like Max Stirner.[29] At worst, as the most honest and intelligent atheists, like Dostoevsky's Ivan Karamazov in the great novel *The Brothers Karamazov* recognize, atheism opens up a moral void in which, with no God, everything is permitted.[30] This includes the crimes long considered most heinous, like parricide or infanticide—and soon enough as the European imperialist period led into the twentieth-century catastrophes, eugenics and genocide.

Finally, to complete the ambiguity around charges that Camus could be a "nihilist," when we finally arrive at the later nineteenth-century German philosopher, Friedrich Nietzsche, we find a different, *fourth* sense of "nihilism." Nietzsche's usage of "nihilism" moreover, and not by coincidence, symmetrically inverts the fundamental bases of the Christian-theological conception of the term. Unlike the earlier modern metaphysical rebels, who set about disproving God's existence or reviling his alleged injustices (see Section 3.3), Nietzsche claimed that God was already "dead" by the second half of the nineteenth century, as Camus notes (see Section 3.4).[31] Nietzsche responded to declining levels of religious belief and church attendance in Europe, occasioned principally by the growing regnancy of the modern sciences, but also by the widespread success of thinkers like Voltaire in challenging the moral and intellectual authority of the churches.[32] Nietzsche believed that the sheer metaphysical enormity of this "death of God"—the principled discrediting of the religious beliefs that had undergirded European civilization for nearly two millennia—had not been taken nearly seriously enough by his contemporaries. As he writes:

> Nihilism is the conviction that life is absurd, in the light of the highest values already discovered; [but] it also includes the *view* that we have not

the smallest right to assume the existence of transcendental objects or things in themselves, which would be either divine or morality incarnate.[33]

The causes of this modern affliction, as Nietzsche sees things, go back much farther in Western cultural history than the eighteenth-century free thinkers. They hearken back to the inception of what he terms the "slave revolt in morals" with the Jewish prophets, Socrates, and Saint Paul.[34] The modern nihilism of the scientific age, as Nietzsche saw it, was the legacy of two millennia of what he would term "life-denial," which he claimed to locate at the heart of "Christian morals."[35] At issue is the Christian belief that the origin of value in our embodied, finite, transient lives and experiences is to be found in the transcendent, other-worldly God of the Bible and the theologians—that is, exactly the theological belief which Christian thinkers believe can alone stave off modern, atheistic nihilism (sense 3).[36] In avowed opposition to the theological understandings of nihilism, Nietzsche (who was notably preceded here by Eugen Dühring and Max Stirner) contends that it was Christianity, not the secular sciences and *philosophes*, that had first calumniated the world, and emptied it of lasting value.[37] By positing an other-worldly God and destiny for human beings, Christianity asked people to sacrifice this-worldly happiness on the altar of a restrictive, guilt-inducing, universal moral code, and fraudulent promises of life after death. As Camus writes of Nietzsche:

> If nihilism is the inability to believe, then its most serious symptom [according to Nietzsche] is not found in atheism, but in the inability to believe in what is, to see what is happening, and to live life as it is offered. This infirmity is at the root of all idealism. Morality has no faith in the world ... [Nietzsche] is severe on the "calumniators of the world" because he discerns in the calumny a shameful taste for evasion. Traditional morality, for him, is only a special type of immorality. "It is virtue," he says, "which has need of justification." And again: "It is for moral reasons that good, one day, will cease to be done."[38]

For Nietzsche as for Stirner, therefore,[39] nihilism is not something to be overcome through a return to tradition or the churches, let alone through the operations of human reason. What is condemnable is only the "passive" or "incomplete" nihilism of modern societies, populated by mediocre spirits who refuse to draw all the consequences from the death of God, instead luxuriating in a peaceful, technological world whilst continuing to uphold values like "equality" derived from Pauline Christianity. Nihilism for Nietzsche therefore needed a kind of push: to be *completed* by being completely embraced, without timid compromises and post-Christian half-measures—those of the modern "last men" *Thus Spake Zarathustra* excoriates, who long only for comfort and ease. What will be needed is an "active nihilism," born of "strength" or "an increased power of spirit." Such heroic, active nihilism will affirm the emptiness of all "goals hitherto" embraced in the West[40] not as cause for lament, but as an opportunity for "higher men" (the gender is significant here) up to the task, to actively overcome Judaeo-Christian "slave morality." "To that extent, nihilism, as the *denial* of a real world, of a *being*, could be a divine way of thinking," Nietzsche argues, and one which could lead to a genuinely post-modern world.[41]

With this more exacting understanding of the complexities which surround claims and counterclaims concerning modern (or postmodern) nihilism in place, we are ready now to critically understand Camus's particular stance toward the subject without fear of mistaking the meanings at issue.

1.3 No, Camus Was Not an Existentialist: From the Absurd to Revolt

Camus at one point in *The Myth of Sisyphus* effectively anticipates, and steps back from, how he has continued to be read, as a "nihilist." "I said that the world is absurd, but I was too hasty," he qualifies (MS, 21). There can be no doubt that Camus's philosophical position is based on a critical non-acceptance of the claims of the revealed religions (nihilism, senses 3 and 4). He does not suppose the existence of a salvific, interventionist, creator God. He thus qualifies as a "nihilist," if we accept the Christian-theological sense (3) of the term. Nevertheless, it is notable that Camus refused the labels of "nihilist" and "existentialist" completely. "No, I am not an existentialist," he would repeat, as we said in the Introduction.[42] As for being a "Godless" "atheist," he claimed that these "words say nothing to me: for me they have no meaning. I do not believe in God, and I am not an atheist"[43] (see Section 6.4).[44]

For Camus, by contrast with "active nihilists" excited by Nietzsche, the world itself is not senseless or without meaning. To make such a total judgment, we would need ourselves, like Gods, to be outside of the world, which we are not. "The world itself is not reasonable, that is all that can be said" (MS, 21). The human mind is driven, in all of its activities, by a kind of desire or *eros* to unify and give sense to our experience:

> Whatever may be the plays on words and the acrobatics of logic, to understand, is, above all, to unify. The mind's deepest desire, even in its most elaborate operations, parallels man's unconscious feelings in the face of his universe: it is an insistence upon familiarity, an appetite for clarity. (MS, 17)

This desire is also a longing to feel at home in our world, to be able to look around and to see a place that is not foreign. "A world that can be explained even with bad reasons is a familiar world ... in a universe suddenly divested of illusions and lights, man feels an alien, a stranger [*étranger*]" (MS, 6). Nevertheless, the existence and legitimacy of this humanizing desire does not imply that it must necessarily be satisfied: contra some "post-truth" opinions, wishing or feeling something to be true does not make it so. Camus echoes modern philosophers from John Locke to Immanuel Kant, arguing that an honest appraisal indicates that, while our reason and understanding can explain many phenomena, and has great descriptive and analytic powers, humans cannot plumb the deepest metaphysical mysteries of existence (see Chapter 6).[45] Is there a God? An immortal soul? Why is evil and suffering necessary?

With that said, Camus is not an epistemic, moral or cultural relativist, as we will see again and again in this book. Although he agrees with the earlier modern philosophers just named (and the classical skeptics before them) that our understanding and reason is finite and fallible, he does not assent to the easy nihilistic (sense 1) idea that we can thereby really know nothing of the world, beyond our own perspectives. For Camus, it is just that "the key words, the final secrets, are not in man's possession"[46]:

> If thought discovered in the shimmering mirrors of phenomena eternal relations capable of summing themselves up in a single principle, then would be seen an intellectual joy of which the myth of the blessed would be but a ridiculous imitation. That nostalgia for unity, that appetite for the absolute illustrates the essential impulse of the human drama. But the fact of that nostalgia's existence does not imply that it is to be immediately satisfied. (MS, 17)

And this is the decisive point, if we are to understand Camus's distance from the existentialist "the world is meaningless" position and its dark romanticism, of perennial attraction to alienated younger cohorts. Absurdity, Camus notes, is a comparative concept. It describes the relationship between two realities: on one hand, human expectations, and on the other, the larger realities at issue. A peasant girl who wants to marry a prince conceives a desire which is, perhaps, absurd. A madman who tries to attack a battleship with a butter knife is likewise, and even more, absurd: "in all these cases, from the simplest to the most complex, the magnitude of the absurdity will be in direct ration to the distance between the two terms of the comparison" (MS, 30). Just so, absurdity, at the philosophical level of interest to Camus in *The Myth of Sisyphus*, is not a description just of a *world* which eludes full rational humanization. It is an evaluation of the comparison which emerges, when the world's mute resistance to total human comprehension and mastery is assessed, exactly *comparatively*, in light of the human desire for such comprehension: "The Absurd is not in man (if such a metaphor could have a meaning) nor in the world, but in their presence together. For the moment it is the only bond uniting them" (MS, 30).

The absurd, as Camus conceives it, is hence a "divorce" between human desire and "the world which transcends it": "it lies in neither of the elements compared; it is born of their confrontation" (MS, 30). As we might depict the resulting post-theological "trinity" (human desire, world and absurdity) visually (MS, 30):

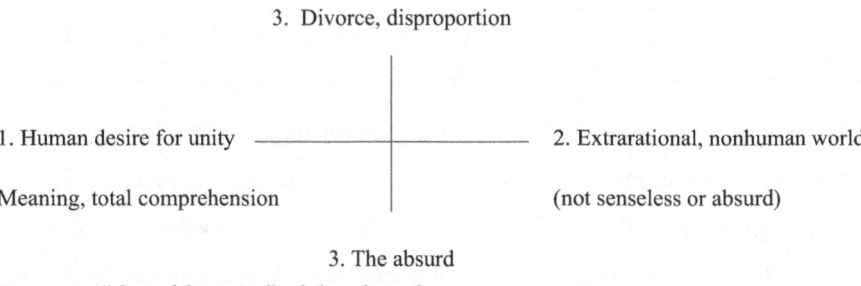

Figure 1 *"the odd trinity" of the absurd.*

For Camus, acknowledging the absurd is a philosophical starting point which resists, or rather emerges on the other side of the most radically modern, skeptical, post-theological assessment of the human desire for meaning. The absurd is not a metaphysical dogma. It is an epistemic concept which aims to describe the *denouement* of all those who would assent only to what we can know concerning ultimate Truth, this side of forms of faith. And recognizing the absurd is a starting point, not a conclusion, Camus repeatedly stressed. To recognize the absurd is to accept a certain "rule of method" in how we approach the world (MS, 50–1). Once we recognize the absurd confrontation as true, in all its components, we must acknowledge that its "first distinguishing feature is that [the absurd] cannot be divided. To destroy one of the terms is to destroy the whole" (MS, 30). There can, on one side, be no absurd confrontation wherever an individual lays claim to total comprehension of the world—whether in the name of a higher Being or unifying principle(s), or by declaiming nihilistically that "everything is *completely* without sense." On the other side, there can be no absurd without honoring our desire for unity and comprehension as a legitimate, inalienable part of the human drama, either. Hence, if a person commits suicide having encountered the irrationality of the world, this for Camus does not consummate, but betrays the absurd. The suicide "leaps," not only perhaps physically, from some window, chair or ledge. She leap/s out of the absurd confrontation, which for Camus is "the sole datum" which a fully lucid stance toward our place in the world, assuming nothing unknowable, can afford (MS, 31).

With this point in view, Camus will argue that thinkers can readily fall prey to what he terms, dramatically, "philosophical suicide." A theologian or philosopher "suicides" metaphorically when s/he "leaps" out of the absurd confrontation into one or other form of comforting, total explanation of the meaning of human existence (MS, 28–50). To repeat, there is no question that Camus agrees with atheists that human beings can never know with certainty that a God exists, let alone a deity concerned with human justice or the fate of individual souls. Such a certainty is beyond the reach of human reason. Indeed, speaking of the phenomenologist Edmund Husserl, Camus expresses comparable skepticism even about the great German-Jewish phenomenologist's supposition that there are quasi-Platonic "extra-temporal essences" of things, allegedly available to human intuition, which would explain how the world makes sense to us (MS, 44). Camus replies skeptically: "that geometrical spot where divine reason ratifies mine will always be incomprehensible to me … I know that I am faced with a metaphysic of consolation" (MS, 46).

On the other hand, Camus's critique of positive theological and rationalist positions does not see him embrace "a philosophy of the non-significance of the world" (MS, 48). Again, despite the press. What instead strikes Camus about the modern age of "nihilism" is how its thought "is constantly oscillating between extreme rationalization of reality and its extreme irrationalization which tends to deify [it]" (MS, 48). If, in contrast to the rationalists, we look at existentialist thinkers like Søren Kierkegaard or Lev Chestov, Camus admires the (ironically rational) power of their criticisms of the attempts of systematic rationalists like Spinoza and Hegel to "explain everything" (MS, 34–6). The problem is that, on this basis, these existentialists in Camus's view make a philosophically suicidal "leap," symmetrical to that of the great philosophical and theological systematizers. It is just that they leap, "by a natural and illegitimate reversal, to the pre-eminence of the irrational" that they have encountered (MS, 36). Having discovered the extra-rational density of the world, its refusal to yield itself up wholly to human understanding, they "do not say 'this is absurd,' but rather: 'This is God: we must rely on Him even if he does not correspond to any of our rational categories'" (MS, 34):

> So that confusion may not be possible, the Russian philosopher [Chestov] even hints that this God is perhaps full of hatred and hateful, incomprehensible and contradictory; but the more hideous is his face, the more he asserts his power. His greatness is his incoherence. His proof is his inhumanity. One must spring into him and by this leap rid oneself from rational illusions. (MS, 34)

Yet, for Camus, to recognize the reality of the extrarational dimension of the world does not license the humiliation of human reason, any more than it licenses suicide and despair. The absurd person who remains faithful only to what he can knowingly assent to, Camus argues, cannot undertake any such *salto mortale*, like Chestov recommends. Instead, "he recognises the struggle, does not absolutely scorn reason, and admits the irrational" (MS, 37). That is all. In truth, what the oscillation of modern philosophy between forms of excessive rationalism and irrationalism shows Camus is that:

> Reason and the irrational lead to the same preaching. In truth the way matters but little, the will to arrive suffices. The abstract philosopher and

the religious philosopher start out from the same disorder and support each other in the same anxiety. The essential is to explain. Nostalgia is here stronger than knowledge. (MS, 47–8)

We can hence see why, for all of his admiration of Nietzsche, Camus does not share the German philosopher's desire merely to turn a passive into a more heroic "active nihilism" (sense 4)—as little as he accepts the idea that he was ever an "existentialist." More like the theological critics of modern nihilism in this regard, Camus sees in irrationalism a modern ailment which must be overcome, albeit without recourse to religious values. "In the darkest depths of our nihilism I sought only reasons to go beyond that nihilism."[47]

Already in *The Myth of Sisyphus*, we see Camus raising a notion which will become central to this lifelong task of overcoming nihilism. This is the idea of "rebellion" or "revolt." In *The Myth of Sisyphus*, it is a principled, ethical "revolt" of the "absurd man" against any forms of totalizing consolation or escape

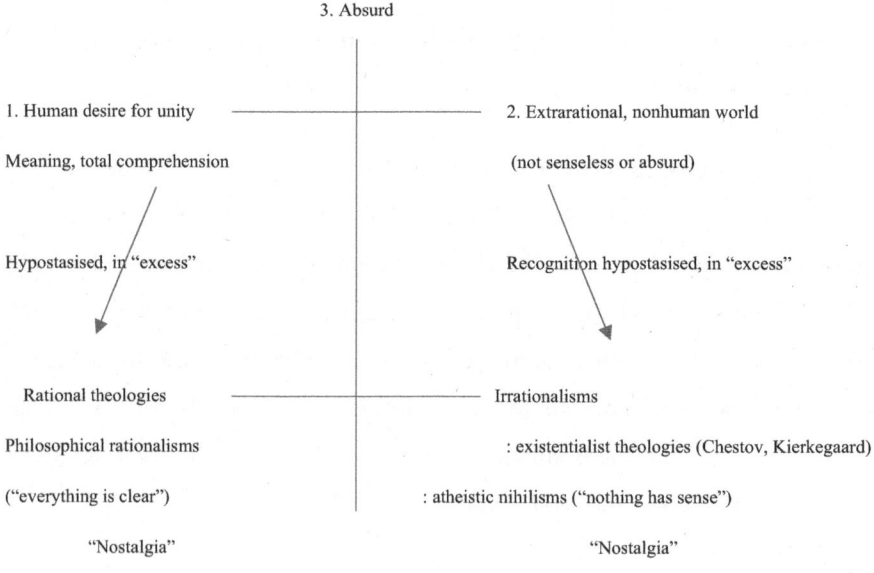

Figure 2 *The rationalist and irrationalist philosophical suicides.*

which would dissolve the absurd confrontation between our longing for unity and "a reality which transcends it" (MS, 55). What is needed, and what Camus finds admirable, is a kind of "discipline" for living lucidly, with and within the absurd, without making the leap of philosophical or actual suicide (MS, 55, 40). This "ascesis" involves a kind of epistemic "decency" which Camus associates with the "lucidity" involved in the modern pursuit of the sciences, as we will stress later (MS, 30–1; cf. Sections 2.3 and 6.3). The point for now is that this individualist Camusian revolt in *The Myth of Sisyphus* is distinctly life-affirming. It is founded less on giving up on all values (nihilism, senses 1–4) than a positive fidelity to the first truth of the absurd, as an Atlassian value upon which to rebuild a post-theological, post-nihilistic way of life:

> It is a constant confrontation between man and his own obscurity. It is an insistence upon an impossible transparency ... It is that constant presence of man in his own eyes ... It may be thought that suicide follows revolt—but wrongly. For it does not represent the logical outcome of revolt. It is just the opposite by the consent it presupposes. Suicide, like the leap, is acceptance at its extreme ... But I know that in order to keep alive, the absurd cannot be settled. It escapes suicide to the extent that it is simultaneously awareness and rejection of death ... The absurd is this extreme tension, which [the rebel faithful to the absurd] maintains constantly by solitary effort, for he knows that in that consciousness and in that day-to-day revolt he gives proof of his only truth. (MS, 54–5)

1.4 If Nihilism Is Murder, What Then?

So: we've seen now that Camus does not base his position on belief in God, although he does not accept the charges of atheism, nihilism or existentialism (nihilism, sense 3). He does not think that the modern unavailability of an absolute, religious or metaphysical explanation of Being licenses relativism, or the inability to establish any reasoned truths (nihilism, sense 1). He shares Nietzsche's stress on affirming this world. But he thinks nihilism is at base a cultural and existential affliction that we should overcome, not something to be actively affirmed or radicalized by "higher men" (nihilism, sense 4). As for the political charge, that all opponents of traditional forms of political life who embrace the modern ideals of liberty, equality and fraternity, without recourse to God, must end by "believing in nothing" (nihilism, sense 2), Camus's rejection of just this claim is the target of his second, extended philosophical work, *The Rebel*.

As Camus states directly in a response to Roland Barthes on *The Plague*, the shift from Camus's works of the later 1930s up to around 1942 ("the absurds") to the cycle of works on revolt inaugurated by *La Peste* in 1947,[48] was a shift from solitary concerns to concerns with concrete political solidarity.[49] *The Plague* enjoyed an unlooked-for resurgence in the years 2020–2, as cities, provinces, and nations locked down to try to stop the spread of COVID-19. In Camus's novel, however, while the human vulnerability to natural evils like epidemics is part of his concern, the same response to Barthes stresses that the novel is also an allegory of the French resistance, and the European struggle between 1939 and 1945 against fascism (Sections 5.3–5.4). Camus himself had played a small role in the resistance, which he was never comfortable with people celebrating (Section 4.2). Camus's experience of lived solidarity between communists, socialists, Christians, and other Frenchmen of good will in the face of the Vichy regime and criminal occupation of the Nazis, left a profound impression upon him. It is no exaggeration to say that it reoriented Camus's work. After around 1943–4, he would look back increasingly critically at the individual focus of *The Myth of Sisyphus*, including the book's celebration of morally ambivalent figures like Don Juan as absurd heroes.[50]

Camus's understanding of "nihilism" would also develop in a notably social and political direction, in light of the European experience of the rise of fascist police states, in a way which arguably marks out his philosophical originality. A reader of Hermann Rauschning's 1939 work on Nazism, *The Revolution of Nihilism*, Camus saw in fascism not a source of spiritual renewal (as other intellectuals and artists like Martin Heidegger or Gottfried Benn did), but a nihilistic outgrowth of cultural despair and irrationalist philosophies of the kind he had critiqued in *The Myth of Sisyphus* (Section 5.3).[51] More than this, Camus made a move that is at most implied in earlier understandings of nihilism, notably that of Dostoevsky's *The Brother Karamazov*. Camus now proposed that what defined modern "nihilism" was not the interwar epidemics of suicide, including in Germany.[52] No, the mark of nihilism, like the mark of Cain, was murder: or rather, the ability of human beings to rationalize the killing of other human beings with scorn, indifference, contempt, or as a necessary means for achieving their own individual or collective goals:

> Europe is sick when to put to death a human being is conceived otherwise than with the horror and scandal which it should arouse, when the torture of men there is admitted as a service which is a little irksome (*ennuyeux*), comparable to resupplying an inventory or the obligation to form a queue in order to obtain a ration of butter.[53]

Human beings have been killing each other, out of malice and passion, since the biblical Cain—which is to say, as long as history has been recorded. Camus was not blind to this.[54] But murder, let alone mass murder, sadism, and torture, had been viewed with sacred and secular opprobrium before the advent of fascism and the Stalinist terror. In the later-modern age, people killed others whom they designated as "enemies" or even "subhuman" without shame, in the name of ostensibly secular ideologies. "It is not today as when Cain killed Abel," Camus reflects in "Time of Murderers" of 1949: "today ... Cain kills Abel in the name of logic and then claims the Legion of Honour."[55] Such indifference to human life amounts to a civilizational crisis. "Yes," Camus affirms, "there is a crisis of man when the death or torture of a [human] being can in our world be examined with a sentiment of indifference or of amiable curiosity ... or with simple impassivity."[56]

We have then come to the point where we can fully gauge the uniqueness of Camus's thinking with regard to the question of nihilism and understand his difference from the other famous existentialist heroes. *The Myth of Sisyphus* had raised the question as to whether, if we no longer accept traditional theological understandings of the meaning of life, the only honest, rationally consistent thing to do would be to take one's life. *The Rebel* opens with a different question. This question, Camus presents as no less existentially pressing, and no less tied to the times in which he lived—a time in which some 50 million people had been deliberately killed by other human beings, in the name of competing ideologies, between 1900 and 1950. It is the question of the justifiability of murder, and whether human beings have an unrelativizable dignity and value, at least for other human beings:

> In the age of negation, it was of some avail to examine one's position concerning suicide. In the age of ideologies, we must examine our position in relation to murder. If murder has rational foundations, then our period and we ourselves are rationally defensible. If it has no rational foundations, then we are insane and there is no alternative but to find some justification or to avert our faces. It is incumbent upon us ... to give a definite answer to the question implicit in the blood and strife of this century. For we are being interrogated.[57]

Nihilism, by the time of *The Rebel*, had evolved in Camus's thinking from an individual question, faced with the extra-human reality of the universe, to one which is inescapably social or political, concerning the lives and deaths of other human beings. For Camus, from now on, any position will show itself to be nihilistic if it claims a warrant to kill other human beings, even in large numbers, without shame or guilt. So, there is another reversal here, relative to the earlier conceptions of nihilism we examined in Section 2. Camus's position suggests that it is not necessarily the absence of any sense of the significance of the world that, by itself, is definitively nihilistic. Anomie may lead to suicide, and it may also lead to passive acquiescence in criminality and evil, by destroying strong reasons to oppose these sordid realities. By itself, however, anomie does not legitimize or motivate death pits and dedicated crematoria, like the kind that burns away by night to the East of Oran in *La Peste*, in a clear reference to the Shoah.[58] Echoing the great early moderns, Michel de Montaigne and Voltaire, Camus's postwar refiguring of nihilism suggests that the human capacity for genocide and dehumanization of others principally comes out of people's excessive sense of self-righteousness: their over-identifications with ideologies which rationalize killing others—whether dissidents, "elites," "illegals," or "displaced persons"—in the name of some higher cause or mission.[59] The ideological fanatic here, utterly certain of their own righteousness, is as nihilistic as the godless cynic who goes along with totalitarian atrocities, out of concern for nothing greater than their own "career," or for sadistic kicks. Moreover, on Camus's model, a position can be nihilistic, whether it takes its premises from revealed religions, from inspired philosophers, from the ideologies of the reactionary political Right, like Nazism, or those of the political Left, like Stalinism. Once a person has accepted that the only thing that matters is achieving the end nominated by their secular or transcendent ideology, then, logically, any means justifies such ends, and cynicism reigns in the practical sphere:

> people believe that nothing has any meaning, or else that historical success alone has one; because human values have been replaced by the values of contempt and efficiency, the will to be free replaced by the will to dominate. You are no longer right because you have justice on your side, but because you succeed. And the more you succeed, the more right you are. Ultimately, that justifies murder.[60]

At this point of the analysis, someone may protest that the mature Camus seems to have gone from a principled rejection of any "metaphysic of consolation," in *The Myth of Sisyphus*, to a kind of "morality of consolation" in *The Rebel*. Doesn't his position lead to a sympathetic and noble, but surely inefficacious and intellectually groundless "red cross morality" that opposes the hard realities of human history, which include the need for violence and killing foes?[61] Camus in his wartime journalism would repeat that, at some level, his own resistance to Nazism and the collaborationists in France came from a revolt born of "the heart": a sense of outraged, almost instinctual indignation at Nazi atrocities.[62] However, by the opening sections of *The Rebel*, Camus's opposition to rationalized, nihilistic murder is grounded, not on the basis of affect, but on the basis of the same quasi-Cartesian premises concerning the absurd which he had developed in 1942 (see Section 1.2). The thought of the absurd, Camus now reflects, represents "the equivalent on the plane of existence of methodical doubt" in Descartes's philosophy. It "wipes the slate clean" of untested, inherited beliefs.[63] *The Rebel* does not step back from Camus's earlier commitment to rebuild a normative position on the basis of the "rebellion" which aims to stay true to the absurd. It remains "absolutely necessary that rebellion finds its reasons within itself, since it cannot find them elsewhere":

> Deprived of all knowledge, incited [in the period of the two wars and total states] to murder or to consent to murder, all I have at my disposal is this single piece of evidence, which is only reaffirmed by the anguish I suffer. Rebellion is born of the spectacle of irrationality, confronted with an unjust and incomprehensible condition. But its blind impulse is to demand order in the midst of chaos, and unity in the very heart of the ephemeral. It protests, it demands, it insists that the outrage be ended, and that what has up to now been built upon shifting sands should henceforth be founded on rock.[64]

We know, from *The Myth of Sisyphus*, that for Camus recognizing the absurd does not license killing oneself, which "would mean the end of the encounter" between our desire for unity and the extra-human world which defines "absurdist reasoning." *The Rebel*'s "Introduction" reasons, therefore, that since to kill another human being is to end their awareness of our shared condition, it too cannot be licensed. As Camus asks:

> How is it possible, without making remarkable concessions to one's desire for comfort, to preserve exclusively for oneself the benefits of such a process of reasoning? From the moment that life is recognized as good, it becomes good for all men. Murder cannot be made coherent when suicide is not considered coherent …[65]

Part I of *The Rebel* thus ends by announcing a primary value which could point beyond nihilism, and toward a civilizational renaissance, after the age of nihilism and ideological *genocidaires*. It is the value of human solidarity: a "we are" which resists the most far-reaching skepticism about big picture theories of everything or of God (*The Myth of Sisyphus*), yet is sustained in living protest against the nihilistic devaluation of human life visited by totalitarian states upon millions of human beings (*The Rebel*):

> In our daily trials, rebellion plays the same role as does the *cogito* in the category of thought: it is the first clue … rebellion is the common ground on which man bases his first values. *I rebel—therefore we exist*.[66]

With Camus's arrival at this "first clue" to going beyond nihilism as he sees it, our work in the first chapter of *Why Camus Matters* is now complete. There is much more to say of this "common ground" and the first, post-nihilistic values which Camus claims to have philosophically recovered. This recovery stands at the heart of his ethical and political positions, and it underlies the drama of his post-1942 literary works. As we will see in the remainder of this book, Camus's attempt to think through and celebrate this commitment to a threatened human solidarity, without any transcendent guarantees, is also what makes his work, in all of its different registers, matter so much today.

2

Beyond Contempt: Camus, Post-Truth and Democracy

2.1 Post-Truth, Polarization and Hyper-Truth

It was 2016, the year when the UK voted to leave the European Union, and Mr. Trump made his first ascent to the US Presidency, that the OED announced "post-truth" word of the year. The UK "Leave" campaign had been fueled by mass disinformation concerning how much money the UK was paying to the European Union, and images of Middle Eastern immigrants trying to enter the green Isle—which turned out to have been images of immigrants trying to enter Europe, not the Brexiting nation. Trump's campaign had featured appeals to Russia to hack his opponent's email accounts, and to "lock her [Hilary Clinton, Trump's democratic opponent] up," as well as heated claims concerning nefarious "globalists," a "deep state," and a Washington "swamp" that the Leader was "the only one" who could "drain." Within months of Trump's election, a subindustry of commentary on "post-truth" or even a "post-truth era" emerged.[1] This was fueled in particular by the opening days of the Trump administration, when the world was asked, despite clear photographic evidence, to believe that Trump's inauguration was attended by more people than Mr. Obama's. It was a matter of "alternative facts."

The lies, exaggerations and motivated misrepresentations did not end after the week following January 20, 2017. The *Washington Post* would document over 30,000 such misrepresentations in Trump's first term,[2] culminating in the explosion of lurid conspiracy theories surrounding the COVID-19 pandemic ("Kong flu," Trump dubbed it, or "the China virus") of 2020–2. At the vanguard of this new cultural phenomenon arose the Q-Anon movement, whose followers ("bakers," they called themselves, of the "crumbs" of hidden truth being revealed by "Q," a supposed "deep state" insider) were convinced that the world was being run by a nefarious cabal of global elites, in league with the Democrats. These folk were operating a global child abuse ring to drain "adrenochrome" from minors, so they could stave off death and aging. The "good news" for the bakers was that these criminals would soon—the dates kept shifting backwards—be righteously exterminated by Trump in a "storm" of military tribunals and extrajudicial executions that haven't yet come.[3]

Viewed from almost all philosophical perspectives, the very idea of "post-truth" seems like a non-starter. A bit like "nihilism," interpreted literally. "Truth" in one sense names everything that is the case. So, unless we senselessly claim that everything stopped existing some time in 2016, we cannot have entered a "post-truth" scenario. If the claim is that politicians like Trump and the UKIP Party, or the tabloid newspapers which championed much of the anti-EU propaganda in 2016, have suddenly begun to lie with impunity, this looks pretty historically naïve. As Hannah Arendt examined in several important articles like "Truth and Politics," politicians and political operatives have always had a conditional commitment to telling the truth, the whole truth and nothing but the truth.[4] They have typically done so only as far as possible, when it accords with their other commitments, and their political desire to win consensus for their causes. The OED offers us the idea that "post-truth" involves a situation where people are moved more to believe things which appeal to their emotions, than to seek out the truth dispassionately.[5] But again, this hardly looks worth assigning a new historical or quasi-philosophical category to. Early modern philosophers like Francis Bacon and John Locke already astutely identified the forms of cognitive bias that have since been subjected to empirical corroboration by psychologists.[6] People tend to believe what they "like" and "share" with others whom they "like," unless they are checked by scientific protocols and ethical controls.

These warranted considerations do not mean that the term "post-truth" has no force. It is a marker of the disbelief many people globally felt about what seemed clear after November 2016. It was not simply that we had politicians inclined to bend the truth and hope they might get away with it, as we've had since Pericles was a lad. A newer breed of politician was on the make. This cohort is more or less indifferent not simply to the factual truth of particular claims they were asserting—"that was the biggest audience we've ever seen," "the UK is paying 350 million pounds a day to the EU." These "post-truth" figures would in no way walk back from these claims, even after they had been falsified, again and again. Instead, they would simply double down, attacking their critics as the truly dishonest "fake news," without any shame—cynically confident that, soon enough, any outrage would pass. The media circus would move on to the next controversy. It was a logic which the world would see writ largest in 2021, when Mr. Trump rallied a crowd of supporters who stormed the US Capitol to stop the ratification of electoral votes to install Joe Biden as President, on the basis of the claim that the Democrats had "stolen" the election through massive voter fraud.[7] This claim was quickly subjected to aggressive litigation by Trump and his supporters. It was found to lack factual validity in over sixty American courts. (In 2024, the maker of a leading documentary underlying the "Stop the Steal" movement, *Two thousand mules*, admitted to the fraudulence of many of his claims.)[8] Yet, "Stop the Steal" morphed between 2021 and 2024 into the basis of the re-election bid of Mr. Trump. In a move with dark historical echoes, the willingness to at least profess belief in this "Big Lie" was used by *Project 25* as a mark of identification to vet potential operatives in the second Trump administration.[9]

"Post-truth," it seems to us, is a potentially misleading, once-fashionable label for this new situation—new for our generation, but not for Albert Camus's—of politicians who no longer consent to play by the grounding epistemic rules of democratic societies. It is true that politicians within liberal democracies often lie. It is true that the "legacy media" often misreports things. On some subjects, it arguably does this systematically, due to biases baked by money and politics into editorial policies. By contrast, "post-truth" politicians know that many of their claims don't have factually defensible bases, and that if the factual bases of their claims and the interests and motivations behind them were known, they could never hope to succeed. What to do? At a "meta" level, they take aim at the mechanisms whereby citizens could adjudicate truth and falsity. The goal—which actually embodies a form of consummately cynical, strategic action, rather than a descent into unintelligibility—is this. The thing is to create a seeming equivalence between their knowingly dishonest or fraudulent positions, and those of anyone who would oppose them or try to hold them to reasoned, evidence-based account. Everyone is dishonest. So, our lies cannot be singled out for accountability (Section 5.4).

The post-truth politicians' antecedents here are the "agnotologists" in the tobacco lobbies. These were spin doctors who worked to create doubt about smoking's harms to human beings for as long as possible. They were funded by big tobacco, so the latter's "business models" did not collapse.[10] Then there is the climate change denial lobby, which uses the same strategies—like pointing to the way that the sciences, being fallibilistic, never operate with 100 percent consensus or certainty, and are always being updated—to manufacture doubt and dissensus around environmental issues. In other words, the post-truth politician "goes nuclear" epistemically. Knowing that they need to misrepresent things in order to manufacture consent to advance their interests, they claim:

1. everybody does it, so we are no worse than anyone else (*and what about all the lies others have told ... fake news ... "lamestream" media ... establishment ...?*)

2. There is no way to establish truth or falsity about anything, in any case, since everything is a matter of opinion, and the play of money and power;
3. Thus, we have as much right as anyone, it is "free speech," to insist on "our narrative," even when all of the available evidence speaks against its truth;
4. Indeed, (since you asked) at least we are not pretending hypocritically that we are different from anybody else, when it comes to the mendacity that makes the world go around.

Those of us who went through universities in the humanities in the heyday of postmodernism will recognize how uncannily this worldly wise cynicism, this "meta"-attack not only the truth and falsity of a particular issue, *but on the very ideas of establishable truth and falsity*, mirrors key claims of the left-liberal postmodernism ascendant in some parts of the university humanities the 1980s and 1990s (Section 3.2). These claims were based in appeals to supposedly "radical" theorists reviled by culture warriors to this day as "cultural Marxists," like Jean Baudrillard, Jacques Derrida, Michel Foucault, Gilles Deleuze, and Jean-François Lyotard. Of course, postmodernists and their well-meaning successors today will claim "but we never meant for Trump … Orban … Bannon … Putin … the Alt-Right." We might honor their *bonne foi* but shake our heads at their naivety. The premises of radical skepticism about truth—the epistemic fallacy that since we cannot know the world except through our ideas, that therefore the only thing anyone can know is their own, or their culture's, subgroups', or tribes' ideas about things—pulls the rug from beneath the *bonne foi*. Unlike Robin of Loxley, relativism does not rob only from the rich. It can equally serve those who have the shamelessness to "flood the zone with bullshit" and create confusion, as Right-wing activist Steve Bannon has named his nihilistic strategy. If there "can only be" a plurality of incommensurable, equally unverifiable perspectives, this flattens the space that authoritarians can occupy with naked self-assertion, backed by appeals to simple, divisive slogans like "lock her/him up!," "stop the steal!," or "smash the deep state!" That's "their narrative," and who are we to fault them?[11]

There are other, extra-political push factors behind commentators' Christening of "post-truth," *c.*2016. The first of these, which Camus could scarcely have imagined, is the ascendancy of privately-owned, now-globally-omnipresent, cross-border social media. Sites like Facebook, after the Arab Spring in 2010–12, were celebrated as vehicles of popular mobilization against authoritarian control. By 2016, it had become apparent that authoritarian governments, led by Putin's Russia, with the consent of the owners of these platforms, had worked out that they were means of surveillance like older generations of secret police could never have dreamed of. To boot, they are also means to spread politically motivated disinformation across international borders in ways Goebbels or Stalin could only have fantasized about.

The business model of these platforms, the world began to work out, was not simply about "making everything transparent" and fostering democratic discourse, as Mark Zuckerberg originally enthused. The platforms harvested data about our activities on their sites, which they then sold onward to third parties, to use for their own profit-making (through targeted advertising) or political purposes (through target political advertising and propaganda).[12] More than this, the way that people's "feeds" work—that is, what information is fed to their interface with the platforms—are governed by non-transparent "algorithms" owned by the big tech companies. However else these algorithms work, it is clear that they are intended to keep people on the sites, clicking on advertisements, for as long as possible. For this is what moves the bottom line, which is about making money. It moreover became clear that the social media companies had worked out, with unabashed cynicism, that the best way to keep people on their platforms, in a suggestible state, is to provoke "activating emotions" in them. The best emotions of this kind are lust, fear, and outrage.[13] These are hardly the kinds of affects we might want people to be experiencing when being asked, democratically, to make informed decisions about matters of shared concern which impact many others, let alone future generations.

On the supply side, as the economists say, this means that "content creators" on sites like YouTube, X, or "Insta" are incentivized to create whatever stories they anticipate will "get most clicks" and "shares." Like the post-truth politicians, who have moreover become adept at broadcasting their own messages on "socials," these incentives operate wholly independently of whether their "content" has been fact checked. It does not matter whether it deftly mixes some modicum of plausibility with outsized dosages of bias-confirming speculation, misinformation, and emotive spin. The whole social media space has become a bonfire of the loudest, most sensational or aesthetically pleasing voices, buzzwords, in-group chatter, "influencers," and "narratives," many of which are openly "monetized."

On the demand side, each of us, when we go onto these sites, gets information and articles "liked" and "shared" by people we have voluntarily "friended," or "followed," because their views have been assessed by the algorithms to broadly accord with ours. Algorithms also select the kinds of things which might outrage or titillate us independently of our existing friends, and select new "content creators" to "follow." We "like" and "share" the content on. In these ways, online "filter bubbles" have been created. These encircle and fortify online tribal subcommunities. It is a matter of increasingly polarized subgroups within democratic societies, sometimes (tragically) cutting across the same families and local communities.[14] To the growing extent that people have abandoned direct consumption of "legacy media"—which has faced decades of impugning from the Right for "liberal bias" and is now formulaically assumed by large populations to be "fake news"—their beliefs about anything beyond the scope of their personal experience is mediated by algorithmically pre-vetted, increasingly partisan information.[15]

Accordingly, the other side to supposed "post-truth"—and another reason to keep our wits about us about that fashionable term—is a kind of "hyper-truth" which characterizes our online age. This is the world of hyper-partisanship online, with its competing communities of information, each wholly convinced of the exclusive truth and rightness of their vision of things—even when that vision is purchased at the price of the most radical skepticism about established experts' views, or ideas that the other side is almost or actually demonically evil. To be clear, it is certain that American, British, Chinese, Russian, and sundry disinformation producers, and programmed bots—as well as Machiavellian operators like Steve Bannon or Putin's GRU—knowingly promote lies and misinformation without shame. We know from the directives of Newt Gingrich in the 1990s ("Language, an instrument of control") to fellow US Republicans that the use of divisive names like "treasonous," "sick," "corrupt," "dangerous," "pathetic," "radical," for their opponents has been part of the avowed rhetorical strategy, to try to rule by dividing audiences and rhetorically humiliating foes.[16] However, the flipside of these "post-truth" producers are millions of "true believers," post-truth consumers and "sharers." These people are less cynical than duped. In good faith, they have been "red pilled" or radicalized online over the last decade by the firehoses of outrage-stoking misinformation that have been spurted by post-truth producers, notably during COVID-19. Such post-truth consumers distrust mainstream media and established authorities. They instead believe conspiracy theories hailing from "alternative media" about the "deep state," "big pharma," "establishment medicine," globalist "elites," nefarious pedophile rings, the World Health Organization, Bill Gates, the UN, Jewish financiers like George Soros, and so on. Many readers of this book, I presume, will find such theories wildly implausible. They are often moreover mutually contradictory and fast-evolving in response to changing events (COVID-19 was a hoax, real but a plot, the vaccines are implanting microchips, causing heart failures …) Our derision does not detract from the deep conviction with which millions *do* believe in these theories.[17] The point is that such true believers are surely not "post-truth," even if they are largely mistaken in what they firmly believe to be true—and although we need to worry that "he who can make you believe absurdities can make you commit atrocities," as Voltaire warned. Whilst they distrust traditional authorities, including scientific and medical experts, they are remarkably uncritical concerning the truth of claims of their own trusted politicians, culture warriors, online personalities, influencers, and even (in the United States) self-professing "MAGA prophets." They each moreover think of themselves as brave, post-enlightenment truth-seekers who "do their own research" to unearth hidden realities. Their online in-group language, saturated with polemical buzzwords to denigrate nonbelievers and foes, *en bloc*, like "SJWs," "soyboys," "libtards," "snowflakes," "lamestream," "normies," expresses not an inability to believe in anything or adjudicate what they think is true and false. It bespeaks an increasingly strident certainty about the dark "hyper-truth" they are "in" on, which is being concealed by "the establishment," and which licenses the pointiest reckoning for the evil ones.

2.2 Nihilism, Contempt, and Polemic

What would Camus think of our social-mediatic, "post-truth" world? What would he say about this uncanny *coincidentia oppositorum* (coincidence of opposites) we now face: of hypercynical, post-truth politicians, influencers, and "political entrepreneurs" (yes, that is a term) and millions of post-truth consumers, increasingly radicalized by conspiratorial hyper-truth narratives which claim that all established institutions are "rigged," so that nothing short of a complete overthrow of liberal democracy will suffice to "drain the swamp"? What would Camus think about the increased polarization that has emerged since the 1990s, as our public discourse is increasingly crowded out by heated "wars of words" on cultural issues concerning identity, race, gender, immigration, and sexuality, whilst our economies become increasingly inegalitarian (see Chapter 3), and the most basic democratic institutions and norms are compromised by rising authoritarianism?

Camus denied that he had any prophetic abilities. But we know (see introduction) that Camus was a journalist from his early adult years in Algeria and was deeply interested in the freedom of the press, and the role that it plays in functioning democratic societies. He would continue to write as a journalist—what he called "one of the most beautiful professions that I know"[18]—until his untimely death. Moreover, after 1942, his literary fiction would increasingly pay attention to what we might term characteristic "deformations in communication" which he saw in his world of democratic crisis, the rise of authoritarian regimes, and descent into global instability, war, and genocide. The final, least-known work of his first "absurd" cycle, entitled *The Misunderstanding* (first staged in 1944) is all about what happens when people accede to lies, half-truths, and misinformation.[19] Its anti-heroines are two hoteliers who, like the ancient Sisyphus, have taken to abusing the norms of hospitality, murdering their guests to steal their wealth. One fine day, unbeknownst to them, the mother's long-lost son, who has learned of their whereabouts, returns like a prodigal son to re-establish connection with his *maman* and sister. In order to add to the savor of the reunion, he however fatally decides that he will not initially disclose his true identity. He wants to strike up a connection with his family members under false pretences, to see what they are truly like. Just as he prepares for the final "reveal," and the joyous reunion, his mother and sister murder him, assessing the (for them) stranger as an easy target. Soon afterward, the man's wife Maria arrives and reveals the truth.

The whole play stands somewhere between tragedy and farse. It highlights the practical human costs of people deceiving others, even for relatively benign motivations. As we will examine in detail in Chapter 5, arguably Camus's greatest and certainly his darkest novel, *The Fall*, is about a man who calls himself a "judge-penitent." Jean-Baptiste Clamence, as he is named, cynically claims for himself the right to mislead others. For he has recognized the hard truth that no one is perfect, and that everybody lies. A post-truth operative *avant la lettre* (before times), he reasons that at least *he* is bitterly honest about the reality of the world, and thereby superior to others (Section 5.4).

It is true that Camus, as we commented in Section 2.1, could not have anticipated anything like social media. But the kinds of deformations of communication we are experiencing in the "post-truth" era were hardly unknown in Camus's time. We saw in Chapter 1 that Camus post-1944 diagnosed his time as a period of nihilism, in which competing ideologies justified the harming, killing and disappearing of large numbers of human beings with complete indifference or a sense of world-historical righteousness. In his 1946 US address, "The Crisis of Man," Camus attempts to identify in more detail the symptoms of this nihilistic condition, in which Gestapo operatives could take lunch and make light conversation with inmates between episodes of brutally torturing them, or ask prisoners to make "Sophie's choices" as to which of their children should be executed first.[20] The first symptom is the use of terror as a political weapon, "following a perversion of values such that a man or a historical force is no longer judged in terms of their dignity, but in terms of their success."[21] Terror often works, at least for a time. The uncertainty created by lawless authoritarian governments, and rolling crises, created a climate of "fear and anguish" in Europe which mitigates against "the spirit of freedom" and democratic culture.[22]

Especially notable for us here, though, is that two of the four other symptoms of Western crisis Camus nominates—alongside the also-today-very-familiar politicization of everything—concern the use of language. The second sign of the civilizational crisis is the impossibility of persuasion and a common language between people, bridging political divides:

Men live and are able to live only with the idea that they have something in common, where they can always meet. You always believe that by addressing a man as a human being, you can get human reactions from him. But we have discovered this: there are men you cannot persuade.[23]

Camus is talking of convinced Nazis, willing to torture and kill inmates in camps. Yet, it is as if Camus had taken a peak through a looking-glass into the social-mediatic world of the 2020s. For the "keyboard warriors" of the culture wars and the filter-bubble-enclosed online enclaves show what Camus's generations learned in war: that once political polarization has proceeded to a certain point, it becomes impossible to find common grounds.[24] Some passages in Camus on this phenomenon, as of 1946, seem almost uncannily prescient, as of 2024–5:

> across most of the world, dialogue is today replaced by polemic. The twentieth century is the century of polemic and insult. Between nations and individuals, and even at the level of formerly disinterested disciplines, polemic holds the place which was traditionally held by considered dialogue. Day and night thousands of voices, each pursuing from its own corner a noisy monologue, unleash on people a torrent of mystifying words, attacks, defences, passions. But what is the mechanism of polemic? It consists in viewing the opponent as an enemy, consequently simplifying him and refusing to see him. When I insult a person, I no longer know the colour of his gaze … Grown three-quarters blind thanks to polemic, we no longer live among men but in a world of silhouettes.[25]

And in this world of culture warring silhouettes, the best justification for the cynical post-truth operator is "whataboutism," with its creating of an equivalence in universal mendacity. It is a matter of what Camus in the years at the start of the Cold War called a "casuistry of blood." The world of polemic and insult, whether online or mediated via the more traditional means of Camus's day, enshrines a "cynical," "infernal dialectic" wherein each side excuses its excesses by pointing to the other side's wrongs. Camus reflected in "Bread and Freedom" of 1953:

> The person pointing to the colonial slave and calling for justice is shown the Russian camp victim, and vice versa … if you protest against the murder in Prague of an opposition historian like Kalandra, two or three American Negroes are thrown in your face. In this disgusting bidding contest, just one thing never changes: the victim, always the same. Just one value is constantly violated or prostituted—freedom—and it then becomes clear that everywhere, along with it, justice too is debased.[26]

The third symptom of the crisis of human beings Camus identified in 1946 was the proliferation of formalized, bureaucratic language and accompanying red tape. This is predicated on the collapse of social trust, and the felt need therefore to monitor, record and account for everything:

> More and more, contemporary man interposes between nature and himself an abstract and complicated machine which thrusts him into solitude. It is when there is no bread left that coupons appear. The French get only 1200 calories of food per day, but they have at least six different documents and a hundred stamps on those documents. And it is the same everywhere in the world, where bureaucracy has continued to proliferate.[27]

Anyone who has worked in a corporation, or even a corporate university, is familiar with the omniscience of what one wit has called "business bullshit" today. So, Camus's claim here will not seem from a foreign world. We mean the pseudo-sophisticated language of "in this space," "moving the needle," "future-orientation," "brilliant," "KPIs," "hubs," "learnings," "leadership groups," and an ever-changing cast of buzzwords, whose use marks speakers off as members or aspirants to the professional-managerial elite.[28] Everyone who has listened to neoliberal, technocratic politicians, or had any more or less extensive dealings with one or other government office or corporate PR team, is familiar with their similar, lifeless, managerial "weasel words." The distance from ordinary communication of such bureaucratese inescapably creates the suspicion that anyone who needs to talk like that must be hiding things. This justified suspicion partly explains why so many people today have been seduced by the promise of "straight-talking" "populists" who claim to speak for "the people," even as their discourse devolves into three-word slogans and bullying name-calling ("wicked," "crooked," "lying," "low energy," etc.) Anything, these people feel, and so falsely infer, is better than corporatese, even open and "honest" abuse of our fellow citizens.

Wherever there is an asymmetrical concentration of power, Camus observed, you will find such deformations of language. It shields leaders from accountability and maximizes their "agility" in decision-making by icing comprehension and, thereby, criticism. Alongside George Orwell in the twentieth century, Camus was one of its most astute, acerbic analysts. In his play *The State of Emergency/Siege* of 1948, for instance, we witness the takeover of the Spanish town, Cadiz (much loved by Camus) by a fascist dictator who identifies himself simply as "The Plague." He is accompanied by a character, "Death," and a Machiavellian assistant named "Nada" (i.e. nothing or nothingness). There is nothing very glamorous about the New Leader, who advises the population that he is a kind of bureaucrat: "when I say I rule ... I rule in a rather special way. It would be more correct to say that I function."[29] In the new Cadiz of this embodied pandemic, every part of subjects' lives and deaths is functionally "administered." When someone is to be eliminated at the Leaders' whim, this is achieved by striking their name off an administrative list. The language of this new regime is a jargon utterly incomprehensible, or vexing, to ordinary citizens, as one member of the "leadership group" frankly explains: "It's intended to get them used to the touch of obscurity which gives all government regulations their peculiar charm and efficacy. The less these people understand, the better they'll behave."[30]

In the light of these signs of crisis (terror, polemic, bureaucratism, and the politicization of everything), and underlying them all, Camus in 1946 finally nominates another cultural phenomenon that hardly sounds outdated in 2025: "the worship of … efficiency."[31] Efficiency is a relative, morally neutral, value. It's about the ability to achieve any goal whatsoever, as fast and with as few resources as possible: whether running a business, a sporting club, a disinformation op, or a death camp. Efficiency is thus, Camus saw, the one agreed value that can and has survived the collapse of all other traditional and religious values. Yet, efficiency sanctifies force or deceit, wherever force or deceit will most effectively achieve whatever goals we have agreed to pursue. On the other hand, appeal to "efficiency" by itself cannot sanction criticism of even the most hateful crimes and injustices, if they have been quickly achieved and proven themselves successful. The "realist" hence becomes a fatalist, and his wisdom defaults into cynicism:

> And that is so true that even today plenty of intelligent, skeptical people will tell you that if by chance Hitler had won this war, History would have paid homage to him and consecrated the dreadful pedestal upon which he had perched. And we indeed cannot doubt that History such as we conceive it would have consecrated Mr. Hitler and justified terror and murder, just as we all consecrate and justify them as soon as we venture to think that nothing has any meaning.[32]

Camus would hence call his period, not one of "post-truth," but a time wherein "human values have been replaced by the values of contempt and efficiency … You are no longer right because you have justice on your side, but because you succeed. And the more you succeed, the more right you are."[33] Camus would have concurred with historian Timothy Synder's assessment that "post-truth" is pre-fascism for the digital age.[34]

2.3 From Rebellion, via Solidarity, to Dialogue

Camus's credentials are therefore clear, as a diagnostician of the kinds of "communication breakdowns" that today trouble nations like Australia, the UK, or the USA, let alone in the authoritarian states like Mr. Putin's Russia. What makes his work on this subject matter especially telling—beyond the power of his writing—is the way that Camus's position is based upon the philosophical premises which we unfolded in Chapter 1. These premises saw Camus move from the most radical skepticism about claims to Absolute Truth, to a position he characterized as that of "rebellion." From the beginning, we saw that Camus is not a radical skeptic about smaller "t" truths available to the human understanding. And he is always deeply opposed to all forms of deceit, even self-deceit. The "leap" of the philosophical suicide, whether absolute rationalist or irrationalist, involves falsely taking as true a perspective that cannot be verified by what our understanding can certify. Rebelling against the "nostalgia" for closure underlying such leaps, Camus maintains, involves a kind of epistemic "decency" or "lucidity." It involves maintaining only what we can know, without any self-deceit about the limits of our powers.

Camus's position here, as he will at different times insist (Sections 6.1 and 6.3), reflects his admiration for classical Greek thought. The Greek philosophers, following Socrates, had supposed that practical wisdom, to live a good life, involved both self-knowledge and the most clear-sighted opinions about others and the world. The best authority on medical matters is not an internet celebrity psychologist or politician, but a trained physician. The best authority on captaining a ship will be someone with the relevant training and tested opinions, and so on. The person who has good intentions, to act courageously or justly, but is ill-informed about what has occurred, will not choose and act wisely. As Dr. Rieux reflects in Camus's *The Plague*, as if he were an ancient Socratic philosopher:

> The evil that is in the world always comes of ignorance, and good intentions may do as much harm as malevolence, if they lack understanding. On the whole, men are more good than bad; that, however, isn't the real point. They are more or less ignorant, and it is this that we call vice or virtue; the most incorrigible vice being that of an ignorance that fancies it knows everything and therefore claims for itself the right to kill. The soul of the murderer is blind; and there can be no true goodness nor true love without the utmost clear-sightedness.[35]

In Camus's second philosophical work, *The Rebel*, we saw that Camus's conception of rebellion, in face of the absurd, was transformed from an individual, toward a more social and political conception of revolt (Section 1.4). Camus claims that the inability of reason to license suicide, even if we admit the irrationalist premise that the world has no knowable global meaning, cannot be "privatized," as it were. If it is illegitimate to kill oneself, it is illegitimate to murder others. The rebel faced with the absurd hence discovers, from out of their own confrontation with the temptation to nihilism and despair, a shared condition with others:

> the first progressive step for a mind overwhelmed by the strangeness of things is to realize that this feeling of strangeness is shared with all men and that human reality, in its entirety, suffers from the distance which separates it from the rest of the universe. The malady experienced by a single man becomes a mass plague (*peste*).[36]

The rebel, Camus elaborates, is not simply someone who says "no" to some perceived injustice, or to the seeming senselessness of their own lives. She is also someone whose "negation" of what oppresses them—whether a boss, a colleague, a government policy, a broken economic system, or a God who seems indifferent or absent—*presupposes* a prior "yes." "Not every value leads to rebellion," Camus writes, "but every rebellion tacitly involves a value."[37] Far from being animated by resentment alone, as Scheler and Nietzsche contend of "slave revolt," it involves a passionate form of affirmation, underlying the negation of something found intolerable. Even if it is only a felt indignation which animates the rebel to protest some measure she might have tolerated previously, this indignation will reflect the sense that some limit has been breached—even if the rebel can't yet give words to that limit, that value, that sense of inviolable dignity. Indeed, Camus claims, the "yes" of the rebel, unless it is just an instance of personal complaint, always involves "something inside him that does not belong to him alone."[38] The dignity that she feels has been breached in her case, is a dignity which is shared by others. Indeed, in many cases, people will only rebel when they see that the ignominies that they have suffered are being visited upon others for whom they care. What is involved in rebellion, Camus claims, is "a perpetual demand for unity," a "desire for the true life," or what he will in 1956 calls a human *royaume* or kingdom, a communion or a homeland.[39]

For Camus, the "I rebel, therefore we are" which he claims to have uncovered through reflection on the absurd, and then on revolt, hence become the philosophical basis for affirming a universal human solidarity—without recourse either to eternal religious, or formal rational values that many people cannot be expected to affirm. He writes:

> Man's solidarity is founded upon rebellion, and rebellion, in its turn, can only find its justification in this solidarity. We have, then, the right to say that any rebellion which claims the right to deny or destroy this solidarity loses simultaneously its right to be called rebellion ... [T]his solidarity, except in so far as religion is concerned, comes to life only on the level of rebellion. And so, the real drama of revolutionary thought is announced. In order to exist, man must rebel, but rebellion must respect the limit it discovers in itself—a limit where minds meet and, in meeting, begin to exist.[40]

What has this to do with our considerations here surrounding post-truth, and the unfolding collapse, as it seems, of the post-war liberal democracies in Europe, the United States and elsewhere? If this community of human beings is the first value of Camus's philosophy, it becomes the basis for a principled defense of pluralistic political democracy. Just as the absurd man, to be faithful to what he has uncovered, must not deny either the human longing for unity, or the extra-human dimensions of the world (Section 1.4), so the rebel should oppose every force which would violate the post-metaphysical solidarity with others: "uncompromising and limited action springing from rebellion upholds the reality [it has discovered, that of inalienable human dignity] and only tries to extend it farther and farther."[41] At issue are a set of limits which ought to be inviolable, preventing murder, but also slavery and *deceit*:

> Every rebel, solely by the movement that sets him in opposition to the oppressor, therefore pleads for life, undertakes to struggle against servitude, falsehood, and terror, and affirms, in a flash, that these three afflictions are the cause of silence between men, that they obscure them from one another and prevent them from rediscovering themselves in the only value that can save them from nihilism—the long complicity of men at grips with their destiny.[42]

Camus's post-war work hence proposes that a universal proscription of capital punishment, the death penalty, ought to be the first statute in any post-war, post-Auschwitz international order. "Capital punishment upsets the only indisputable human solidarity—our solidarity against death," Camus explains: "it kills the small part of existence that can be realized on this earth through the mutual understanding of men."[43] Camus makes his case for this position at greatest length in his 1957 "Reflections on the Guillotine."[44] Only theological values, or certainty about the Meaning of History or the Immortality of the Soul, could justify murder, Camus argues. By contrast, Camus writes, echoing earlier modern arguments by figures such as Pierre Bayle and Voltaire in favor of religious toleration, "he who does not know everything cannot kill anyone ," while claiming a justice to the action.[45] Likewise, we should reject political regimes which license political murder of opponents, like the fascist regimes of interwar Europe or the Stalinism of the Great Terror, and today, the dictatorship of a Putin (ch. 4–5). Instead, democratic pluralism is recommended, as the only political regime consistent with the kind of epistemic modesty, respectful of human limitations, upon which Camus's philosophy is based:

> The men who do not have the absolute Truth do not wish to kill anyone and they ask that others do not kill them. They ask only to search for the truth and as a consequence they have need of a certain number of historical preconditions which permit them this search.[46]

It is appeal to the same primary value of human solidarity that, for Camus, speaks against the "realism" which would accept the right to lie to our fellows—for the sake of whatever cause, "since everybody does it … that is the way of the world … everyone has their own narrative … their own truth."

The person who conceives culture as war assumes the right to lie, to advance their partisan cause. By contrast, Camus argues against principled deceit. By concealing or misrepresenting information that could assist others in making up their own minds intelligently and exercising their dignity, "the man who lies shuts himself off from other men."[47] "Lies, even well-intentioned lies, separate men from one another and relegate them to the most futile solitude."[48] Today, we know that systematic disinformation, promoted by cynical politicians and then spread in enclosed communities online, shuts off entire populations from their fellows. Some "free speech" advocates like billionaire platform owner Elon Musk argue for absolute freedom to speech, including the right to spread whatever lies or misinformation a person feels motivated to share. Whether for fame, money or fanaticism, or simply to cause mayhem and harvest "LULZ" (cynical laughs). "The freedom we must win," Camus by contrast asserts, "is the right not to lie"[49]:

> In order to emerge from solitude and abstraction, it is necessary to talk. But it is necessary to be frank, and on every occasion to speak all the truth one knows. But one can speak the truth only in a world where this is defined and based on values common to all men … And it is necessary to rediscover the values which sustain that [common] conscience, destroyed today by terror. This means that, outside political parties, we all have to create communities of reflection which will initiate dialogue, across frontiers; and which will assert … that this world must cease being one of policemen, soldiers and money to become one of men and women, productive work and considered leisure.[50]

The twentieth century had become a century of monologues, of rival ideological warriors so certain of the Rightness of their Causes that they assumed the license to kill, cheat, lie and betray. By contrast, Camus argued, if we are to move beyond such a world of polemic, insult, and contempt, what we need to foster is a "civilization of dialogue," "a community of reflection which will initiate dialogue," "the free exchange of dialogue."[51] "Socrates was right," Camus comes to affirm, contra Nietzsche, after 1945: "there is no man without dialogue. And it seems that, for Europe and the world, the moment has come to bring the forces of dialogue together against the ideologies of power."[52]

2.4 Why Camus Matters, Beyond "Post-Truth"

The troubling reality about the advent of the phenomena associated with "post-truth" is that the ability of people to speak truth to power, and the ability of a public to hold their leaders to account by recourse to established, agreed norms and facts, is basic to a political democracy. Once all public faith breaks down in the ability of the media, academia, and the judiciary to honestly seek out the truth and hold leaders' proverbial feet to the fire, then democracies must falter and fail. We have seen so far in this chapter that Camus matters in this period of "post-truth," for at least two reasons. Firstly, he identified symptoms of the same anti-democratic malaise in the public culture of his own time, the immediate post-war years in France and Europe (Section 2.2). Secondly, Camus's criticism of the normalization of "polemic and insult" is grounded in a unique philosophy of rebellion, which draws from his work on the absurd, and which effectively proposes a new ground for political democracy: the solidarity of human beings, circumscribed by prohibitions against terror and political murder; against all forms of enslavement—hardly an idle consideration in the years after the Nazi camps and Soviet gulag; and finally, against all forms of premeditated deceit, no matter how many "clicks" it might attract (Section 2.3).

There is a third reason why Camus is such a unique voice in our "post-truth" discussions, amongst the philosophers of the last century. This is his feet-on-the-ground experience as a journalist, from his earliest years in Algeria onward, when Camus distinguished himself by a series of dispassionate, almost ethnographic articles on the sufferings of the people of the Kabylia highlands.[53] Camus's commitment to the descriptive, versus the explanatory, powers of human intelligence informed not simply his theoretical reflections. They also informed his understanding of his role as a journalist, as well as the style for instance of the great 1947 novel, *The Plague*. Doctor Rieux, the narrator, explains the manner of his chronicle of the yearlong lockdown of Oran, once bubonic plague had manifested itself in the dying of rats in the streets and under the stairwells:

> To some, these events will seem quite natural; to others, all but incredible. But obviously, a narrator cannot take account of these differences of outlook. His business is only to say: "This is what happened," when he knows that

it actually did happen, that it closely affected the life of a whole populace ... The present narrator has three kinds of data: first, what he saw himself; secondly, the accounts of others ... and, lastly, documents that subsequently came into his hands. He proposes to draw on these records whenever this seems desirable, and to employ them as he thinks best.[54]

Camus's reflections on the function of fact-seeking journalism in a healthy democracy are concentrated in the heated period between the end of 1944, with the liberation of Paris, and mid-1945. In this period, Camus, writing as editor and columnist in the resistance newspaper, *Combat*, is animated by the hope that a revolution could take place, renewing French democracy after the shame of the Nazi occupation. He feels the responsibility, in this moment, to prescribe directives for a new press in France, that would not fall prey to the shortcomings of its pre-war and Vichy predecessors. These directives can also speak to us today, as we face the formidable questions surrounding how public culture, and basic faith in democratic institutions, could be restored in this new age of looming authoritarianism.

The function of the journalist is to inform the public. They are a kind of historian of the present, Camus maintains. As such, no journalist can truck knowingly in deceit: "truth must be his primary concern."[55] But finding truth in passing events is "elusive." Hence, anyone writing to inform the public should accept an ethical code, aiming at "objectivity and prudence," and at the same time, be scrupulously aware of their own limitations.[56] The problem, which was already reemerging in the months after the liberation, is that the press instead was seeking more to move copy by spying out exciting "scoops." The commercial argument, then as now, was that sensational articles laced with clichéd expressions, aiming to titillate readers, are "giving the people what they want"—rather than contributing to creating forms of manufactured pseudo-consensus and an ill-informed, if entertained population. Camus proposes that such "simple-minded," emotive journalism is underlain, in truth, by a kind of condescending contempt for the ability of readers to reflect critically, as democratic citizens. It licenses "mediocrity and fabrications," and harms democracy.[57]

In an extended piece on "Critical Journalism," Camus argues that, alongside factual reportage, papers should include articles in which journalists inform the public as to the context of the events reported on. They should also examine the limitations of their sources (including contradictory testimony) and assess the likelihood that each piece of information used is true, wholly or in part. It is journalist's job, Camus argues, since they are better informed than their publics, to "indicate the extent to which news is based on sources which he finds dubious."[58] They should moreover inform the public as to the mechanisms whereby news is sourced and reported, "awakening their critical faculties rather than appealing to their baser instincts."[59] A serious and sober tone should be adopted, not without the irony which comes from accepting the informational challenges of the task, and human fallibility. False and dubious reporting, Camus claims, should not be presented as news, but clearly marked off from it.[60] Language should be "clear" and "virile." Terms should be defined, so misunderstandings do not compound:

> All thought, all definition which risks adding to the deceptions or entertaining them is unpardonable. It is enough to say that in defining a certain number of keywords [for instance, "democracy"], in rendering them sufficiently clear today so that they will tomorrow be effective, we are working towards liberation.[61]

Every effort should be made to avoid the language of "hatred," with its typecast terms for perceived enemies. Camus for instance in "Dialogue and Vocabulary" chastises a communist critic who accused him of being a "fascist" in such a way as to contribute to rendering that term effectively meaningless, and make dialogue between the men impossible for want of a *lingua franca*.[62]

The temptation to indulge in hatred and dehumanization of the other, Camus claims:

> is what we first need to conquer. We must heal those poisoned hearts. And tomorrow, the hardest victory we have to achieve over the enemy must be won within ourselves, through the exceptional effort that will transform our appetite for hatred into the desire for justice. Not yielding to hatred, conceding nothing to violence, not permitting our passions to become blind—this is what we can still do for friendship and against Hitlerism.[63]

It would be hard to overstate the distance between Camus's prescriptions for responsible journalism, therefore, and today's world of social media "influencers" and YouTube "thought leaders." There are very real financial pressures that have contributed to the decline of "legacy media" in the age of the internet—such as the need to compete with independent media, diminishing revenue pushing cuts to staff and capacities, and the need to bid for "clicks" to please online advertisers. Camus was not blind to the material preconditions of anything like a responsible, democratic free press—as against a sensationalized, monetized media environment. In his 1944–5 articles on truth in journalism, Camus stresses that the precondition for anything like the press reforms he hopes for is the need, through political reforms, to liberate the press from "the power of money," so that it attains "real independence from the power of capital."[64] For Camus, the fight against Hitler had also been the fight against the power of money. It had not ended with the fall of the Vichy regime.[65] Where "money is King," Camus writes,[66] and where press barons can readily outcompete and buy out smaller outlets without restraints, we can expect sensationalism and "giving the people what they want"—or what an empowered few "with fear in their hearts and money in the bank" suppose they should want—to crowd out and shout down more responsible, critical and investigative journalism, to the detriment of informed public debate and decision-making.[67]

For his part, and in his time, we can see Camus beginning to despair as early as March 1945 of the prospects of a robustly independent media, not shackled to big money in postwar France. We have only continued to see the phenomena he feared in the age of tabloids and culture warring mast heads, then the advent of social media algorithms and their billionaire owners.

3

Beyond Political Romanticism: Camus and the *Avant Gardes*

3.1 Commodified Dissent: How Revolt Became the Norm

Albert Camus's longest political and philosophical work was his book on rebellion, or man in revolt.[1] Camus correctly saw how central rebellion against inherited forms of authority has been to the modern Western experience: from 1789 to 1917, via 1848—and we might today add 1989–91, with the end of the Soviet Eastern bloc. So, perhaps Camus would not have been surprised that the decade of the 1960s at whose beginning he tragically died is lauded or lamented as one more period of cultural and political rebellion: from the student rebellions in the United States to May 1968 in France and across Europe. Nor might he have been wholly surprised at the aestheticist dimensions and directions of the sixties counterculture, as we'll see. But one thing Camus might well not have been able to anticipate was the strange ways in which counter-cultural revolt of the 1960s, with its rock music, its exploration of alternative lifestyles, its challenges to bourgeois mediocrity (and mundanity), its celebrations of the different, the exceptional, and the transgressive would be so readily accommodated by liberal-capitalist societies—"the Man" that both its progenitors, and its severest reactionary critics, took this revolt to be upsetting. To read Camus as a philosopher of rebellion today is hence to have to start with the paradox of the normalization of the counterculture. In more recent liberal capitalist societies, rebellion has become commodified in the markets and almost obligatory in some corners of academia, rather than representing the dangerous threat that Camus saw culminating in the gulags or the Nazi death camps. So, we'll start this chapter by looking at the commodification of dissent in capitalist marketing and managerial discourses in the decades following 1960, before looking in the next section at the rebellious paradoxes surrounding what is usually reviled or embraced as "radical theory."

At the time of Camus's death in January 1960, in the United States, maverick marketing agency Doyle, Daniel, & Berbank (DDB) was undertaking its own counter-cultural revolution at the very heart of liberal capitalism, within the advertising industry. 1950s advertising in nations like the United States or Australia had been largely conformist, aiming at White middle class suburban families. Ads pitched products based on the staid authority of good science; men in white coats informing audiences of the virtues of the products. They played, unironically, and in a way which today seems quaint, to the desire to fit in and get ahead in the thriving suburban world of the post-war recovery. Into this world, as Thomas Frank has examined in his invaluable work, *The Conquest of Cool*, came DDB's revolutionary advertisements for the humble Volkswagen Beetle. Instead of extolling the car's real and affordable virtues, the ads adopted a highly ironical stance toward "the bug." The VWs, it confessed disarmingly, were "ugly," "monsters," and "shoeboxes." With a winking intimacy with the audience—who all clearly knew how other advertisements lie—one DDB advert confided to their prospective buyers about an experimental model that was "something awful. Take our word for it."[2] In other adverts, DDB went further, directly mocking the ideal of 1950s suburban conformism of look-alike houses, with their picket fences and well-kept lawns. Instead, it tried to sell the Beetles, precisely as being *different* from this world. So, buying one would be a social statement and affirmation of individuality and authenticity. "If the world looked like this [white picket fences, etc.], and you wanted to buy a car that sticks out a little, you probably wouldn't buy a Volkswagen," the ad copy addressed its viewers: "But in case you haven't noticed, the world doesn't look like this. So, if you wanted to buy a car that sticks out a little, you know just what to do."[3]

The significance of this campaign, in which sophisticated irony, knowing mockery of lifeless conformism, and the pitching of products to consumers as potential tokens of their authentic identities and rebellion against the mainstream, can hardly be overstated. In one of the many enthusiastic works by the new admen (or "madmen") who emerged in DDB's wake, Jerry Delia Femina's 1969 *From Those Wonderful Folks Who Gave You Pearl Harbor*, the author waxes biblical about the VW campaign:

> In the beginning, there was Volkswagen. That's the first campaign which everyone can trace back and say: 'This is where the changeover began.' That was the day when the new advertising agency was born, arid it all started with Doyle, Dane, Bernbach ... Volkswagen was being handled in the United States by Fuller and Smith and Ross. Doyle, Dane took over the account in 1959. One of the first ads to come out for Volkswagen was the first ad that anyone can remember when the new agency style really came through with an entirely different look. That ad said simply: "Lemon." The copy for "Lemon" said that once in a while we turn out a car that's a lemon, in which case we get rid of it. We don't sell the lemons. And we are careful as hell with our cars, we test them before we sell them, so the chances are you'll never get one of our lemons.[4]

The flower children of the later 1960s, the anti-Vietnam and civil rights protest movements, and the events of May 1968 would inscribe the sixties into Western cultural memory as the age of counter-cultural revolt. What has been less remarked upon, but is picked up in cultural critics like Frank, Boltanski and Chiapello, and Michel Clouscard,[5] is that the 1960s were also a period of transition within "mainstream" society: one in which, uncannily, core counter-cultural themes promoted by the "primary ideologist" of the allegedly "logocentric" or "homogenizing" capitalist order, marketing, became normalized.[6] As Frank puts it in *The Conquest of Cool*:

> For all the sophistication of recent cultural theory, many of its practitioners still tend to identify the sins of consumer order as "homogeneity" or an obsessive logocentrism. In the advertising industry, that order's primary ideologist, however, these values were everywhere under attack by the mid-1960s. As a creative revolution followed in the wake of DDB's artistic and commercial success, the advertising industry began to recognize creativity, even more than science or organization or standardization or repetition or regulation, as a dynamic element of advertising and, ultimately, of the permanent revolution of capitalism itself.[7]

The archetypal adman of the 1960s was less scientist than artist and rebel, half-avant-garde surrealist and half James Dean, as wonderfully portrayed in the tele-series, *Madmen*. "If you are not a bad boy, if you're not a big pain in the ass, then what you are is mush, in this business," George Lois informs us—railing as he goes, like the radical students, against the lifeless, over-rationalized, over-bureaucratic culture of "big business" which picked up his tabs.[8] As a 1970 column in *Madison Avenue* reflected on this new commodification of rebellion, if in ordinary society people might "strive for ... acceptance, conformity, anonymity," advertising from DDB forwards has learned to appeal to people's drive to "stand out, to excel, to be idolized [and] adulated."[9]

Even as the mechanization of production and the concentration of product markets led to the homogenization of actual products, advertising was busy working to stimulate demand for particular "brands" by associating them with the values previously restricted to intellectual and artistic *avant-gardes* and political rebels: individuality, dynamism, difference, pluralism, and revolt. "To be afraid to advertise in a way which talks about real problems and real differences is to be afraid to look in the mirror," *Madison Avenue* sermonized: "To balk at communicating differently from competition is to balk at moving ahead of competitors."[10] As the late Marxist critic, Frederic Jameson would hence be able to comment by the 1990s, talking about the postmodern integration of the celebrated rebellious motifs of the artistic counterculture into later capitalist consumerism:

> Not only are Joyce and Picasso no longer weird or repulsive, they have become classics and now look rather realistic to us. Meanwhile, there is very little in either the form or the content of contemporary art that contemporary art finds intolerable and scandalous … commodity production and in particular our clothing, furniture, buildings and other artifacts are now intimately tied in with styling changes which derive from artistic experimentation: our advertising, for example, is fed by modernism in all the arts and inconceivable without it.[11]

Boltanski and Chiapello identify this "new spirit of capitalism" after the 1960s, one informing the subsequent supplanting of forms of social democratic by neoliberal economics, with what they call an "artistic critique" of society— albeit one that has become integral to consumerist society itself. Such a critique turns away from the earlier socialist Left's characteristic concerns for equality, solidarity, and collective organization. This saw them criticize capitalist society for promoting deep inequalities, as well as economic and social alienation (Section 4.2). It replaces these concerns with the concerns of the artistic *avant-gardes* for individual creativity, expressivity and singularity. These are values which were already being promoted in the 1960s with the birth of consumer culture, and which would later make their way into managerial discourses aiming to justify the new business practices of the 1990s, including the continuing deunionization and "flexibilization" of the workforce with the growth of casual and temporary positions, without leave, forms of social or health insurance, and other entitlements.[12] According to the most up-to-date managerial theory of the 1990s, such changes were not to be seen as reactionary step backwards for society, or for workers. No, as Frank again comments, this time in *One Market Under God*, his work focusing not on advertising, but managerial discourses:

> Whatever recommendations individual gurus might make regarding the structure of the workplace, the management literature of the nineties almost universally insisted that its larger project was liberation, giving a voice to the voiceless, 'empowering' the individual, subverting the pretensions of the mighty, and striking moral blows against hierarchy of all kinds.[13]

In an uncanny echo of the integration of rebellion which the previous generations had seen within the marketing industries, the enemy of the new "agile" managers in the fast-moving economy of the 1990s, it turns out, was always really the enemy of the rebels of the New Left. The villain of their manifestoes and declarations was the soulless "Fordist" corporation, in which individuality had been drummed out of line workers, impersonal "hierarchies" reigned supreme, and the kinds of individual creativity needed to unlock new sources of shareholder value had been oppressively stifled. In the authoritarian "controlling organizations" of the benighted Taylorist past, management guru Peter M. Senge explains in the bestseller, *The Fifth Discipline*, all decisions and "learning" came from the top-down.[14] All that now had to change, and it *was* changing. The solution, however, was not anything like bottom-up organization to redemocratize workplaces and ensure that no worker was left behind. What was needed were top-down deconstructions of these organizations, championed by vanguardist managers dedicated to the liberating tasks of "delayering," "downsizing," "reengineering," or "disintermediation." New, more flexible, non-hierarchical modes of organization had to be imagined. And with them, new workers needed to be educated and fostered, unburdened of retrograde longings to be insulated from "the violent winds of the marketplace" which needed "to be driven into every nook and cranny in every firm."[15] Where once there was solidarity, now there should be competition between colleagues. Where once there were collectively arbitrated contracts, now there should be individualized, temporary arrangements. Above all, where once people could base entire lives around holding down a stable position with a single company and trade, now employees needed to become "change agents" and "life-long learners"—positively leaping at every opportunity to move from place to place, position to position, and contract to contract, should their position be rendered redundant.

At the height of this extraordinary managerial revolution, *Oracle*'s bizarre 1998 marketing campaign went as far as to show its employees dressed as AK-bearing Khmer Rouge cadres, demanding the liberating "disaggregation" of their workplace.[16] However, as against 1789 or 1917—and the kinds of revolutionaries about which Camus wrote in *L'Homme Révolté*—the revolutionary vanguards in the 1990s "stepping righteously into battle against the elites were the country's highest paid management consultants and CEOs."[17] And what this well-paid corporate *avant-garde* was saying was clear. Actions that might formerly have been perceived as just plain firing people were the means to enable the triumphant, Nietzschean yes-saying of the new "knowledge-workers," enabling their burgeoning class consciousness. "Organizations have to get used to the idea that not everyone wants to work for them all the time even if the jobs are available," Handy warned complacent CEOs as the Berlin wall was coming down in 1989. *Fortune* magazine's 1997 "Declaration of Independence" of the "Free Agent Nation" announced that, in the new economy, "free agents are gladly swapping the false promise of security for the personal pledge of authenticity."[18] Handy's best-selling *Empty Raincoat* did not stop short of concluding that, in the very period in which Marxism as we had known it seemed forever retrenched, it was in the capitalist societies which Marxists had reviled that we had actually attained "what Marx dreamt of ... the 'means of production,' the traditional bases of capitalism, are now literally owned by the workers, because those means are in their heads and at their fingertips"[19]

3.2 Post-Structuralism (or "Postmodernism") as Aestheticized Revolt

On one hand, the uncanny commodification of dissent in post-1960s advertising, and then the embrace of motifs from countercultural revolt in the service of managerial reforms in the 1990s, provide one more confirmation of the validity of Camus's identification of the modern age as, decisively, the age of revolt. On the other hand, the collapse of rebellion against the mainstream into a newly aestheticized, highly individualized and commodified mainstream culture represents a paradox. It can seem, and it has seemed to many, to suggest the ultimate dead end or exhaustion of this modern project of permanent revolt. How then did radical theory develop, in the decades after Camus's death?

When Camus passed, the PCF (French Communist Party) was still a leading political force in France. The cold war was just getting to its most perilous, nuclear point. His own work was amongst the first to force a reckoning of the Marxist Left with Stalin's legacy, precipitating his break with Jean-Paul Sartre and the *Temps modernes* group.[20] He could not have foreseen how, over the course of the next decades, the radical intellectual Left in Paris would widely jettison Marxism, everywhere but in the imaginings of conservative culture warriors. If we look for instance at Michel Foucault (whom Sartre labeled in the 1960s as "the last barricade of the bourgeoisie against Marx"),[21] we see that his famed conception of power was constructed in explicit opposition to what he perceived to be the intellectual hegemony of Marxism in the French progressive academy.[22] Like the other post-structuralist thinkers who would in due course be taken up in anglophone academia as "French theory," Foucault eschewed

Marxism's political economics, tracing political and cultural forms back to their economic conditions. He likewise conceived of power as "everywhere," reaching down into the smallest, "micro" dimensions of life, rather than being concentrated in the State, or in social classes, or within relations of production. In Jean-François Lyotard's highly influential 1979 work, *The Postmodern Condition*, Marxism is aligned with other modern "metanarratives" of progress which Lyotard argues have been terminally discredited by the developments of Western liberal-capitalist societies in the age of computer technologies, and the shadow of Auschwitz.[23] In Jacques Derrida, and the thinkers of *Tel Quel*, there was a decisive shift away from anything like materialist analysis of political economics into the analysis of texts and signifiers, adapting methodologies drawn from structuralist linguistics. By the time Derrida returned to Marxism in the 1980s, the latter had become a kind of utopian "spectre" pointing, ghostlike, toward an amorphous "democracy to come."[24] Nostalgic polemical attempts to paint deconstruction as a continuation of "Marxism" by other means (as in culture warrior, Jordan Peterson),[25] bear no relation to any really existing Marxist movements.

On what bases then did these theorists present their radical criticisms of the contemporary world? Following the discrediting of Marxism, from 1960 to 1990, these intellectual radicals looked for bases for social and political critique that would position them as able to decry both the failures of Soviet Marxism, and the liberal-capitalist societies the former were conceived in political-economic opposition to.[26] The two principal figures from the history of ideas they appealed to were, strikingly, Friedrich Nietzsche, who had been a principal inspiration of the European fascist movements and their leaders; and Martin Heidegger, who had been a Nazi Party member from 1933 to 1945.[27] In Nietzsche's and Heidegger's works, however, the bases for radical cultural and philosophical criticism could seemingly be expanded. Beyond targeting the injustices, contradictions, and crisis tendencies of liberal capitalist societies, as Marxism had done, critics would now target all modern technological societies: a critical curse, so to speak, on all the liberal, socialist, and fascist houses. Here, the Marxist criticisms of alienation, commodification, and reification (per Gyorgy Lukács),[28] still tied in Marxism to progressive and revolutionary aspirations, represent a kind of bridging point. Via Nietzsche and/or Heidegger, criticisms of these dimensions of capitalist society could be opened up, as in the Frankfurt School, onto criticisms of the dehumanizing and ecocidal effects of instrumental rationality and *Technik*, allegedly traceable back to very roots of Western reason itself: or outflanked and supplanted in "deconstructive," post-Heideggerian work challenging Western "metaphysics" or "logocentrism," as in Derrida; or broken open by neo-Nietzschean critiques of post-Christian denials of the vital, dynamic, affective, feminine, elusive becoming of terrestrial life and the limitless horizons of human desire; or regrounded in criticisms of a Western "humanism" with roots reaching back to Socrates or Plato, which has inevitably devolved into a "philosophy of the subject" that is unregenerately hostile to all things singular, undecidable, and unpredictable.[29]

There are evident intellectual attractions to these positions, based as they are in sweeping reassessments of the West's rational legacy which, moreover, is hardly wholly unimpeachable. The failure of Marxism-Leninism in the Soviet bloc to avoid devolution into forms of dictatorship (Section 4.3), as well as the tendencies of capitalism to cheapen and commercialize all forms of higher culture, alike became impugnable to shared, previously-unthought-through preconditions. For the post-structuralists, the problem was not capitalism, as Marx shallowly supposed. It was Western thinking's obsessions, in which Marx participated, with reason, closure and coherence. At issue was the West's epochal project, since the ancient Greeks, of reducing all uncertainty within ever-newer forms of exactitude and objectification. There was also a retargeting of critique, in this way, at the "transcendental" or "ultra-transcendental" level, as Ian Hunter has examined.[30] These intellectually radical stances moreover opened avenues onto both forms of feminist critique, targeting the patriarchal androcentrism of Western thinking since the same Greeks, and post-colonial critique, which slated Western imperialism's devastations of non-Western peoples and life-worlds to the occidental overvaluation of its own allegedly "superior," more "rational" or "enlightened" forms of culture.

Nevertheless, cracks in the presumptively radical political prospects of "postmodernism" are readily evident. Derrida's deconstruction is on one hand devoted to showing how the attempts of canonical works of philosophy to close down the infinite "sliding" of the signifier—and the indeterminateness of all meaning—all fail, leaving telltale marks of self-contradiction. On the other hand, many of Derrida's strongest demonstrations are of how thinkers who promise an escape from the "logocentrism" of post-Socratic Western thinking fail in this attempt also—whether in Bataille's celebrations of excess, or Emmanuel Levinas's ethics of pure Alterity. A similarly closed emancipatory horizon greets the Foucault reader, by the time that we learn that power is everywhere, and everything is therefore "dangerous," at the same time as Foucault impugns modern "disciplinary" and "biopower" for their creation of self-monitoring, "docile" modern bodies peopling what his friend, Gilles Deleuze, would call the "society of control."[31] If metaphysical totalization and disciplinary power were so ubiquitous that even their most radical and decorated French critics could not escape their reach, where could genuine resistance and sources of renewal be found?

As the 1970s passed into the 1980s and 1990s, the answer was becoming at once increasingly clearer, and successively opaquer and more ineffable.[32] Derrida had always praised "difference" with an "a," resisting all closed signification. Deleuze and his followers posited a non-relative "difference" underlying and undermining all claims to rational identity, or the acentric movements of a completely dehumanized "desire." The earlier Foucault, like the younger Lyotard, had been attracted to the most rebellious celebrations of the unfathomable workings of desire, creativity and transgression. As early as *Being and Event* (French publication 1988), Alain Badiou (whose anglophone celebration in some quarters would only come much later) had begun repackaging radically "indiscernible" and irrational "Events" as the basis of "Truth," making an esoteric appeal to set-theoretical mathematics as the basis of all ontology (understanding of being, or what is).[33] Yet, the relationship between such celebrations of the ultra-transcendental, unheralded, and ineffable to any concrete progressive political program, let alone the day-to-day issues at play in functioning democracies, is very unclear indeed. In place of politics in any recognizable sense, these intellectuals mostly turned their energies toward acts of radical interpretive virtuosity; for instance, explorations of recondite modern art, with its world-shattering non-representational capacities; and celebrations of the marginal, minoritarian, and excluded as such (rather than as potential agents of principled political resistance or reform). Then there has been a conjoining fascination with rupturous revolutionary "Events," less for any vision of a better world they might open up, than on grounds of their transgressive or violent *elan*; before, increasingly, thinkers turned away from secular reason toward ostensibly "post-secular" forms of theology and messianism.[34] In what is perhaps the most unlikely endpoint of all for these ostensibly Leftist "projects," the new millennium even saw a brief vogue for excavating the subterranean revolutionary potentials of the *Epistles of Saint Paul*.[35]

Whether any of these intellectual acts of subversion ever achieved "escape velocity," sufficient to break with the dominant logics of the global, neoliberal order—or to provide a reasoned account of why this venture should be undertaken—can be contested. Meanwhile, as a thinker like Gabriel Rockhill has examined, "theory" had itself become one more "edgy" commodity, integrated into academic syllabi across different humanities programs, and packaged in radical publications with prestigious university and academic publishing houses.[36] This theory continues to be presented, and interpreted, within many circles as deeply transgressive and system-shaking—that was and is its attraction to younger people. At the same time, publishers have seen the commercial promise of these texts introducing readers into the "revolutionary" textual acrobatics of deconstruction, Deleuzian "lines of flight" into unfathomable idiosyncratic self-explorations, the Lyotardian exploration of irresolvable "differends," Badiouian Evental mathematics, etc. Far from being politically mobilized, the students radicalized by these *avant-garde* discourses typically no longer have anything but scorn for the vulgar "economism" or "materialist reductionism" of the Marxists, let alone any ongoing connections with anything like industrial trade unions. Their foundational commitments to difference, creativity, idosyncrasy, and subversion tend instead to make anything like solidary organization with others look hopelessly "reactionary"—if not a ceding to the totalizing, hydra-like ubiquity of Western "logocentrism," "metaphysics," "reactive forces," or "Power."

What few of the theorists stopped to notice was how the more pessimistic declamations of a Derrida about the inescapability of "metaphysics," or Foucault on "power," or Deleuze on "capitalism," applied uncannily to their own material practices and products. These everywhere promised political resistance, but delivered interpretive and conceptual virtuosity available to ever-shrinking audiences of students and tenured intellectuals.[37] Indeed, with the simultaneous advent of avowedly postmodernist forms of marketing and managerial discourses—let alone later, the artful corporate sponsorship of the causes of ecological and identity politics to boost their brands[38]—the paradoxical circle of institutionalized counter-cultural rebellion had become closed, even in the much-feared "radical academy."

3.3 Sympathy for the Devil: Camus Against *Avant Gardism*

Camus's criticism of the total regimes of the interwar period places his critical position in some proximity to the later "theory of the sixties," as post-structuralism has sometimes (contestably) been called. Camus's early emphasis on the absurd and the limits of human rationality can be read as anticipating key directions, notably, in Derrida's deconstructive thought. Camus's repeated use of the plague as a metaphor for forms of administrative control suggests parallels both with Foucault, and the Frankfurt School's "critique of instrumental reason."[39] His own admiration for Nietzsche, another anticipator of the post-1960 Nietzschean turn in French theory, will be addressed in the next section. Camus was moreover an artist, a Nobel Prize-winning *litterateur*. He is consistently sympathetic to the ways that artistic creativity and the experience of beauty represent fundamental sources of humane value, which resists the dehumanizing dimensions of modern forms of power (see Chapter 6). He also is attentive to the ways in which modern art has been shaped, in analogy with forms of political rebellion, by the real (and in his view, legitimate) desire to explore alternative modes of life and perception in rebellion against the commercial cheapening of culture in liberal-capitalist and mass societies.[40] Nevertheless, it is possible to read Camus also as a critic of the kinds of *avant-garde* antinomianism which were taken up both by post-1960 French theorists—and their many global legatees—and within later capitalist marketing and management practices.

In fact, it is notable when we read *The Rebel* that Camus dedicates two important but often-neglected sections in Part II of the book on "Metaphysical Rebellion" to the forms of revolt characteristic of modern artists: firstly, the romantics ("the dandies' rebellion") and secondly, later poets such as Lautrémont, Baudelaire, Rimbaud, and the surrealist, Breton ("the poets' rebellion").[41] Unlike the post-structuralists, Camus tended to be highly critical of forms of modernist artistic rebellion which, aiming to create objects which resist massification, challenge representation itself, or which celebrate transgression or violence as aesthetic ends in themselves. Faced with the exhaustion of the postmodernist Left, indeed, Camus's criticism of the romantics and then the later *avant-gardes* can today be reread as a pre-emptive criticism of the messianic and nihilistic directions this later theory has steered generations of students toward.

Camus addresses the romantics, significantly, under the heading of "absolute negation" (R, 36). In the nineteenth century, in the same period in which Left Hegelianism was opening the path toward Marxist historical revolt, Camus notes that "men of letters," poets and writers (or maverick poet-philosophers, like the Marquis de Sade (R, 37–46)), played a primary role in the development of modern metaphysical rebellion against the remnants of divine authority remaining after 1789. The romantics' revolt, the revolt of men of letters, intellectuals, as against workers or *sans culottes*, Camus notes, "is separated from earlier forms of rebellion by its preference for evil and the individual" (R, 47). The great inspiration for such romantic rebellion against God is Milton's *Paradise Lost*. As William Blake recognized, many of Milton's most powerful lines in this epic are given over to Satan, rather than to God or His army of benignant angels (R, 48). Milton's Satan considers himself the wronged Party in the Creation, who has Justice on his side. If he renounces good, it is first of all from out of an outraged sense of having been violently mistreated by the Creator and granted "the greatest share of endless pain." But God has no right to treat him so: "whom reason hath equal'd, force hath made supreme above his equals" (R, 47–8). The "Prince of Darkness" sees nevertheless that God commands all talk of good at the same time as he suppresses revolt against His will. Does He not deny even knowledge of good and evil to human beings? Such goodness is surely a con. Satan's rage hence soon becomes directed not simply against God, but against the notions of goodness or innocence itself which He commands. An "excess of despair" in this way leads his revolt against divine injustice into its own sanctification of evil: "So farewell hope, and with hope farewell fear, farewell remorse ... Evil be thou my good" (at R, 49). As Camus puts it:

> since violence is at the root of all creation, deliberate violence shall be its answer. The fact that there is an excess of despair adds to the causes of despair and brings rebellion to that state of indignant frustration which

follows the long experience of injustice and where the distinction between good or evil finally disappears. (R, 48–9)

This is the "Satanic" heart of romantic artistic rebellion, in Camus's view: "in order to combat evil, the rebel renounces good, because he considers himself innocent, and once more gives birth to evil" (R, 47). It is a matter of what psychologists might call identification with the oppressor. Since evil seems part of God's/nature's order, so that people—or at least, geniuses—suffer so unjustly, then we should actively accept and take on the evil that is in any case visited upon us: "so many injustices suffered, a sorrow so unrelieved, justify every excess," Milton's Satan laments (R, 49). Romanticism hence oscillates between the most idealistic affirmations of the outraged goodness of the human race, and disgust at human vice, folly, and weakness, leading into profound misanthropy in poets such as Lautrémont, Rimbaud, or Baudelaire (R, 82–3).

After Milton, Camus notes, Satan goes from being the horrifying, distorted figure of medieval depictions into a figure of exquisite beauty in the romantics' nightcast imaginings: "young and charming" (Vigny), "beautiful, with a beauty unknown to earth" (Lermontov) (R, 49). Metaphysical aestheticist revolt, originating in a sense of justice, takes on the visage of aestheticized, glamorized evil. It is precisely actions and figures who defy justice who from now on will be heroized:

> Without exactly advocating crime, the romantics insist on paying homage to a basic system of privileges which they illustrate with the conventional images of the outlaw, the criminal with the heart of gold, and the kind brigand. (R, 50)

Since the divine or natural order is such a con, a stance of permanent rebellion against all order becomes a heroized attitude, even a way of life—or at least one staged for the delectable experience of outraging God and the forces of any establishment which might look to impose itself (R, 52). Uncivilized instincts, the bestial dimensions of humanity which were previously the signature of vice, become lauded as cyphers of freedom: "exquisite sensibilities evoke the elementary furies of the beast" (R, 49). Lautrémont will picture his hero Maldador as copulating with a shark to strike out at the order of nature (R, 85). Since the sentence of death hangs over us all, romanticism enjoins its devotees to extol passing, extreme experiences wherein it is possible to feel most ecstatically alive: "the brief and vivid union of a tempestuous heart united with the tempest (Lermontov)" (R, 49). Violence itself, even apocalyptic violence, ceases to be feared or judged according to any moral principle, including consequences on any targets or bystanders. Criminal violences—and soon enough, political revolt, when it is violent—are enjoined as aesthetic acts: "an absolute value in which everything is confounded—love and death, conscience and culpability" (R, 49).

But such permanent revolt is demanding. Each outrage creates a precedent that the next blasphemy must surpass. And every act of blasphemy presupposes the outrageous authorities who need, in their turn, to be duly outraged by the impish spectacles of artistic revolt. Hence, the aesthetic of the dandy "is an aesthetic of singularity and of negation" (R, 52). And so, we arrive at the very values that we find, not by chance, at the other end of the Derridean deconstruction of metaphysics, the Foucaultian excavation of power, the Lyotardian annunciation of the end of totalizing "metanarratives," or Badiouian mathematics of "Events" whose criteria for veridiction can only be seen *aprés coup*, and then only, by those faithfully interpellated as their revolutionary subjects. Here is Camus:

The dandy is, by occupation, always in opposition. He can only exist by defiance. Up to now, man derived his coherence from the creator. But from the moment he consecrates his rupture with him, he finds himself delivered over to the fleeting moment, to the passing days, and to wasted sensibility.

Therefore, he must take himself in hand. The dandy rallies his forces and creates a unity for himself by the very violence of his refusal ... The dandy, therefore, is always required to astonish. Singularity is his vocation, excess his way to perfection ... Their rebellion thrusts its roots deep, but from the Abbé Prévost's *Cleveland* up to the time of the Dadaists—including the frenetics of 1830 and Baudelaire and the decadents of 1880—more than a century of rebellion was completely glutted by the audacities of "eccentricity." (R, 52)

As Camus writes of André Breton and the surrealists, who inherit the romantic stance of God-defying, counter-cultural revolt in the twentieth century, for them—as against the Marxists, for example—even political revolution was not to be looked to as the means toward a better future, the end of history, a "more perfect union," and so on. Like all good artists, the surrealists mostly had nothing but patrician scorn for the "abominable material comfort" that socialist dreamers, like the execrable bourgeois, sought to deliver to the many (Breton, at R, 96). Political revolution is instead for the *avant-gardist* "man of letters" to be ardently desired as a rapturous, violent, extraordinary Event. It is a kind of test of existential authenticity, to "further the surrealist adventure," by "preventing the completely artificial precariousness of the social conditions from screening the real precariousness of the human condition" (Breton, at R, 96). It is, and this is all, *interesting*. Even reactionary violence, in this purview, is "better"—because less ordinary, and more shocking—than the tedium of liberal-democratic societies with their sciences and public discussions (R,96): "these frenetics wanted 'any sort of revolution,' no matter what, and as long as it rescued them from the world of shopkeepers and compromise in which they were forced to live" (R, 94). Breton would frankly celebrate treason and declare that "violence is the only mode of expression"—by which he clearly meant, the most authentic mode of expression for the aestheticist rebel (R, 94).

Modris Ekstein is the author who has arguably written the invaluable history of how *avant-gardism* in the decades surrounding the World Wars came to valorize artistic shock and violence. He takes his title, and his beginning, from the scandal deliberately instrumented around the opening night of Igor Stravinsky's ballet *The Rites of Spring*. This was a spectacle staged to outrage the bourgeois patrons who would attend it, and whose success was measured by its shock value. Ekstein's analysis shows how this turning of art into war (as in "avant-gardes," advance guards or forces) against bourgeois mediocrity and prudishness, within a decade, proceeds to the aestheticization of war which we find in fascist literature, led by Ernst Jünger's *Storms of Steel* (see Ssection 5.3).[42] Camus anticipates Ekstein, both as an historian of post-romantic aesthetic modernism, and in his clear-sighted recognition of its ethical and political limitations and ambivalences. Born of a rebellious desire for vindication and unity, in defiance of an unjust or tawdry world, the works of romanticist rebels tend, via an aestheticist route, toward valorizing violence, eccentricity, singularity, and permanent revolt against all structures, in place of other, older values and virtues informing ethical and political life. The post-structuralist radical theorists and their admirers, although hailing from the most elite higher education institutions after 1960, have carried forwards this normative orientation. Post-structuralism, certainly in its global reception as "French theory," is a repackaging of post-romanticist revolt for the new generations of the *trentes glorieuses* and the birth of consumerism, in the recondite languages of post-Nietzschean/post-Heideggerian "critiques of modernity," or of "disciplinary power," "logocentrism," or "ontotheology." The concrete implications of such an orientation, however, should such "men of letters" look to engage in the fallen world of sociopolitical life, are at best underdetermined, as the genealogy of post-structuralism from Heidegger to De Mann clearly shows. At best, the game of performative radicalism can and has been readily commodified in later capitalism (see Section 3.1). But it is already intriguing that both Lautrémont and Rimbaud later reverted from the most strident revolt to the most obtuse forms of conformism (R, 84–6, 89–91).⁴³ At worst, political romanticism leads to the licensing of murder and enslavement of the very kinds which Camus thinks modern revolt, including romantic revolt, was born from protesting: "their works are bathed in blood and shrouded in mystery. The soul is delivered, at minimal expenditure, of its most hideous desires—desires that a later generation will assuage in concentration camps" (R, 50).

3.4 Camus's Nietzsche and the Fascism Question

Camus's closest genealogical proximity to later *avant-garde* French theory comes in his avowed admiration for Friedrich Nietzsche. We know that he was carrying a copy of *Gay Science*, by the German philosopher, in the car at the time of his death. At that time, as his chapter on Nietzsche in *The Rebel* suggests, Camus could not have foreseen the remarkable ways in which Nietzsche's post-war reception would transpire in the cold war. In fact, in the decades after Camus's death, the philosopher who claimed that his thought was "dynamite" would go from the disgraced intellectual progenitor celebrated by fascists and Nazis, to being presented as a gentle, apolitical or even progressive quasi-libertarian figure, an artist philosopher. In the Unites States, this occurred via Walter Kaufman; in France, through Gilles Deleuze, Sarah Kaufman, Michel Foucault, and others.⁴⁴

It is impossible to know what Camus would have made of what critics have called the "hermeneutics of innocence"⁴⁵ which attended this gentrification of Nietzsche's texts for consumption in the universities of the liberal-democratic nations which had just decades before taken the field against the Axis powers in the Second World War. In a recent criticism of the "Left Nietzscheanism" of figures led by Deleuze and Foucault, Aymeric Monville positions Camus, alongside George Bataille and Maurice Blanchot, as a predecessor of these later

French Nietzscheans, whose positions are predicated on the total dismissal of any real links between the philosopher and the fascist regimes which claimed his ideas as their own.[46] Is this reading, which positions Camus with a Bataille, correct?

It is true that Camus does proclaim, in *The Rebel*, that "we can never confuse Nietzsche with Rosenberg," the leading Nazi ideologue who claimed a Nietzschean lineage for his programmatic *Myth of the 20th Century*. (R, 76) "We shall never finish making reparations ... for the injustice done to [Nietzsche]," Camus claims, for the way the Nazis "set him up as the master of lies and violence," to claim elevated justification for their mendacity and criminality (R, 75).[47]

Nevertheless, it is untrue to suggest that Camus completely whitewashes the philosopher, as can arguably be said for later "Left Nietzscheans," looking to claim the German thinker for their own Left-libertarian projects.[48] Neither does Camus's continuing admiration for Nietzsche's personal struggles and passionate authenticity blind him to the dark political dimensions of the latter's work. For Camus, in contrast to the post-structuralists, that Nietzsche's dream of supermen gave rise to a race of jackbooted sub-men is "a fact which doubtless should be denounced, but which also demands an interpretation" (R, 76). Indeed, the weight of Camus's chapter in *The Rebel* on Nietzsche is critical. It is geared toward his book's larger question, as to how seemingly elevated philosophical doctrines like Nietzsche's could in twentieth-century Europe vindicate forms of oppression and genocidal atrocities. In ways which his French successors would sheepishly avoid, Camus inquires whether the kinds of spiritual elevation that Nietzsche extolled do not also implicate a kind of aristocratic radicalism which "perhaps, explains the bloody travesty of his philosophy" (R, 76). As Camus asks, and then answers:

> Is there nothing in his work that can be used in support of definitive murder? Cannot the killers, provided that they deny the spirit in favour of the letter ... find their pretext in Nietzsche? The answer must be yes. (R, 76)

Readers will find no such clear assertion in any later "Left Nietzschean." As we saw in Chapter 1, Camus admires Nietzsche first as what he calls a "diagnostician" of the "nihilism" of nineteenth-century Europe (R, 65). Unlike the romantics, who exhausted themselves defying God (Section 3.3), Nietzsche finds that God has died in the hearts of his contemporaries. His project, as Camus identifies it, is one aiming at a rebuilding, or even a renaissance, which would come to terms seriously with this epochal event (R, 68–9). To revalue all values, however, Nietzsche proposed first the most radical critique of modern social and cultural forms: "instead of methodical doubt, he practiced methodical negation, the determined destruction of everything that still hides nihilism from itself, of the idols that camouflage God's death" (R, 66). For Nietzsche, the fallen God and religious morality could not furnish any antidote to nihilism, as Christian critics of modern revolt were already claiming. In that inversion of religious diagnoses of nihilism that we saw Camus registering in Chapter 1, Nietzsche saw Judeo-Christian and post-Socratic values as the basis of the spiritual malaise to be overturned:

> Moral conduct, as explained by Socrates, or as recommended by Christianity, is itself a sign of decadence. It wants to substitute a mere shadow of a man for a man of flesh and blood. It condemns the universe of passion and emotion in the name of an entirely imaginary world of harmony. If nihilism is the inability to believe, then its most serious symptom is not found in atheism, but in the inability to believe in what is. (R, 67)

There can be no question of Camus's debts to Nietzsche's project of clear-sightedly affirming the world as we find it, and to his sense of nihilism as involving a turning away from the world of our lived experiences in favor of some other-worldly idyll: "a nihilist is not one who believes in nothing, but one who does not believe in what exists" (R, 69). Instead, she would subordinate this present life, and other people, to abstract ideals or imagined Deities. Yet, Camus cannot be rightly lined up with liberal and post-structuralist apologists for the German thinker who, ignoring Nietzsche's own most inflammatory declarations, present him as a gentle philosopher-artist, uninterested in what he nevertheless termed "great politics (*Großpolitik*)." Camus lucidly assesses how Nietzsche's criticism of Christianity did not prevent him from admiring "the cynical aspects of the Church" as a political institution, including Jesuitism: "only the God of morality is rejected" (R, 68).[49] He moreover clear-sightedly identifies how for Nietzsche, Christianity is to be condemned, particularly, for promoting the equality of souls before God. For this is the idea that would in due course inform modern socialism "and all forms of humanitarianism" (R, 69). Camus is equally under no misapprehension that Nietzsche, in his later works, reviled the freethinkers of the enlightenment who paved the way toward the French revolution (R, 79): "the equality of souls before God leads, now that God is dead, to equality pure and simple. There again, Nietzsche wages war against socialist doctrines insofar as they are moral doctrines" (R, 76). Finally, unlike his later *avant-garde* Francophone enthusiasts, Camus is not misled by Nietzsche's own solitary persona into missing how he nevertheless clearly articulated a metapolitical program based squarely on philosophical premises, and the key motifs of the revaluation of all values in overcoming slave morality: "Nietzscheanism—the theory of the individual's will to power—was condemned to support the universal will to power. Nietzscheanism was nothing without world domination" (R, 76). Far from an unworldly contemplative, Camus denounces how the later Nietzsche consciously assumed the mantle of the prophet or prophet-legislator, who wanted to fundamentally change the world:

> Since the world has no direction, man, from the moment he accepts this, must give it one that will eventually lead to a superior type of humanity. Nietzsche laid claim to the direction of the future of the human race: "the task of governing the world is going to fall to our lot." And elsewhere: "the time is approaching when we shall have to struggle for the domination of

the world, and this struggle will be fought in the name of philosophical principles." (R, 77–8)

For Camus, accordingly, the many extreme statements that litter Nietzsche's work, especially after 1882, are not incidental anomalies, somehow tangential to his wider thinking. Indeed, disarmingly and from the very start, Camus assesses that "we can draw no conclusions from Nietzsche except a base and mediocre cruelty, unless we give first place in his work—well ahead of the prophet—to the diagnostician" (R, 65). The basic issue for Camus is how, after Nietzsche diagnoses the modern dethroning of the Christian God, and decries the putative nihilism of attempts to posit counter-factual ideals or norms, there is nothing left for him *qua* prophet but to propose a totalizing affirmation of this "sad and suffering world," without reserve:

> From the moment that it is admitted that the world pursues no end, Nietzsche proposes to concede its innocence, to affirm that it accepts no judgment since it cannot be judged on any intention, and consequently to replace all judgments based on values by absolute assent, and by a complete and exalted allegiance to this world. (R, 72)

It is a matter of the famous Nietzschean *amor fati*, love of fate, and the eternal recurrence. Camus admires the consistency of Nietzsche's reasoning, to arrive at this fatalism. He also appreciates the ethical heroism involved in striving, against reason itself, to accept everything that happens as necessary (R, 72). Yet, he remains critical of the implications of this "absolute affirmation," as he describes it: "this magnificent consent, born of abundance and fullness of spirit, is the unreserved affirmation of human imperfection and suffering, of evil and murder, of all that is problematic in existence" (R, 72). At this point, Nietzsche's modern revolt against divine injustice issues—as in the romantics, but via this very different theoretical route—into "the exaltation of evil" (R, 75). In Camus's formulation, "it [evil] is accepted as one of the possible aspects of good [that is, the innocence of becoming] and, with rather more conviction, as part of destiny" (R, 75). Slavery, all manner of Machiavellian ruthlessness, cunning and violence: all once more find in Nietzsche a philosophical sanction, for those ruthless enough to embrace them:

> To say yes to everything supposes that one says yes to murder. Moreover, it expresses two ways of consenting to murder. If the slave says yes to everything, he consents to the existence of a master and to his own suffering ... If the master says yes to everything, he consents to slavery and the suffering of others, and the result is the tyrant and the glorification of murder. [As Nietzsche writes:] "[i]s it not laughable that we believe in a sacred, infrangible law—thou shalt not lie, thou shalt not kill—in an existence characterised by perpetual lying and perpetual murder?" (R, 76–7)

In the light of this reasoning, Camus is in fact quite clear as to his assessment of Nietzsche's philosophical responsibility for the "barbarians of the 20th century", and their attempts to elevate themselves by force and fraud to being racial and imperialist masters of the world.[50] Nietzsche had extolled the body and the innocence of becoming, asking the individual to "bow before the eternity of the species and submerge themselves in the great cycle of time"; the fascists vulgarized these motifs into the vitalistic biologism of racialist theory, and the sacrifice of the individual to the *Volk*. Nietzsche himself, who never enjoyed the robust physical health he symptomatically idealized, was not a directly political man. However:

> From the moment that assent was given to the totality of human experience, the way was open to others who, far from languishing, would gather strength from lies and murder. Nietzsche's responsibility lies in having legitimised, for reasons of method ...the opportunity for dishonesty ... But his involuntary responsibility goes further ... He himself conceived of a

system in which crime could no longer serve as an argument and in which the only value lay in the divinity of man [i.e. in the overman]. The grandiose initiative also had to be put to use. National Socialism in this respect was only a transitory heir, only the speculative and rabid outcome of nihilism … Placed in the crucible of Nietzschean philosophy, rebellion, in the intoxication of freedom, ends in biological or historical Caesarism. (R, 79)

Far from being a one-sided apologetics for Nietzsche, we have to therefore protest that Camus is actually one of his first, clear-sighted post-war critics who would in no way have been surprised at the philosophers' recurrence in contemporary neofascism's "thought leaders" as a heroized inspiration.

4

Beyond Identitarianism: Camus and the Future of the Left

4.1 Post-Equality: What We Missed While We Were Culture-Warrin'

In his great 1947 novel, *The Plague*, Camus comments that even death in a pandemic is not blind to social distinctions. Those who are poorer suffer most.[1] For they have least access to clean, quality accommodation, and live in closer proximity to each other than the rich, who can afford more space and higher walls. In 2020–2, the world learned the truth of Camus's observation. It is not simply that countries with higher levels of economic inequality suffered higher levels of mortality, or that within the United States, the burden of mortalities fell disproportionately on the less wealthy.[2] As the global economy shut down, and millions of people were left with time on their hands to go down myriad conspiratorial rabbit holes, the US stock market was surging. As the death toll in the world's post-war hegemon crested 100,000 in mid-2020, the S&P 500 index pushed past 3,000. By the time in 2021 that 500,000 Americans had perished of COVID-19, amid widespread disbelief in the reality of the disease, the S&P had climbed over 5,000. As Chris Brown, founder of the Ohio-based hedge fund Aristides Capital wrote to his investors in June 2020: "The cognitive dissonance is overwhelming at times."[3] If there ever could have been a real-time demonstration of the disconnect between the success of global business or Wall Street, and the welfare of ordinary people on Main Street—and anyone was still unconvinced after government bailouts of banks, not homeowners, after the 2008–9 financial crisis—it was this.[4]

This plague however not only cast a dark spotlight on trends in the world economy from 1970 to 2020. These trends have fundamentally reshaped our world and now facilitate the ascent of authoritarian ethnonationalist strongmen in the United States, Europe, Brazil, Argentina, the Philippines, Russia and Turkey (Section 5.1). The author is neither an orthodox nor a political economist. Yet, we can lean on the data from people who have studied and documented these intersecting phenomena. There is the decoupling of wages from productivity, including in the advanced Northern economies (the gap between the growth rate of median wages and that of GDP per person). In the United States, for instance, whereas productivity has grown by 80.9 percent between 1979 and 2024, median wages have grown just 29.4 percent.[5] There is, in line with this, the declining "labour share" in total national and global wealth. Between 1970 and 2014, this share dropped some 14 percent in Spain and 12 percent in Italy, 11 percent in the United States, 9 percent in Japan, with smaller declines of about 6–7 percent in other advanced economies. Between 2004 and 2017 alone, the global labor share as percentage of GDP dropped from 53.7 percent to 51.4 percent.[6] These figures need to be read alongside the extraordinary growth in inequalities within the ranks of wage earners. Whilst global rates of profit in non-financial sectors have largely stagnated or declined in recent decades, and the entire wage pool has been shrinking, CEO pay has risen some 1322 percent globally since 1978. CEOs were paid 351 times as much as a typical worker in 2020. In the United States, as of 2015, this cohort earned on average some 829 times the average American worker.[7] Meanwhile, official statistics suggest that global unemployment has remained at relatively constant, relatively low levels. Yet, levels of "underemployment"—the number of people working insecure, casual, part-time and/or fixed term jobs who would rather have full time continuing positions, with more basic rights and protections in their workplaces—have ballooned, alongside managerial discourse celebrating the postmodern "flexibility" of economies unshackled from unionism and the scourge of public regulations (Section 3.1).[8]

With this increasing "flexibilization" of labor, wage levels have stagnated for people in the lowest 90 percent of workforces. In the United States, where the political efforts by pro-business forces to deunionize labor and deregulate capital have been most well-financed and aggressive, the figures are staggering. Between 1979 and 2018, real wages for the top 10 percent of earners grew very handsomely, by 37.6 percent. But if you were in the bottom 10 percent, your real wages grew by just 1.6 percent. Wages at the 50th percentile grew by 6.1 percent.[9] These patterns varied, regressively, by gender and ethnicity. From 1979 to 2017, the income share of the bottom 20 percent fell from 5.3 percent to 3.5 percent of GDP. Yet, the share of the top quintile rose nearly ten points, from 41.9 percent to just over 50 percent. A September 2020 *Time* article,[10] based on RAND research (hardly a "pink" outfit, by any stretch) suggested that the American "experiment in radical inequality" had effected a $50 trillion wealth transfer from the bottom 99 percent to the top 1 percent of Americans from 1975 to 2018—extrapolating, as a baseline, against the 1974 distribution of incomes.[11] By 2012, the top 1 percent of Americans owned 42 percent of the United States' wealth. This is up from just 30 percent in the years of the postwar boom presently being advertised as "great," and 23 percent as late as in 1973, when America was at its most economically egalitarian, and the OPEC crisis struck.[12]

Meanwhile, since the 1970s oil and stagflation crises, governments have come to accept almost universally, across the floors, the wisdom of "free market" or "neoliberal" economic orthodoxy which has been vociferously pushed by a global network of privately funded think tanks, via compliant media. This wisdom maintained that the best way to achieve optimal economic performance by nations was to deregulate business, including financial markets, open borders to the flow of moneys (if not always to workers), cut taxes on capital gains and corporate profits, reduce social spending, and privatize any and all public assets, including those delivering basic services to populations such as water, electricity, health, insurance, even assistance to find work. In the United States, as recently as 1956, during the Republican Eisenhower administration and at the height of America's imperium, the tax rate was 91 percent for all income over $3.4 million a year. In 1976, 70 percent taxation still applied to all income over $80,700; presently the top income tax rate is 37 percent.[13] Since around 1970, corporate tax rates have been slashed, from over 50 percent in 1968 to just 21 percent by 2012—with Mr. Trump's first and second "populist" administration driving further cuts. In 1980, this money represented over 6 percent of local and state revenues; by 2015, this figure had dropped below 4 percent.[14] Nevertheless, ever larger sums of private income and capital—at least $21 trillion as of 2010—has come to be "parked offshore" in "tax havens" (places around the world wherefrom it cannot be taxed by the national government) by business leaders who often clutch the flag, and denounce others for being unpatriotic, without any sense of irony or shame.[15] The level of regulations on business activities, to minimize "externalities" and protect the public from the deleterious effects of private transactions, has also been reduced across the board. By 2006, all regulations had been removed from US oil and gas extraction, railroads, airlines, trucking, and, notably, the financial sector[16]—which would in 2008–9 collapse catastrophically, only to be bailed out by public moneys, being "too big to fail."

Whether these neoliberal reforms, predicated on a radically asocial, individualistic vision of the world ("society does not exist, only individuals and their families," Margaret Thatcher intoned), have supercharged the real economy is nevertheless questionable—putting aside the massive inequalities they have visited upon countries. The promise of freeing all markets, as against stodgy public enterprises, was supposed to be to foster competition, leading to greater innovation, hence cheaper, higher quality and more various products and services. In reality, as the world sees writ large in the clique of tech billionaires who own the companies which deliver our search engines, social media, and computer operating systems, the neoliberal period has seen remarkable increases in industry and banking concentration[17]: what critics call monopoly capitalism.[18] Between 2000 and 2014 alone, economic concentration—that is, the reduction in the numbers of firms competing to deliver a product or service—increased in 77 percent of European industries, and 74 percent of North American industries, by on average 4 percent and 8 percent respectively.[19] Moreover, just as economic theory would predict, while "firms in industries with the largest increases in product market concentration show higher profit margins and more profitable mergers and acquisition deals,"[20] their ability to insulate themselves from competition leads to lower efficiencies. It also affords greater leeway to "markup" prices, without fear of losing customers, as the world has seen in the post-COVID recovery. The neoliberal era, despite its glittering promises, will not be remembered for the achievement of cheaper, better services, infrastructure, or forms of social insurance, should our fellows or we ourselves fall on hard times.

We commented above that rates of profit in the neoliberal era have remained relatively stagnant, outside of the financial sector. The neoliberal period has instead seen more and more of the profits generated by economic activity concentrated in finance. This has created strong incentives to redirect money away from investment in productive or service industries, to investment in financial instruments—which make money from money and from calculations of risk—or in residential property. Wall Street's slice of total US profits rose from around 16 percent, as recently as 1962, to some 43 percent of all US domestic corporate profits by 2002.[21] (These figures are to be read against an historical average of about 12 percent prior to this period.) As Michael Hudson has commented:

> In America the easiest way to make money is not by "creating jobs" but by loading the economy down with debt, inflating asset prices on credit, privatizing natural monopolies and extracting economic rent in the form of higher access charges. None of this increases real output. But it does increase the cost of living and doing business.[22]

Then there is the advent, enabled by financial deregulation since the 1980s, of such noble figures as corporate raiders, private equity companies, and hedge funds, who—in the words of Les Leopold:

> have turned corporations into financial strip mines. They buy up companies, load them up with debt, extract fees and dividends and then use the earnings from the target company to pay off the debt. They also tie CEO compensation to the value of the company's stocks. This gives the CEO and other executives a big incentive to use company earnings to buy back stocks, [not investing in anything like R&D but] increasing the value of stock options and enriching themselves.[23]

Global debt levels, notably private debt (including households') have risen steeply since the 1970s. Whereas total US debt tracked GDP as recently as 1970, by the GFC, it was trebling the national GDP, over $40 trillion. Total US household debt as a proportion of income had soared from 70 percent to around 130 percent between 1980 and 2008.[24] America is far from alone in such figures. Houses prices globally, relative to stagnant incomes for those in the middle- and lower-income brackets, have widely soared, albeit unequally in different nations. In Australia, where the resulting housing affordability crisis has become especially acute since the turn of the millennium (worse only in neighboring New Zealand), median house prices in capital cities now exceed $1 million.[25] The median income remains around $70,000 per annum.[26]

We ask the reader's forbearance for presenting such a tranche of political economic data in a book on why Camus matters. We plead the precedent of Camus's own journalism, most notably in the series of articles on the Kabylia region that we'll return to below. These articles include detailed sociological analyses, as well as his own vivid depictions of the people's conditions.[27] The point here is to propose a basic sketch of the profoundly inegalitarian world we have come to inhabit by 2025, in which the disorienting statistics attesting to social distress with which this book opened have become possible (Section 1.1). The widespread alienation, anomie, deaths of despair and distrust in public and private authorities have not been produced in a socioeconomic vacuum. It's not solely "the economy, stupid," as someone said. But the economy cannot be discounted if we are to understand and redress the deep problems besetting our world, including the pathologies of our "post-truth," increasingly authoritarian-friendly culture (Sections 2.1 and 5.1).

4.2 Why Camus Matters to the Left Today: Balancing Freedom with Justice

It is one thing to grasp these material realities. Then there is the task to understand, in this period of this $50 trillion wealth transfer to the top 1 percent in the world's leading democracy, why the political Left in the United States and elsewhere has been so singularly inefficacious in opposing these changes—and more recently, the devolution from neoliberalism toward authoritarianism (Chapter 5). In the United States, UK, Australia and elsewhere, the social-democratic Left as was, with its representative Labor or Democratic Parties, have not only widely failed to oppose neoliberal restructuring. They early on accepted its inevitability and championed its fatalistic "there is no alternative" (TINA) closing down of options for democratic governance. Often, they have proven neoliberalism's more responsible stewards, not opposing the mass layoffs of working class jobs and their offshoring to places with lower labor regulations,[28] the global rolling back of trade unions, the lowering of corporate taxes, the "populist" demonization of recipients of public benefits as parasites on the public purse, the privatization of social services through the creation of "quasi-markets," and the rethinking of the role of the State as to market entire nations as attractive sites to park footloose international capital, the reconception of people's homes as financial investments or ATMs ... There is bitter truth in Margaret Thatcher's *bon mot* that her greatest achievement was Tony Blair: a "New Labor" leader who carried forwards the anti-social democratic economic settings she had introduced into Britain after 1979.

The artistic and intellectual Left, meanwhile, influenced by the forms of *avant-gardism* we examined in Section 3.2, have widely redirected their critical energies away from the material concerns of most people on "Main Street." Politics has been shunted into culture. Forms of liberalism and Marxism widely gave way to poststructuralism, feminism and post-colonialism in the humanities faculties of the Northern universities. This new postmodern Left, whose carriers are no longer blue-collar industrial laborers (whose numbers are depleted following relocation of secondary industry to the global South), but white-collar professionals and managers, contest what the Right in the 1990s came to dub "culture wars" surrounding competing claims to identity, cultural representation, and recognition of sexual and racial groups which have long been disadvantaged in advanced economies. Their interest in threatened claims to identity in conditions of socio-economic destabilization has been eagerly taken up and thrown back at them by corporate media commentators, and in the social media age, the "Alt-right" and the "populists." But it is surely no coincidence that Right-wing commentators and corporate media networks have shown themselves only too enthusiastic to engage endlessly with "the Left" on these cultural issues, while the neoliberal economic elephant was running through longstanding democracies, leaving anxiety, anger, and alienation in its wake. It pays to choose one's enemies, and what is left in silence. In the scathing assessment of Michael J. Thompson of the "cultural turn" in new Leftism, following the 1960s:

> social movements have lost political momentum; they are generally focused on questions of culture and shallow discussions of class and obsessed with issues of identity— racial, sexual, and so on—rather than on the great "social question" of unequal economic power, which once served as the driving impulse for political, social, and cultural transformation. As these new radical mandarins spill ink on futile debates over "desire," "identity," and illusory visions of anarchic democracy, economic inequality has ballooned into oligarchic proportions, working people have been increasingly marginalized, and ethnic minority groups are turned into a coolie labour force ... political discourse [on the postmodern intellectual Left] has become increasingly dominated by the impulses of neo-anarchism, identity politics, postcolonialism, and other intellectual fads. This new radicalism has made itself so irrelevant with respect to real politics that it ends up serving as a kind of cathartic space for the justifiable anxieties wrought by late capitalism, further stabilizing its systemic and integrative power rather than disrupting it.[29]

Indeed, we will not be the first to note how the suite of cultural sensitivities which the aggravated Right denounce as "woke," far from upsetting corporate capital, has made it into the commanding heights of corporations' advertising, public relations, and human resources platforms. It is a matter of what Nancy Fraser has called "progressive neoliberalism."[30] The older Left, based in the now-vacated industrial heartlands and rustbelts of cities of the global North, had politicized the economy. It had undertaken strikes and marches to demand greater economic as well as political protections, rights and equality. The newer Left of the tertiary-educated, professional managerial classes has politicized "signifiers," embraced "speech codes," and some in the social media age have taken to justifying "cancelling" those who, sometimes unwittingly, violated these standards. This New Left has also widely promoted "difference" from the mainstream as an end in itself—all in ways which made their Rightist criticism as elitist, moralizing, censorious, irrationalist, and "out of touch" with ordinary people resonate widely across the threatened middle and working classes of the "new divergence": that is, our increasingly polarized social and political societies.[31]

Why might Camus matter, amid the agonies of the global Left in the era of Putin, Erdogan, Trump, Duterte, Orban, Le Pen and the rising fortunes (backed now by billionaires) of *Alt für Deutschland* in the land that gave Nazism to the world? We have by now some pointers to address this question. From Chapter 1, we know that Camus opposes any political positions that license, directly or indirectly, the murder of human beings, based upon a nihilistic assessment of their lack of any inalienable dignity and worth. From Chapter 3, we know that although Camus always identified as an artist, that he nevertheless rejected romanticism and *avant-gardism*, which place a premium on negation, creativity, difference, and becoming as ends in themselves. In Chapter 2, above all, we stressed that Camus is a defender of dialogue and pluralism, versus monologue and polemic. At the same time, he is an avowed moral universalist, not an individual or cultural relativist,[32] who thinks that limits on killing, enslaving, and lying to our fellows are non-negotiable, if the modern West is to recover from nihilism, and our democracies are not to devolve into forms of tyranny (Sections 1.4 and 2.3).

On this basis, as we are about to examine, increasingly after 1946, Camus became a staunch critic of Stalinism in the USSR, while remaining a person of the Left. And this is why Camus matters for the Left today. Here we have a principled thinker concerned to balance the kinds of freedom of concern to the new Left and the liberal-conservative Right, with economic and social justice, of concern for the older socialist Left. Indeed, this aim to balance liberty with justice, the political freedoms won by past social struggles with forms of economic collectivism, the "aristocracies" of labor and of the mind,[33] despite the powers of money and police, becomes his political *leitmotif* after 1944. In Camus, the Left today can find a man who looked to chart a democratic socialist way forwards, without ceding to cynicism and authoritarianism, and between the mutual recriminations and "whataboutism" which characterize the culture wars today.

So, let's first give the *bona fides* surrounding Camus as a non-aligned socialist, throughout his short existence (Section 4.4).[34] Camus entered political life as a young man, joining the Algerian Communist Party in 1934, aged twenty-one.[35] He was tasked with handing out leaflets to the Islamic population. He in addition formed a radical theatre group, the *Theatre de l'Équipe*, and a pro-communist cultural group, the *Maison de la Culture*. Camus in 1936 became a supporter of the Popular Front government in France, which aimed to bring together different anti-fascist forces, secular and religious, to oppose the rising "populist" Right on the continent. The precise date is disputable, but Camus left the Communist Party by 1937.[36] Camus nevertheless did not become "anti-communist," as some have claimed, including some Marxists: most famously, Sartre and his associates at *Les Temps modernes* after the 1951 publication of Camus's *The Rebel*. As late as 1944, he would denounce anti-communism of the kind which became widespread in the cold war as the beginning of authoritarianism.[37]

After leaving the Communist Party, Camus continued to hope for a revival of the Popular Front after its defeats in May 1936 and then March 1938, with the election of the conservative Daladier government. In October 1938, Camus began work as a journalist at the self-styled "Popular-front newspaper," *Alger-républicain*, writing at the paper until its ban under wartime censorship in early 1940. Camus moved to Paris, where he briefly worked at *Paris Soir* until the German occupation. The Nazis' killing of communist journalist Gabriel Péri was decisive in the resolve of the author of *The Myth of Sisyphus* to become *engagé*. "I didn't think of myself as being elsewhere, that is all there is to it," he would say with *pudeur* in 1948.[38] In Lyon, Camus associated with the resistance group which published *Combat*, defying the law under the Laval-Petain Vichy government, from December 1941. In 1943, he clandestinely published (in Italy) the anti-Nazi "Letters to a German Friend" which we'll examine in Chapter 5. Camus became an editor at *Combat* by late 1943 or, at latest, March 1944, then editor in-chief from August 1944.[39] Between August 1944 and June 1945, Camus wrote articles under pen names on a range of subjects, from journalism itself (Section 3.4) to events from the front lines of the war.

All the powers of Camus's rhetoric during the period surrounding the liberation of France from Nazism is directed to the hope that the solidarity that the resistance had forged, between communists, socialists, democrats and some Christians could become the basis for a full-scale "revolution." This revolution would instate "a true people's and worker's democracy,"[40] bringing together a "collectivist economy and liberal politics"[41] in ways which generations raised after 1970 have been taught is frankly impossible—"collectivism?—liberal?" Indeed, it must be underlined how *radical* Camus's proposals at this time were, relative to our own oligarchic period. The war against Hitler, Camus claimed, was also a war against money—far from fascism being a "socialism" (Section 5.2).[42] For Camus, the widespread complicity of French big business in the Vichy regime, and its crimes against the French people and the French Jews, showed this only too clearly.[43] The *résistants* had not fought the Nazis to reinstate the "resignation," "mediocrity," and "scandalous fortunes" of the "one hundred families," like today's 1 percent (or 0.1 percent):

> We shall call justice a social state in which each individual receives every opportunity at the start, and in which the country's majority is not held in abject conditions by a privileged minority.[44]

To speak only of freedoms, Camus noted, is to give freedom to the unlimited accumulation of money. It is also to sever freedom from obligation, rights from duties, and this is to enshrine injustice.[45] Camus accordingly repeatedly called for the collectivization of the ownership of industry, with working class management of enterprises, praising initiatives such as Marcel Barbu's working group at Valence.[46] Camus supported the establishment of French *comités des enterprises*, in which trade unions would have been directly involved in shaping national economic policy, as well as union training for workers to actively participate in economic governance.[47]

In brief, Camus's commitment to civil and political liberties did not "crowd out" his concerns for economic justice. We need to remember, as we read Camus's impassioned writings from 1944 to 1945, that rebellion's primary value, solidarity, prevents all forms of enslavement, as well as murder and deceit (Section 2.2). "[The rebel] is not only the slave against the master, but also the man against the world of master and slave," Camus contends. For, in contrast to the solidarity of people at grips with their destiny:

> There is ... nothing in common between a master and a slave; it is impossible to speak and communicate with a person who has been reduced to servitude. Instead of the implicit and untrammelled dialogue through which we come to recognize our similarity and consecrate our destiny, servitude gives sway to the most terrible of silences.[48]

Camus maintained that, if any person or family in a society does not have enough economic security to save or enjoy creative leisure, then that is enough for us to maintain that that order is unjust, and in need of amelioration. For the effective freedoms of these people to live well, educate themselves, and enjoy leisure and beauty, are denied with their material and social impoverishment. If the price of my freedom is your barely being able to sustain yourself and your loved ones, then my freedom is unjust. Justice itself hence serves for Camus to circumscribe and guarantee effective freedoms for people, far from being its abstract opposite: "There is no possible freedom for a man tied to his lathe all day long who when the evening comes crowds into a single room with his family ... this fact condemns a class, a society and the slavery it assumes."[49]

In 1947, Camus stepped back from and then resigned from *Combat*, increasingly feeling that the resistance movement's ability to revolutionize French politics was passing.[50] This was also the year when, in October, he met Arthur Koestler and learned of the extent of Stalin's gulags (forced labor and reeducation camps), falling out bitterly with Maurice Merleau-Ponty about whether such camps could ever be justified in a way that anticipated his spectacular break with Sartre in 1951–2.[51] Yet, in 1948, Camus still supported Jean-Paul Sartre's organization, the *Rassemblement Démocratique Révolutionnaire* (RDR) which aimed to rally progressive intellectuals unaligned to the Communist Party (as Sartre, like Camus, remained at this time). Camus himself set up the *Groupes de liaison international* (GLI) (International Liaison Groups) to help political prisoners in Franco's Spain, the Soviet Union, and other authoritarian regimes. From 1951 until his death, he would continue to write for non-aligned socialist outlets: for *La Révolution prolétarienne* from 1951, from 1954, for *Témoins*, and between 1955 and 1956, for Servan-Schreiber's *L'Express*.[52] In 1955, for the only time in his life, Camus made public his electoral support for Pierre Mendes-France, leader of the *Parti républicain, radical et radical-socialiste* in his failed bid for the French Presidency.

For all of his criticisms of Stalinism, we see that Camus's political position always remained a man of the Left: someone who thought that a better world was possible, beyond one in which "money is King."[53]

4.3 Beyond Messianism: Camus's Critique of Authoritarian Communism

It is notable that the political-economic and laborist dimensions to Karl Marx's work have largely been sidelined by the postmodernist thinkers (Section 3.2). What if anything has been carried over into their more Nietzsche- and Heidegger-inspired work is Marxism's prophetic side, stripped from all faith in rational human progress. What remains of "Marxism" in someone like Jacques Derrida, for instance, is a spectral promise of a democracy to come, a kind of opaque messianism without any specifiable sociopolitical parameters.[54] Marx's talk of revolution has morphed in a Slavoj Žižek into the valorization of radical voluntaristic Acts or, in Alain Badiou, into the amorphous promise of rupturous Events which do not develop imminently out from, but break radically with, previous political conditions, demanding from "subjects" a "fidelity" which cannot be rationally communicated to, nor understood by outsiders (Section 3.2).[55]

Camus from the start identifies that there are different dimensions of Marx's work that mitigate against its wholesale polemical dismissal, along the lines either of post-structuralist charges of "reductive economism," or invariant Right-wing claims that "this all leads to the gulags." On one hand, there is Marx the political philosopher who, above all prior philosophers (Camus also admires, in his own time, Simone Weil) valorized work and dignity in work as basic to the human condition:

> To him we owe the idea which is the despair of our times ... that when work is a degradation, it is not life, even though it occupies every moment of a life. Who, despite the pretensions of this society, can sleep in it in peace when they know that it derives its mediocre pleasures from the work of millions of dead souls? By demanding for the worker real riches, which are not the riches of money but of leisure and creation, [Marx] has reclaimed, despite all appearance to the contrary, the dignity of man.[56]

On the other hand, there is Marx the political economist and social scientist, looking to scientifically understand the society of the nineteenth century, in which rapid industrialization and urbanization had displaced entire populations, generating both untold material wealth and new forms of social inequality and alienation. Camus's criticism of Marxism hails from the claim that Marx, or at least many of his followers:

could blend in his doctrine the most valid critical method with a utopian messianism of highly dubious value. The unfortunate thing is that his critical method, which, by definition, should have been adjusted to reality, has found itself farther and farther separated from facts to the exact extent that it wanted to remain faithful to the prophecy.[57]

When he raises "utopian messianism," this third dimension to Marx's oeuvre as he reads it, Camus means the famous Marxian prediction that the crisis tendencies of industrial capitalism, with the concentration of wealth and of those with nothing but their labor to sell, would *necessarily* precipitate a proletarian revolution and give rise to a classless, post-capitalist society. By 1950, it was clear that this global revolution had not and would not come to pass according to such an unswayable, predetermined historical dialectic. Marx did not, and could not have, foreseen capitalism's ability to adapt from the relatively primitive industrial state which Engels and he observed in England. Nor could he anticipate the twentieth century compromises between business, unions and states between the great depression and the 1970s, which would produce forms of limited social democracy across Northern nations. If Lenin's Bolshevik Revolution succeeded in predominantly agricultural Russia, Camus observes, this was in violation, not confirmation, of Marxism's credentials as a predictive science of history, which had in fact seen the revolution as inevitable only in Europe's advanced economies.

What remained in the social sciences' place, after "the failing of the prophecy,"[58] was Marxism as a messianic vision of the end of alienation, class struggle and of all human "prehistory." Stalinism for Camus hence involved nothing like social science. It involved a species of unfalsifiable "historic reason." The determinist faith that economic development, by itself, would meaningfully liberate all human beings Camus sees as a "bourgeois" inheritance which Marx shares with Turgot, Renan, and Comte.[59] The supposed "guarantee" that the impoverished, alienated modern proletariat will be the agent of revolutionary liberation came from an adaptation of Hegel's philosophy of history.[60] Just as Christ needed to lose all human hope at Golgotha to fulfill his salvific mission, Marxist messianism postulated that:

> capitalism, by driving the proletariat to the final point of degradation, gradually delivers it from every decision that might separate it from other men. It has nothing, neither property nor morality nor country. Therefore, it clings to nothing but the species of which it is henceforth the naked and implacable representative ... "Only the proletariat, totally excluded from this affirmation of their personality, are capable of realizing the complete affirmation of self." That is the mission of the proletariat: to bring forth supreme dignity from supreme humiliation. Through its suffering and its struggles, it is Christ in human form redeeming the collective sin of alienation.[61]

As Nietzsche argued, so Camus hence sees in Marxism not a godless atheism, as many Christian critics have worried.[62] Marxism-Leninism for Camus was a secularized political eschatology (conception of the last and highest things). In its messianic dimension, as against its social scientific and laborist sides, it transposes religious hopes for the Kingdom of Heaven into the human future. As Marx wrote of the hoped-for end of human prehistory, almost oneirically, in the 1844 *Economic and Philosophical Manuscripts*:

> Communism in so far as it is the real appropriation of the human essence by man and for man, in so far as it is the return of man to himself as a social being—in other words, as a human being—a complete conscious return which preserves all the values of the inner movement. This communism, being absolute naturalism, coincides with humanism: it is the real end of the quarrel between man and nature, between man and man, between essence and existence, between externalization and the affirmation of self, between liberty and necessity, between the individual and the species. It solves the mystery of history and is aware of having solved it.[63]

For Camus, however generous this utopian vision is, its great distance from the sufferings and struggles of ordinary men and women is problematic. Like Nietzsche, Marx denied all traditional and religious sources of value, as "opium for the people." But whereas Nietzsche dreamed of aristocratic supermen unashamed by slave morality to undertake vast "collective programs" of "breeding" to overcome modern slavishness,[64] Marxism proposes that the eschatological end of prehistory will come with the revolution of the workers whom Nietzsche wished to re-enslave. In this way, Camus argues, Marxism in its prophetic dimension removes all standards for judging actions good or evil, except insofar as they are deemed to promote or to oppose the achievement of the one thing needful, the revolution:

> Marx destroys all transcendence, then carries out, by himself, the transition from fact to duty. But his concept of duty has no other origin but fact. The demand for justice ends in injustice if it is not primarily based on an ethical justification of justice; without this, crime itself one day becomes a duty. When good and evil are reintegrated in time and confused with events, nothing is any longer good or bad, but only either premature or out of date. Who will decide on the opportunity, if not the opportunist? Later, say the disciples, you shall judge. But the victims will not be there to judge.[65]

In this way, just as in Nietzscheanism and fascism, murder, enslavement and deceit are again justified, albeit for progressive rather than reactionary ends (Section 5.3). The primary value discovered by modern revolt, as an appeal to justice and affirmation of the "we are," as against a utopian "we shall be," is once more violated:

> The results are the same. If it is true that History obeys a logic and a fatality—if it is true that the anarchic State must be succeeded by the feudal State, then feudalism by nations, nations by empires, and empires by the Universal Society—then everything that serves this march of History is

good and the achievements of History are definitive truths. All one has to do is wait for them to arrive. Since they can arrive only by the normal means—wars, lies, tricks and individual or collective murders—all acts are justified not insofar as they are good or bad, but insofar as they are effective or not.[66]

It is remarkable, if we look as far back as Camus's explanation to his teacher, Jean Grenier, for leaving the Algerian Communist Party by 1937, how early he seemed to object to what he called the "all sorts of nonsense" that socialism had taken on, via Marxism-Leninism, from "German ideology."[67] Camus was certainly horrified and saddened, but he was not surprised when he learned of the Soviet gulags in 1946, constructed in the name of Soviet communism; the repression of workers by the Communist Party in East Berlin in 1953; and the brutal suppression of the Hungarian revolts by Kadir in 1956. But he had struggled alongside communists in the resistance. Camus would write, against reactionary critics, in October 1944 that "we vigorously reject anti-Communism because we know what inspires it and where it leads"[68]: namely, to the "whataboutist" rationalization of the crimes of the West and the legitimization for instance of a General Franco's military regime, which from 1952 became a UNESCO member.

Nevertheless, there are two broad kinds of socialism, in Camus's assessment. And it is this two-sided, non-polemical, nuanced assessment—and the way that it breaks with the "either-or" logic of the culture wars, in which even moderate social democratic measures are heatedly depicted as "Marxist ... communist"—that makes Camus's position matter today. On one side, there is what Camus sometimes calls a "liberal socialism."[69] This starts from the ground up, in concrete struggles and workplace organization, and does not lean on metaphysical philosophies and prophetic eschatologies. It is the socialism that Camus associated with British trade unionism, the Scandinavian democracies and French anarcho-syndicalism. On the other side, there is Marxist-Leninist communism, embodied in the French Communist Party and the Soviet States, of which Camus explained in 1944:

> Most of our comrades' collectivist ideas and social program, their ideal of justice and their disgust with a society in which money and privilege occupy the front ranks, we share. But as our comrades freely recognise, their adherence to a very consistent philosophy of history justifies the acceptance of political realism as the primary method for securing the triumph of an ideal shared by many Frenchmen. On this matter, we very clearly differ. As we have said many times, we do not believe in political realism [i.e. the idea that political "reality" licenses deceit, murder, or enslavement (cf. Section 2.4)].[70]

If there is to be a revived Left today, and the long drift Rightwards toward neofascism is to be arrested, balanced and reversed, such two-sided thinking is one of the preconditions. There will also be the willingness, illustrated by Camus's thinking and in the French resistance, to work alongside people with whom we share fundamental orientations, even as we disagree about particular issues, in face of common adversaries. The better, however imperfect, is not the enemy of the good.

4.4 Beyond Libertarianism: Balancing Liberty with Equality

Camus's position is therefore that the Left needs to defend a collectivist economy, with worker's management of enterprises, alongside political liberty. This is a combination which we've been assured for decades is impossible, and which the New Left has shunned, focusing instead on cultural issues and accepting neoliberal economics as the only game in town. If Camus's commitment is clear therefore to economic reforms to re-empower the working classes, while avoiding falling into what he perceives to be the shortcomings of Marxism-Leninism, someone will however ask: How can this be achieved in any way that is consistent with sustaining the kinds of political liberty characterizing liberal-capitalist societies, in which workers most definitely do not have a say in management and economic governance? What role can there be for freedom in a philosophy which advocated for a "people and worker's democracy," with economic collectivism, and the nationalization of productive and banking capital, as Camus suggests, so that it serves common interests?

Especially after 1950, with the Soviet repression of workers' revolts in East Berlin, then in Hungary in 1956, Camus came to place ever more emphasis on the necessity to maintain freedom, while pursuing a more just socio-political society. His political position, he would protest, is simple: "social justice can easily be achieved without an ingenious philosophy."[71] The civil and political freedoms that are conditionally assured in liberal-democratic nations—in contrast to the freedom of *pleonexia*, to accumulate unlimited fortunes—are necessary, even though they're far from enough to guarantee a good society. They are the products of long progressive social struggles, pursued principally by working people: "freedom is the concern of the oppressed, and its traditional protectors have always emerged from oppressed peoples."[72] The liberal freedoms have only been won from those with social and political power begrudgingly—for instance, after the great depression in the United States and elsewhere, as well as the rise of the USSR, forced business to concede rights and social securities to working people to avert communism.[73] In our imperfect world, Camus argues: "one might even have to fight a lie in the name of a quarter truth. That is our situation today. However, the quarter truth contained in Western society is called liberty ... without liberty, heavy industry can be perfected, but not justice or truth."[74] The freedoms which emerged from the eighteenth-century liberal revolutions (of conscience, worship, publication, association, and against arbitrary imprisonment without *habeus corpus*) are also necessary if justice and other human values are to be championed, without the need for protestors to risk their lives and wellbeing, and that of their families, by facing down the oppressive arms of the State. In particular, Camus stresses, the need to fight for freedoms of conscience, assembly, and from arbitrary treatment by public or private authorities comes from how, "even when justice is not realized, freedom preserves the power to protest and guarantees human communication."[75]

Underlying Camus's political position on freedom, and its balance with justice, is his philosophy of rebellion. Does the primary value, the "we are" discovered in rebellion, sanction the unlimited freedom for anyone to say and do as they please? It does not:

> The most extreme form of freedom, the freedom to kill, is not compatible with the sense of rebellion. Rebellion is in no way the demand for total freedom. On the contrary, rebellion puts total freedom up for trial. It specifically attacks the unlimited power that authorizes a superior to violate the forbidden frontier. Far from demanding general independence, the rebel wants it to be recognized that freedom has its limits everywhere that a human being is to be found—the limit being precisely that human being's power to rebel.[76]

The upholding of human solidarity is hence a matter of justice, which rightly limits freedom. Allowing a monarch, governor or President, like the emperor Caligula of Camus's celebrated 1944 play (written 1938–9) of that title, to have unlimited freedom kills justice. There is no possible community between an autocrat with Godlike powers, and those He can command, enslave, or eliminate at Will. Likewise, as we saw, the freedom to lie to others needs to be limited, not defended blindly as "freedom of speech," at the price of dishonoring all other values, starting with dignity and mutual respect. The freedom of each finds its limit in the demands for just treatment and respect for the agency and dignity of others: "chaos is also a form of servitude. Freedom exists only in a world where what is possible is defined at the same time as what is not possible."[77] Such respect for the freedoms of others is undermined by the accumulation of "scandalous fortunes."[78] Camus and *Combat* hence loudly called for the dividing and redistribution of the fortunes of the "1 percent" of his day—armed with the memory that big French industrialists like Renault had collaborated, to their own profit, with the Nazis under Vichy.[79] On the other hand, the demand for social justice, and every means to its achievement finds its limit in others' basic freedoms:

> These two demands [for justice and freedom] are already to be found at the beginning of the movement of rebellion and are to be found again in the first impetus of revolution. The history of revolutions demonstrates, however, that they almost always conflict as though their mutual demands were irreconcilable. Absolute freedom is the right of the strongest to dominate. Therefore, it prolongs the conflicts that profit by injustice. Absolute justice is achieved by the suppression of all contradiction: therefore, it destroys freedom.[80]

This "tension" between justice and freedom is one example of that philosophy of *mesure*, balance or moderation, which Camus found in ancient Greek drama and philosophy, and which we'll return to in Chapter 6. On one hand, he charges the Right with defending the freedom of money, and thereby in time, of the strong, at the price of impoverishing others: unlimited capitalism devolves into oligarchism and dictatorship, as we are presently rediscovering. On the other hand, Camus charges the pro-Stalinist Left, moved by their legitimate desire to end needless oppression, with betraying the demands of freedom, also at the heart of genuine revolt. The Marxists of his day, Camus contends, mistake the legitimate, needed criticism of bourgeois freedom, in its ideological function—the freedom to accumulate, and serve one's own ends and those of one's shareholders without wider public regard—with freedom per se. But this is a fallacy:

> When, after Marx, the rumour began to spread and to be reinforced that freedom was bourgeois claptrap, a single word was misplaced in that

dictum, but we are still paying for that ... in the convulsions of the century. What should have been said was that bourgeois freedom was claptrap, not all freedom. What should have been said was that bourgeois freedom was precisely not freedom, or in the best case not yet, but that there were freedoms to be won and never again relinquished.[81]

Camus does not demand absolute equality in economic outcomes, a drab, monotone, lifeless world. For those who excel in and wish to make more money than they need can surely be allowed to do this, within the limits presented by living in a society with other human beings whose material and social needs cannot rightly be scorned and neglected. But the unlimited accumulation of wealth, such as we see in the Unites States today, limits opportunities for most people, destroys social mobility, eliminates effective freedom of the press, and pulverizes any sense of the common good—beyond demagogic, sports-stadium invocations of "the nation," "real Americans/Australians/French," and "the people" which do not translate into people's workplaces and local communities, after the rally is over. To preserve freedom of opportunity means limiting the freedom of endless accumulation. But to pursue more just social arrangements, in Camus's view, should be undertaken through peaceful, principled protest and reform, wherever possible. Violence should be only a last resort, when all other alternatives are exhausted. And then its consequences, in destroying human community, bloodying people's hands and minds, and creating legacies of bitterness and cycles of vengeance, must be seriously weighed. The revolution is not a party or aesthetic spectacle for intellectuals to savor. At best, it is a grim necessity.

As for the much-hyped anxieties about "wokeism," and its speech codes around divisive cultural issues, these New Left preoccupations have been embraced triumphantly by the Right as a battleground, to rationalize their own illiberal radicalization. My sense is that Camus would understand and honor the passion for justice that underlies these calls, given his staunch antiracist statements (Section 4.5). But he would, I believe, caution against the punitive enforceability of speech codes against language which falls short of incitement to violence and worry that all the emphasis on "signifiers," and what people write and say, is a displacement of powerlessness concerning wages, conditions and economic governance. Hateful speech was odious to Camus, a poison polluting public debate, and destroying the possibility of dialogue. Similar considerations apply for the possibility of spreading disinformation and hatred on social media. Given his stance on breaking up the wealth of the hyperwealthy, we can likewise appeal to Camus in calls to publicly limit, monitor or even disband the big platforms which have become megaphones for extremist positions and movements long deemed beyond the pale after 1945.

4.5 Race, Camus, and Algeria

We close this chapter by turning to Camus's positions on race, given its continuing political relevance in 2025, and to Camus's contested stances on Algeria. Camus was a French Algerian with Spanish blood, a working class *pied noir*, the first one literate in his family, who grew up poor in the searing sunlight of Algiers. When the Algerian war for independence of the indigenous populations against French colonial rule broke out, Camus found himself sorely divided. He was sympathetic with the justice of the Algerians' causes against French colonialism. Yet, until his death in January 1960, with the war still raging, Camus maintained his belief that "the 1 million French and 8 million Arab and Berber Algerians were condemned to live together."[82] The "French reality" of a community, his own, settled in Algeria for over 100 years and numbering over one million people, he would claim "can never be eliminated,"[83] and "should not be sacrificed to the immense sins of French colonization."[84] It is this position which has seen Camus criticized by the French Left, including the communists, who supported the Algerian independence struggle, and since his death, by post-colonialist critics. Drawing on his famous 1957 comment that, if it is a matter of non-combatants being blown up by independence fighters on trams, he would support his mother over such "justice," this is seen as Camus compromising his ethical and philosophical position.[85]

Criticisms of Camus on this issue must credit that, from the mid-1930s, Camus had been a public advocate attracting ire from the Algerian and French Right for supporting the cause of justice for Algerians. On the back of his searing indictment of the conditions in which Berbers were living in the Kabylia region, at a time when no one on the mainland Left was concerned, Camus advocated for economic measures to redress people's material distress.[86] He also proposed the full instatement of Algerians' political rights, on a par with other French citizens, protesting the conditions of "a country where 900,000 inhabitants [Muslims] are deprived of schools," and denouncing the "unprecedented poverty" of the Arab population, as well as the way that the colonists "bullied [them] by special laws and inhuman regulations."[87]

In the heated days of 1945, indeed, in the immediate weeks after victory in the Second World War, Camus dedicated a series of articles in *Combat* to endorsing Ferhat Abbas's Manifesto calling for an Algerian constitution guaranteeing immediate and effective political participation and legal equality for Muslims.[88] If the French did not learn from the Arab peoples, Camus warned, and did not accord them the respect and dignity that they deserved, then the French would have no one to blame but themselves, should the Algerian people revolt. This diagnosis proved prophetic. After November 1954, with the war raging, Camus's interventions in Algeria became increasingly forlorn. He denounced the torture by the French of the Algerian militants as both inhumane, as well as likely only to aggravate enmity against their cause. He denounced the violence directed against civilians of the Algerian FLN (National Liberation Front), fighting for independence. In 1956, he tried to broker a "civilian truce": a moratorium on killing noncombatants, contemporary with peace talks. The event was broken up by French "ultras" throwing rocks through the windows. Camus's final position, unheeded, was to argue for an Algerian-French Federation based on the Lauriol Plan. This would recognize that "the era of colonialism is over."[89] Camus argued for reparations to the "eight million Arabs who have hitherto lived under a particular form of repression."[90] With the aim of a "union of differences" in Algeria, he proposed Algerian representation in the French national assembly, as well as an Algerian regional assembly "to represent the distinctive views of Algeria," coupled with a federal, metropolitan-Algerian senate.[91]

What are we to make of Camus's Algerian agony? Were these historically failed positions just the sanctionable, inefficacious genuflections of a "well-meaning coloniser," trying to appease his own guilt? Can we agree that the relocation of a community of over a million people, many of them poor like the Camus family, is a simple matter of justice, as Camus's critics suppose?

In 2024, as the bombs of Israel rained down on crowded civilian areas in Gaza in response to the Hamas terrorist attacks of October 7, 2023, calls from around the globe came for a moratorium on killing civilians, so that the parties could start peace negotiations—just as Camus had proposed, so scandalously, in 1956. In the end, this process took over fourteen months, all the while the death toll in Gaza rising, up to January 2025. Then the war resumed. All talk of ceasefire was long decried by many on the Israeli and US Right as far too radical to countenance. If it is true that Camus was a well-meaning colonizer, the evidence suggests that this must be balanced with his clear statements that "the era of colonialism is over, and the only problem now is to draw the appropriate consequences."[92] In 1946, Camus would advocate for seats in the UN or a World Parliament for colonized nations, a radical anti-colonial position.[93]

As Camus's anti-Nazism highlights—as well as his own record of political advocacy in pre-war Algeria—there also can be no question of a racism on Camus's part. In 1947, in an editorial entitled "Contagion," Camus sought "to draw attention to signs of a racism that dishonours so many countries already and from which we need to protect ourselves" in France. Such prejudice, Camus maintained, "point[s] up what is most abject and senseless in the human heart."[94] In 1945, in his articles for *Combat* on the Algerian Crisis, Camus called for Europe to "accuse itself, since with all of its upheavals and contradictions, it has managed to produce the longest, most horrible reign of barbarism the world has ever known."[95] Advocating renouncing "our feverish and unbridled desire for power and expansion," Camus advised that Europe has "something to learn from the wisdom of Arab civilization ... to understand and to serve it," "granting that we have nothing to teach."[96] These are not the words of a *nouvelle droite* Europeanist or a racist colonizer. Anticipating the language that liberal-relativistic forms of postmodernism would adopt and underscoring his continuing relevance in our multi-cultured world, Camus would explain that he believed only in differences, not uniformity, "because differences are the roots without which the tree of liberty withers and the sap of creation and civilization dry up."[97]

5

Camus Against Fascism

5.1 The Spectre of Twenty-First-Century Neofascism

On January 6, 2021, a mob of Donald Trump supporters including groups of armed citizen militia breached the US Capitol building, surging and breaking windows to enter. Their aim was to stop the ratification of the democratic election of President Joe Biden after his victory in the 2020 election. Once inside, violence transpired against police, protestors defecated on the desks of elected representatives, and the House was successfully occupied for a time. Outside the building, gallows were erected, as some protestors chanted "Hang Mike Pence," the Republican Vice President who refused to obey Trump's orders not to ratify electors. Trump, on social media, impugned his VP as a traitor, too "weak" to do what was necessary. The whole insurrection had been fueled over the previous twelve months, first, by anticipatory claims that the election would be stolen if Biden won, and then, after he did, that the election was stolen due to massive voter fraud instrumented by the Democrats. Trump and his followers filed some sixty lawsuits alleging such fraud around America, with no legal success. The evidence of such fraud did not exist, since the fraud had not taken place. The actual attempt to steal the election was what followed, on January 6, 2021, after Trump had told his followers to gather *en masse* in Washington, promising that "It will be wild!" In a speech before the rioters at the Ellipse, he had told his supporters that they needed to "fight like hell" to save their country from the evil Democrats. He then watched the chaos unfold for hours on his favored news channel, Fox News, which had provided a megaphone for the election-steal misinformation in preceding months, as well as airing the Far Right "Great Replacement" conspiracy theory which intersected with it. Only hours into the chaos was Mr. Trump compelled to tell his followers to "stand down," delivering them a tender message of support. By that hour, several police officers lay dead, with many more people injured.

January 6, 2021, was a turning point for many people, including this author, who had long hesitated to call the "MAGA" (Make America Great Again) movement "fascist." Many still refused after the riot, and presently still (mid-2025) hold out. Sure, the latter people must concede, this movement has increasingly been built around a Leadership cult. Sure, the Leader and his lieutenants have promised national "palingenesis" or rebirth, to "make America great again."[1] Sure, they have alleged in "populist" fashion that the United States had been betrayed by liberal "elites" who are "globalists," and who promote multiculturalism, "DEI" (Diversity, Equity, and Inclusion), and non-European migration at the expense of "real Americans." Sure, Trump had made clear even before the 2016 election that, if he lost, he would consider the system "rigged" and not commit to the peaceful transition of power. Sure, he had started chants at rallies to "lock her up!" about his opponent, Hilary Clinton, as early as 2016. Sure, he had also encouraged violence at these spectacular rallies against journalists. Sure, Trump's Machiavellian second, Steve Bannon—a self-described Right-wing "Leninist"—had called the "lamestream media" "the enemy of the people," echoing the darkest chapters of the twentieth century. (Trump calls any critical reporting on his actions "fake news"). Sure, Trump had not denounced the Neo-Nazis and Right-wing extremists who had flocked to the MAGA cause online, calling him the "God Emperor." Sure, he had said that "there were very fine people on both sides" after the Charlottesville "Unite the Right" rally ended in the death of a liberal protestor, after a night-time torchlight rally in which white men in columns chanted "The Jews will not replace us!" Sure, Trump had praised Right-wing dictators led by Russia's Vladimir Putin and Hungary's Victor Orban. Sure, but … no one could call "MAGA" fascist or even neofascist (one well-meaning centrist commentator suggested "fascoid"!) And if anyone did, although the MAGA movement was predicated on celebrating the Leader's schoolyard name-calling of opponents (with many online emulators), it was they who would be being illiberal—if not hysterical, suffering from "Trump derangement syndrome."

And so things went. After the January 6, 2021, riots, there was a week in which some Republicans whose safety was directly threatened in the Capitol insurrection denounced Trump. But, within a month, it became clear that they were in a minority and that some would even walk back on categorically condemning attacks which saw elected representatives cowering under their desks and being prevented from doing their democratic duty until late that evening. (Many MAGA Republicans, tellingly, refused to vote to ratify Biden on the night of January 6, 2021). Meanwhile, online, on Fox and other Right-wing media, a host of mutually inconsistent conspiracy theories gradually emerged to try to soften the blow of January 6, and the clear and present danger to Trump and the Republican (now "MAGA") cause that it represented. The rioters were peaceful protesters. Or else they were tourists, not protestors. Or else, they were in truth violent, but that was because they were "Deep State" plants sent to act out in ways which would harm MAGA, not real MAGA followers. Or they were violent "Antifa," carrying out a "false flag" (the "anti-fascist" group whom Mr. Trump had been demonizing in 2020). As Freud joked of the dishonest, neurotic man who gave back a broken kettle: *when he got it, it was broken; he gave it back intact; and besides, it wasn't him who broke it anyway.*

Very soon in 2021, it became clear that Trump and MAGA would not be discredited or in any way waylaid by the January 6 violence. The clear example it gave of how Trump's "movement" (as Bannon called it, evoking the German

Bewegung) was now openly illiberal and antidemocratic, willing to sanction violence to achieve its ends, hold onto power, and punish its enemies would amount to nothing. The Democrats and the judiciary, let alone the divided American Left, were clearly incompetent to do anything to prosecute the case against Trump and disband the insurrectionary movement. The old Republican Party was dead, with its old republican values like the rule of law, the peaceful transition of power, and loyalty to Constitution and country over Party or sect. Trump and his followers started speaking of those imprisoned after "J6," including members of armed militia groups "The Three Percenters," "The Oath Keepers," and "The Proud Boys" as "political prisoners" or "hostages" of the invisible, wicked "Deep State." The political mainstreaming of openly anti-democratic conspiracy culture was complete, and with it, the vertiginous power to deny and reframe what millions of people had watched live on television. Footage of the "J6" prisoners singing as a choir in jail would be played at MAGA rallies leading up to the 2024 election. The "Big Lie" around the "steal" of the 2020 election started to function as a loyalty test for MAGA followers, and people who wished to advance in the Republican Party. Into 2024–5, it would become a leading question recruiting for "Project 25," the wish-list of the American Right framed by the Heritage Foundation for "Trump 2.0," following the anticipated win or takeover after the 2024 election. This is a "project" predicated on replacing the neutral public service with dedicated MAGA cadres who will not oppose any orders from the President, soon enacted under Trump's renewed rule in 2025.

For, run for President in 2024 Mr. Trump did, despite J6, and despite all of these "signs and wonders" attesting to the lurching of the MAGA movement toward neofascism for a new, social-mediatic age. Many learned commentators (here in uneasy alignment with agitated culture warriors wanting to deny with their left hand what they sponsored with their right) continued to reassure themselves, and anyone who would listen, that all of this was still not enough to use the "f-word." Even after Trump called his domestic enemies "vermin" and spoke of the "blood poisoning" from immigrants; even after Trump underlined that "internal enemies" like the Democrats and the nefarious "elites" were more dangerous than any external threats; even after Trump praised the "good genes" of his predominantly white followers; even after decades of the American Right-wing fear-mongering about the protection of basic social services as "communist" or "Marxist" (as in Trump's "Comrade Kamala" slur about Democrat Kamala Harris); even after the Supreme Court that Trump had stacked with a majority of appointees found in July 2024 that the President could do anything in his office as President, even the extrajudicial killing of those he deemed foes; even after Trump failed to commit, again, to a peaceful transition of power; even after he legitimized the January 6 violence at rally after rally; even after Trump absurdly claimed at a Presidential debate that Haitian immigrants were "eating pets," based on racist Far Right propaganda spread online; even after he touted a "mass deportation" of between eleven and twenty million "illegals," including women and children, to countries unspecified, and his supporters held up "mass deportation" signs at the Republican National Convention in pride; even, finally, after Trump held a rally at Madison Square Garden in the last week before the 2024 election in direct emulation of interwar "America First" Nazis—these experts calmly reassured us that this was not, or was not even leading toward, "fascism."

The remaining non-MAGA US media, impugned from the Right for decades for "Leftwing bias," bent over backwards to present Trump as just another democratically legitimate candidate. Democracy as usual. In fact, reports emerged suggesting that Trump 2.0 would be good for ratings. When Trump's victory neared, several newspapers' editorial policies shifted away from a critical stance toward the Leader. At the same time, even after Trump was indicted over eighty times for criminal offences, including for inciting the mob on "J6" to insurrection; even after he was found liable in a civil court for sexual violence, and then, for publically defaming his victim; even after he was found criminally guilty of financial fraud during the 2016 election campaign, to cover up his extramarital affair with a porn star—nothing mattered. Trump's base remained faithful, even energized. MAGA media dismissed all criticisms in advance as politicized "witch hunts" and "fake news." His support from American evangelicals hardened, depicting the convicted felon, adulterer, and fraudster as an unjustly persecuted, Christ-like figure sent by God to save the United States from the terrifying evils of the Democrats, DEI, and "wokeism."

On November 6, 2024, Trump, still at that time under absurdly drawn-out (and soon dropped) investigation for defrauding the American people in 2020–1, won the popular vote and became the first convicted felon to be the US president. Reports suggested that Americans were more worried at the polls about the price of eggs—which Trump had promised to bring down with his usual fact-free bravura—than the MAGA threat to their centuries-old republican system of government. On January 6, 2025, the Democrats who had been projectively accused for nearly a decade of using any and all means to end fair elections lamely sanctioned the electoral college votes. Mr. Trump was inaugurated on January 20, 2025, inside the Capitol his followers had stormed in violence four years prior, now surrounded by the world's richest men. In the following days, amidst a rush of Executive Orders, Trump would quickly begin consolidating the new regime with politicized appointment after appointment including known conspiracy theorists, shameless tech billionaires led by South African Elon Musk (who threw a provocative Nazi salute at Trump's inauguration) and patently unqualified Fox News personalities. Within weeks, inspector generals from different government departments had been unceremoniously fired. Public servants had received notice that "DEI" initiatives were no longer to be funded (and shouldn't be talked about, "free speech" aside), and that their positions were on notice under "Schedule F." Trump had started threatening to invade Greenland and thereby the EU, as well as the Panama Canal, and to send military forces into Mexico to break up drug cartels, in violation of Mexican sovereignty. Reports of Immigration

Customs Enforcement raids targeting "blue" (Democrat-voting) states, targeting even schools, began to roll in, alongside of the imminent opening of a new offshore Internment Camp for "illegals" deemed "criminal" by the regime at the notorious American military base in Guantanamo Bay, Cuba—soon after, to be replaced by offshore facilities in El Salvador and a shortlived "alligator Alcatraz" in Florida.

The struggle against tyranny is the battle of memory against forgetting, the Czech novelist Milan Kundera opined. What the neofascism this time makes clear is that, even with all the historical knowledge available, we must also fight derealization, denial, and the desire to assure ourselves despite every evidence that things will turn out OK, until well after they have not. To measure the developments we've just laid out, even against the unquestioned norms and standards of the year 2000 in the West is to experience cognitive vertigo. So far has the "Overton window" shifted, as Right-wing operatives can rightly gloat—although, when needed, they also present themselves as "freedom" and "democracy" itself.

Yet Trump 2.0, and with it the collapse of US democracy into a kind of Constitutional twilight zone, awaiting the lurching consolidation of the New Regime ("like we've never seen before," as Trump says), is also far from being an outlier. Whereas in 1990, next to no Far-Right political movement had any share of power in Europe, "populist," anti-immigration, ethnonationalist parties are now in power in Hungary, Italy, and Russia. Far Right Parties are more popular than they have been since the interwar in France and Germany. They are on the rise in Portugal and Spain, Poland and Austria.

Much of the world as of 2025, hence, seems on an unstoppable course toward a second, "neo"-fascist era. But this time, the international Axis of Right-wing authoritarian states will be led by the nation whose soldierss took back Italy and North Africa, then stormed the beaches of Normandy in June 1944 and were instrumental in the downfall, firstly of Mussolini's fascism, then of German National Socialism.[2]

5.2 Competing Theories of Fascism

Part of the confusion surrounding whether to call the "MAGA" movement "fascist" or not reflects decades of inconclusive specialist debates in "fascism studies."[3] This is a recondite academic subdiscipline given over to the question of how, if at all, we can provide any definition of fascism, whether this definition should include Nazism, whether "fascism" was a singular historical phenomenon, and related questions. Then there is the way the "f-word" has been thrown around, often irresponsibly, to name any kind of authoritarian gesture, person, or political phenomenon: from a neurotic local schoolteacher to Joseph Stalin. After 1945, the outrage at "the crimes that stank in the nostrils of the world" committed by the Nazis[4] made fascism almost synonymous with evil and political illegitimacy. Accordingly, the term is used politically, including by those on the Far Right, to designate anyone people disagree with. In this way, it is sometimes even used synonymously, for instance by Mr. Trump, with "Marxist," to denigrate people like the neoliberal American Democrats beyond all reason.

Camus was one of the first philosophical authors, alongside Hannah Arendt, to write at length about Nazism and fascism. Firstly, he responded to Hitler's reign as a journalist at *Combat* in 1944. Then, after 1945, he addressed fascism, its causes, features, and dangers in the novel *The Plague*, a series of important public addresses ("The Crisis of Humanity," "Witness of Freedom," and "Time of Murderers"), *The Rebel* of 1951, and finally, the dark masterpiece, *The Fall* of 1956 and near-contemporary short story, "The Renegade," in *Exile and the Kingdom*. Camus's ideas hence precede the decades-long scholarly debates about "fascism"'s or "Nazism"'s precise extensions amongst theoreticians. They hail from a period in which the Holocaust and Second World War, as well as the occupation of France and other European nations in the Nazi *Grossraum* from 1939–45, were living memories. Camus matters today, as a clear-sighted critic of fascism, who aimed in his writings to warn contemporaries and future generations like ours. As he has Dr. Rieux reflect in the moment of liberation from the plague in *La Peste* of 1947 (and as we quoted at the very start of this book), as far as Camus was concerned, interwar fascism was not a once-off. It was, under the right conditions, a permanent human temptation:

> And, indeed, as he listened to the cries of joy rising from the town, Rieux remembered that such joy is always imperilled. He knew what those jubilant crowds did not know but could have learned from books: that the plague bacillus never dies or disappears for good; that it can lie dormant for years and years in furniture and linen chests; that it bides its time in bedrooms, cellars, trunks, and bookshelves; and that perhaps the day would come when, for the bane and the enlightening of men, it would rouse up its rats again and send them forth to die in a happy city.[5]

To understand Camus's position on fascism, its causes, and the sources of its recurrent attraction to human beings and societies in the kinds of distress we've examined (Sections 1.1, 2.1, and 4.1), we need to place it in relation to other theoretical perspectives on this subject. It seems to us that, outside of the more complex but recondite field of "fascism studies," there are two broadly competing orientations in this field.

5.2.1 Fascism as Hypertrophy of Administrative Reason and "Modernity"

On one hand, we have positions which see fascism as the culmination of broadly "totalitarian" tendencies within modern society, hidden in its commitments to rationality, the sciences, technology, and the bureaucratic administration of human affairs. Probably the most influential version of this perspective, in the neoliberal era, is that of Friedrich Hayek, in his 1944 work *The Road to Serfdom*.[6] Hayek argued that Far Right regimes, no less than Far Left authoritarian regimes like that of Soviet Russia, resulted from the superimposition of artificial, centralized administrative regulation on the "catalaxy" of free markets. For Hayek, located individuals "on the ground" are always in the best position to make decisions as to what to buy and sell. Distant decisions made by regulators in capital cities pervert people's incentives and create manifold inefficiencies, reducing overall productivity in a society and driving down living standards. They also limit people's freedom to choose to pursue whatever courses in life, or at least, to do business that they might desire. From this point of view, Nazism and Stalinism can be viewed as different, ostensibly Rightist and Leftist versions of "State socialism." Their ideological opposition was strong enough to send millions to their deaths in Europe in Second World War. But it conceals their deeper, shared illiberal features, clear to the neoliberal theoretician.[7]

It is remarkable how closely Hayek's position comes to core directions that come out of "postmodernist" and New Left thinking on this subject. In 1942, in exile in California, the critical theorists Theodor Adorno and Max Horkheimer wrote their fragmented work, *The Dialectic of Enlightenment*.[8] Horkheimer particularly retained some commitment to enlightenment ideals, that the advancement of human knowledge, by dissolving myths, would advance the cause of human liberation. Yet, this text argues that "the enlightenment" of the eighteenth century carries forwards a baleful civilizational addiction to "instrumental reason" looking back to the Homeric epics, notably the *Odyssey*. Western humanity, animated by an unspoken fear of the natural world, has used reason and cunning to try to dominate nature. In doing so, we have enslaved our own, internal natures, and devised social systems which use reason to exercise total control over each other and eliminate all human freedom. The enlightenment rationality which was supposed to overcome irrational, mythical fatality has meanwhile become its own unavoidable fate, removing everything unpredictable, incalculable, and spontaneous from human experience. The modern enlightenment in its triumph, the two theorists hence claim, "radiates disaster [calamity] triumphant."⁹ Kantian deontological ethics, with its categorical imperative, has led via Sade's cruel visions into the universe of the modern concentration camp. British thinker Francis Bacon's dream of alleviating the estate of man, for the glory of God, has led to the glory of the German Führer and universal enslavement.[10]

Despite the Marxist provenance of Horkheimer, this pessimistic vision of "modernity" ends by flattening all distinctions between liberal, socialist, and fascist societies under the sign of a civilizational "instrumental reason." In this way, like Hayek's, these critical thinkers' vision—who have so ironically been seized on by Right-wing conspiracists as engineering an anti-capitalist demise for America—comes into proximity to that propounded by the openly Nazi thinker, Martin Heidegger, at least after around 1936–8.[11] Heidegger embraced Nazism in 1933, seeing in it the only "exit" from the reign of modern technology. The latter, he argued, had roots in Western rational "metaphysics" going back to Plato. Modern technology ends by nihilistically objectifying everything, including human beings, as "standing reserve" (or *Gestell*).[12] Nazism, by contrast, with its stress on the specific destiny of the German *Volk*, in its relationship with the German homeland or *Heimat*, promised a new "inception" of the West. After around 1936, Heidegger's attempt to win influence as the philosopher of the regime failed—his ideas, considered idiosyncratic by the regime's leaders, were largely ignored. From then on, the celebrated "great thinker" withdrew his early activist enthusiasm. Heidegger became convinced that Nazism was an insufficiently radical attempt to break from the reign of modern *Technik*, which his *Black Notebooks* reveal he associated with the advance of Western Jewry (*Judentum*).[13] After 1945, as Germany lay in ruins, divided by the liberal and socialist Allies, Heidegger intoned that actually existing Nazism was one more manifestation of modern technological society. The Holocaust was like mechanized agriculture or the nuclear bomb.[14] Hence, it was not a distinctly German, distinctly Nazi crime, animated by fanatical belief in the irrationalist myth of a "Jewish world conspiracy." It was a hypertrophy of modern rationalism—again, as in Hayek, and Horkheimer and Adorno. As such, Nazism had more supposedly in common with liberal democracies and socialism than real differences. With that said, unrepentant, Heidegger would uphold until his end the idea that Nazism "moved in the right direction," as against liberalism and socialism, if only it could have been reconceived according to his lights.

5.2.2 Fascism as Politicized Irrationalism

There is a second orientation, in response to fascism and Nazism, however. It is associated with figures like the younger Herbert Marcuse, Aurel Kolnai, Ernst Bloch, and György Lukács.[15] This orientation is much closer to the ideological texts and statements of the fascists themselves about their political movements. In decisive contrast with the first kind of theory of fascism, it successfully captures the specificity of these Far-Right regimes, in contrast to the liberal regimes they despised, and the forms of socialism with which they positioned themselves at cultural, then real, war. This orientation argues that the genealogy of modern fascist regimes, and the rationales for their crimes, do not hearken back to Plato's metaphysics or Homer's epics. Although the Far Right regimes in power of course employed modern technologies, fascism as a political movement is characterized principally by its irrationalist vision of human nature and human history. Its ideological antecedents look back to German romanticism and the generation of thinkers like Schelling, after Kant, then pass through forms of vitalism such as that of Nietzsche, a common heroized reference for fascist ideologues across national boundaries (Section 3.4).[16] These thinkers pitted passion against reason, and intuition, art, and "genius" against the kinds of methodological procedures for certifying truths characteristic of the modern sciences. They argued that the advent of modern rationalism had cut human beings off from the prerational, deep sources of value which lie in people's primal roots, ethnicity, soil, tradition, destiny, will, or "historicity." They maintained that the world is not experienced in the same ways by different people, from different places and heritages. It "shows itself" (as Heidegger says) differently at different times and places. The kinds of modern reason extolled by liberals and socialists alike, with its baleful universalism, is hence depicted by fascists as an "ethnocidal" disaster, uprooting people and delivering them over to a reign of bloodless abstractions, technology and "asphalt," as the Nazis used to say.[17] Its implicit egalitarianism, captured in the slogans of 1789 ("liberty, equality, fraternity"), is based in the sense that reason is given to all people. Accordingly, such modern thinking unnaturally denies the inequalities, both within people—wherein some only are born for genius, creativity, and leadership, and the majority to serve; and between peoples, each of which has a particular, distinctive destiny, and a few of whom are superior to others, fated with higher "missions" justifying imperial claims. Fascism, as a violently antiliberal, antisocialist political movement, polemicized and popularized these romanticist ideas, tying them to "populist" narratives of national or racial greatness, and of elite or foreign betrayal, like the "stab in the back" myth of Germany after the First World War:

> stripping them of everything "private" and "spiritually high-flying" and converting what was left into a determined and uncouth form of popular corruption. Everything that had been said on irrational pessimism from Nietzsche and Dilthey to Heidegger and Jaspers on lecture platforms and in intellectuals' salons and cafes, Hitler and Rosenberg transferred to the streets.[18]

Hannah Arendt's celebrated works stand interestingly between these two traditions, in ways which invite comparisons with Camus such as that of Jeffrey C. Isaac.[19] On one hand, Arendt sees in Nazism and the concentration camp system it engendered a break with Western tradition. This unites her position with those of Kolnai, Marcuse, and Lukacs.[20] Fascism was predicated on the devolution of modern populations, under conditions of imperialism, war, and economic uncertainty, into a "mob" open to the demagoguery of figures like Hitler, Mussolini, and their lieutenants.[21] Its rule was hardly rational, the culmination of scientific progress and technique. It was less like a crystal palace, in fact, than an irrational dynamo[22] which swept away all the protections of law and tradition, leaving entire peoples disoriented and delivered over to the whims and wills of the Leader-figures.[23] On the other hand, Arendt's use of the category of "totalitarianism," notably in Part III of *Origins of Totalitarianism* (written later than Parts I and II), suggests proximity to the Hayek-Horkheimer & Adorno-Heidegger perspective. Indeed, as Emmanuel Faye has saliently contended, when Arendt argues that the totalitarian ideologies (like those of Nazism) gave to the disoriented masses a new "consistency" in worldview that they desperately craved, she comes close to equating this ideological "consistency" and "logic"[24]—the logic of conspiratorial narratives like that found in *Protocols of the Elders of Sion* or today in irrational panics like QAnon—with the epistemic virtues at the basis of ancient philosophical and modern scientific rationality.[25] Her contention, developed in the controversial text on Nazi administrator, Adolf Eichmann, comes increasingly to suggest that the evil of Nazism, like that of Stalinism, hailed not from its irrationalist ideology celebrating strength, will, force, race, and domination. It came from the "banality" of administrators, working in offices, scheduling trains to death camps, as administrators in socially liberal nations schedule welfare payments to the needy or disadvantaged.[26]

How we understand fascism and "totalitarianism" is vital, presuming that it remains agreed with Camus in 2025 that, whatever the proposed problems, embracing such regimes is always worse.[27] The Kolnai et al. view of Nazism as a form of irrationalist reaction suggests the importance of criticizing reason in its thoughtless misapplications. But it stops short of abandoning modern commitments to the sciences, liberty, equality, and fraternity—unlike the Hayek, Adorno and Horkheimer, and Heidegger directions. It also seems far better placed than its neoliberal-reactionary competitor to comprehend the plague of conspiratorial fantasies, pseudo-masculine aggression, and scorn for legal and administrative rationality that have surrounded the neofascist re-ascendancy of our times. Arendt by the end of her analysis can be adduced, alongside Hayek and the critical theorists, to argue that all we might need to do to honor the "Remember!" scratched into the bark of a birch by an unknown victim at Birkenau is to oppose the further advancement of modern rationality. That pathway, we will see, is not Camus's.

5.3 Irrational Terror: Camus's Critique of Fascism

How does Camus stand in relationship to these two competing orientations toward fascism, in this period in which entire nations seem committed to revisiting the rhetoric, ideologies, and many of the policies of the interwar fascist regimes, whilst denying the undeniable historical echoes that their endeavors set up?

Camus broke from the Algerian communist party when, following directives from Moscow, it sought to prioritize anti-fascism over addressing the concrete social issues facing the Algerian population. With the outbreak of war in September 1939, Camus seems for a time to have been bewildered, even despondent. Nevertheless, by 1943–4, we see his writing addressing the fascist spectre: notably, in the play *Caligula*, about a nihilistic tyrant who effectively commits suicide by behaving so hatefully that he provokes his own killers, and in "Letters to a German Friend" (Section 5.4). In *Combat*, in late 1944, as Allied forces began invading Germany to signal the end, there are several articles on Hitler, Germany, and Nazism.[28] Camus depicts Nazism as a form of nihilism for which might is right, and success at any cost the only measure of value. It rested on an irrational idolization of the Fuehrer, perceived as a "genius" or "great man" to whose vision of national regeneration every other value was sacrificed: "art, philosophy, and morality."[29] For Camus, Hitler was not a genius. He was a mediocrity elevated by circumstance, "who screamed his hatred above thousands of helmeted heads," and under whose regime "the word 'man' ... lost all meaning...., thus debasing forever the very idea of 'greatness,'" replacing it with an ecstasy of "humiliation and suffering."[30] In key postwar speeches, Camus would carry forward this diagnosis, impugning Nazism and fascism for having introduced amoral "realism" into European civilization, shamelessly licensing deceit, enslavement, and murder in ways which amounted to a crisis of humanity.

It is however in *The Rebel*, in the context of his history of modern revolt against divine injustice and its devolution, that Camus gives his longest theoretical accounting for the regimes of Hitler and Mussolini. The chapter's title, "State Terrorism and Irrational Terror" demarcates Camus's nuanced position in debates concerning fascism's identity, and its relationship with the "totalitarian" regimes of the communist bloc. "It is not legitimate to identify the ends of Fascism with the ends of Russian communism," Camus contends. Fascism is the result of "rushing blindly into history in the name of the irrational" (R, 246). It involves, as for Kolnai or Lukács, "deifying the irrational, and the irrational alone, instead of deifying reason" (R, 177–8). Marxism-Leninism proposes its own, historicized, post-Hegelian form of "absolute rationality," as the End to be pursued (Section 4.3). Fascism, as we saw in Section 3.4, "wants to establish the advent of the Nietzschean superman" by exalting a particular people or race, "liberating a few by subjugating the rest" (R, 246–7). Communism aims at liberating all human beings in a post-historical universal Society, and one must "grant the grandeur of its intentions," Camus maintains (R, 247). It is at the level of the means employed, once such great historical Ends are nominated, that Camus's opposition to Marxist-Leninism begins: "on the other hand, it is legitimate to identify the means employed by both with the political cynicism that they have drawn from the same source, moral nihilism" (R, 247; cf. Section 4.3).

If we look at the means employed by fascism in power, Camus maintains, the same willingness to kill, deceive, and enslave that was found in Soviet Russia under Stalin is manifest: "terror and concentration camps" (R, 247). In both cases, we have the assertion of the will to power, and the willingness to do everything necessary to subjugate the internal population of the nation through terror and propaganda, as well as to destroy its external enemies through war. Ernst Jünger, Camus maintains (rather contestably), was the only literary and intellectual figure able to give any philosophical substance to fascism's political project. In *The Worker* of 1930, Jünger envisages a wholly militarized dystopia of soldier-warriors, living under total mobilization, "removed from the sphere of negotiation, from pity, and from literature and elevated to the sphere of action. Legal obligations are transformed into military obligations" (R, 181). These figures, without individuality or any morality transcending that of obedience to the orders of their superiors, would give body to "a religion of anti-Christian technology" (at R, 181). Such a society, Camus observes, amounts to "the factory and the barracks of the world" (R, 181). Hermann Rauschning described Nazism in 1938 as "the death of freedom, the triumph of violence, and the enslavement of the mind" (R, 181). What this translates to is a craven political theology in which the Leader, elevated beyond good and evil and claiming a mainline to an obscure Providence, presents Himself as a "jackbooted Jehovah" (R, 182). In classically tyrannical fashion, he destroys all intermediaries between He and his clique, and the masses. The latter, usually in choreographed public spectacles, are reduced to shouting slogans and carrying out His every barked order. "One Leader, One People" (a central Nazi slogan) for Camus signifies "one master and millions of slaves" (R, 182). There is no possibility of free agency or criticism from below. In place of the intermediaries provided by a relatively free press, a relatively independent judiciary, and anything like a legislature or executive accountable to the people through elections, there is the Party or "apparatus," "which is the emanation of the Leader and the tool of his will to oppress" (R, 182). All individual responsibility is abdicated by functionaries, as the Nuremberg trials demonstrated:[31] "honor lay in obedience, which was often confused with crime" (R, 183).

Human beings are reduced to tools or "cogs" in the vast machine of such a hyper-militarized totality. Or else, they become "enemies" or "heretics" to be eliminated, "a waste product of the machine" (R, 183). "Irrational terror transforms men into objects, 'planetary bacilli', in Hitler's formula" (R, 183). Through "propaganda and terror," fascism takes aim at everything in human being that is not reducible to such mindless tools or obstacles: "it proposes the destruction, not simply of the individual, but the universal possibility of the individual, of reflection, of solidarity, and of absolute love." What remains from this "systematic degradation" is "identification with the cynical criminal and forced complicity," a phrase which might sound uncanny in 2025 (R, 183).[32]

Camus hence accepts a comparison at the level of means between Nazism and Stalinism, and as such, in terms of the lived experience of subjects and victims. This is ethically decisive. Both regime-types pervert the longing for justice at the heart of modern revolt into a revolutionary or counter-revolutionary fervor which takes aim at total, Godlike control over millions of human beings. Each, once it becomes totalitarian, instates forms of oppression every bit as unjust as that of a tyrannical deity:

> Totality is, in effect, nothing other than the ancient dream of unity common to both believers and rebels, but projected horizontally onto an earth deprived of God. To renounce every value [beyond achievement of the ideological End] ... amounts to renouncing rebellion in order to accept the Empire and slavery ... The German nation frees itself from its oppressors, but at the price of the freedom of every German. The individuals under a totalitarian regime are not free, even though man in the collective sense is free. Finally, when the Empire delivers the entire human species, freedom will reign over herds of slaves, who at least will be free in relation to God. (R, 233)

Yet, the "irrational terror" in Camus's title of his chapter on fascism also marks his distance from any thesis which posits an equivalence between the deformation of communism under Stalinism, and the fascists' open exaltation of will, blood, soil, race, and violence as ends in themselves. If we examine what the fascists declared about their movements, Camus agrees with Kolnai or Lukács, what we find is a vitalistic exaltation of movement and dynamism, not of reasoned deliberation, historical rationality, or the sciences:

> Hitler's untenable paradox lay precisely in wanting to found a stable order on perpetual change and a negation. Rauschning, in his *Revolution of Nihilism*, was right in saying that the Hitlerian revolution represented unadulterated dynamism … At the Nuremberg trial, Frank spoke of 'the hatred of form' which animated Hitler … this man was nothing but an elemental force in motion, directed and rendered more effective by calculated cunning and by a relentless tactical clear-sightedness. (R, 178–9)

Rosenberg, the official Nazi intellectual, would comment—in words echoed by other ideologues—that Nazism was the exaltation of action alone, as its own expressive End: "like a column on the march, and it is of little importance towards what destination and for which ends this column is marching" (R, 180). As Herbert Marcuse quickly realized, at issue in these movements is a kind of black political existentialism.[33] Fascism rejects all sources of moral, reasoned and transcendent value. So, it can only look to find significance in the very movement of life itself and the exaltation of action and power. It is in this connection that Camus, notably, frames fascist biologism of the kind we see reestablished in "Alt"-corners of the internet, and making its way into the discourse of Trump and others. It is not for Camus the defining mark of fascism or Nazism. It is rather a rationalization and attempt to give some substance to the ruthless Machiavellianism at issue: "the exaltation of the dark powers of blood and instinct, the biological justification of all of the worst things produced by the instinct of domination" (R, 179).

The underlying psychological source of attraction to fascist irrationalism amongst the masses, Camus maintains, is despair—of the very kind, and with the very features (including heightened levels of suicide (R, 178)) which we opened this book by documenting in the United States and more widely around the globe (Section 1.1). "In Germany, shaken to its foundation by a calamitous war, by defeat, and by economic distress, values no longer existed," he comments (R, 179). And "to those who despair of everything, not reason but only passion can provide a faith, and … it must be the same passion that lay at the root of the despair—namely, humiliation and hatred" (R, 179). The result of this politicized irrationalism, rooted in despair and humiliation, was that the nation of Goethe embraced "the ethics of the gang" (R, 179). And, as Camus explains in words which ring prescient in our era of Trumpism: "gangster morality is an inexhaustible round of triumph and revenge, defeat and resentment" (R, 179). For such an amoral "ethics," despite its self-presentation as triumphant self-assertion and "strength," an enemy is always necessary. This a doctrine which, like so much else, can be found in Nietzsche, and is asserted openly in fascist thinkers even of the highest calibre, such as Heidegger and Schmitt:[34]

> They could only define themselves, psychopathic dandies that they were, in relation to their enemies, and only assume their final form in the bloody battle that was to be their downfall. The Jews, the Freemasons, the plutocrats, the Anglo-Saxons, the bestial Slavs succeeded one another in their propaganda and their history as a means of propping up, each time a little higher, the blind force that was stumbling headlong towards its end. Perpetual strife demanded perpetual stimulants. (R, 179)

Ultimately, Camus claims, far from being the necessary result of modern Western rationality, Nazism's originality came in how, "for the first time in history, the rulers of a country … used their power to establish a *mystique* beyond all ethical considerations" (R, 184). Ernst Jünger outed the desire for annihilation that stalked this craven, supra-moral political theology in which "the commandments of the Leader, standing in the burning bush of spotlights, on a Sinai of planks and flags," was the only lawless Law (R, 183). "One of the great and cruel pleasures of our time is to participate in the work of destruction," Jünger confided (R, 178). The result of a "doctrine of such total destruction being able to seize the levers of command of a civilized nation" was, by 1945, "crimes without precedent in history" (R, 184). These crimes culminated, via the crematoria of the death camps, in the Leader's willing of annihilation down upon the defeated German *Volk* itself, to accompany his own suicide (R, 185).

We are a long way in Camus from seeing in fascism the alleged epochal-inevitable triumph of Western rationalism looking back to the Greeks, or any confusion between liberal-democratic, socialist, and Far Right parties, politicians, movements, and regimes.

5.4 After the Fall: Camus and the Psychology of Fascism

Intellectuals work with ideas as their daily bread. We are prone to supposing that, if only the true theory of a phenomenon is discovered, then real world change must follow. If for instance "fascism" could be defined, it could be prevented. This idealism is poorly matched to politics. The triumph of the Far Right in America in 2025, for instance, is the result of concerted political organization hailing back to the Powell memo and "Southern strategy" of the Nixon years, to which countless millions of dollars (at least) have been devoted—as well as of connected, continually growing conditions of political-economic inequality (Section 4.1).[35] Camus himself supposed that the West's vulnerabilities to the plague of cynicism, "realism," and imperialistic, totalitarian excesses could only be overcome through a second renaissance, beyond nihilism (see Chapter 1). The causes of fascism, in his time, lay not only in the ideas that Camus traced back to Hegel and Nietzsche. They also came from the shocks of war and depression, as well as the reign of money in the liberal democracies, including over the press. This had engendered a shallow, commercialized culture, in which truth and dialogue took a back seat to spectacle and titillation (Chapter 2). In the interwar world as in our neoliberal age, material inequalities were allowed to foster forms of effective servitude and dig deep wells of desperation, resentment and alienation (Chapter 4). To prevent the reemergence of fascism, Camus counsels us from the 1940s and 50s, societies need to be created in which these causes cannot be allowed to take root. Social and political movements need to be formed which could oppose their formation.

Yet, Camus's perspective on fascism as "State Terror *and Irrational Terrorism*," and the challenge it poses to the accounts hailing from thinkers like Heidegger and Adorno and Horkheimer, is important. What most presents itself about the new forms of fascism today, is after all not their hypertrophy of administrative or scientific reason. It is their florid irrationalism: from the lurid conspiratorialism of QAnon to the higher end recourse of organic Alt-"thought leaders" to forms of vitalistic accelerationism associated with the "tech bros" on one hand, and the essentializing pseudo-traditionalism of figures like Julius Evola, Jordan Peterson and Aleksandr Dugin on the other. If people in nations wherein forms of authoritarian ethnonationalism have not yet consolidated power are to forestall this, we must cease mistaking Right-wing authoritarianism for anything like forms of democratic state formation, in which markets are limited, and basic social protections are ensured for all. Fascism mimics socialism before it wins power, presenting itself as a radical alternative to mainstream lassitude and corruption to garner popular support. In power, it supports the most regressive measures which do not benefit the base, beyond their mobilization against internal and external foes in endless *Kampf*. But we must also develop an empathetic—not sympathetic—understanding of why millions of people are attracted in conditions of crisis to grandiose claims of "national regeneration," proposed by would-be salvific Leaders whose principal qualification seems to be an outsized sense of their own genius and an unavailability to shame.

Here, Camus's work as a *litterateur*, not only a theoretician, separates his work from other twentieth-century philosophical voices who sought to understand the disasters of Hitler's and Stalin's terrorism. He is amongst other things a discerning psychologist of the human attraction to forms of evil and perversion. Camus initially baulked at the idea, suggested by the triumph of the authoritarianisms, that there is a longing for servitude in many intellectuals and perhaps knitted into human psychology more widely. How can a being that desires happiness, and connection with others, be drawn to embracing the Leadership of figures and ideologies that deprive them of freedom, and offer instead the promise of glorious sacrifice and the chastisement of enemies? By 1951, he had come to an assessment:

> "The human being needs happiness, and when he is unhappy, he needs another human being." Those who reject the agony of living and dying wish to dominate. "Solitude is power," says Sade. Power, today, because for thousands of solitary people it signifies the suffering of others, bears witness to the need for others. Terror is the homage that the malignant recluse finally pays to the brotherhood of man. (R, 248)

Camus addresses the psychology of the embrace of fascism principally in two places, the wartime "Letters to a German Friend," then in *The Fall* of 1956. The latter novel is arguably his profoundest, although most bitter work. It was written amidst the darkness of his intellectual isolation from the Parisian *rive gauche*, the civil war in Algeria, and his failures as a husband to his second wife. As I've argued elsewhere, Camus's "Letters to a German Friend" has been wrongly accused of presenting an overly sympathetic response to Nazism.[36] The four letters address a nameless German companion, who has come to embrace Nazism. As the letter format would suggest, it is true that Camus does not from the start stridently condemn his friend. He instead concedes seeing a number of flawed, but partly valid reasons why his friend had been drawn into Hitler's *Gefolgschaft* (following): the loss of faith in intelligence, the love of country and, notably, the nihilistic *denouement* in which many young people of the interwar generation had found themselves.

There is always something in our natures, Camus moreover concedes, "that yields to instinct, to contempt for intelligence, to the cult of efficiency."[37] In *Combat*, he will note that there are always many people for whom "success is a law and brutality a temptation."[38] But the struggle against fascism, Camus maintains, is at one level a struggle for a few fine distinctions which fascist ideologies and propaganda work to confuse in the minds of followers:

> We are fighting for the distinction between sacrifice [legitimate where necessary] and mysticism [fascism], between energy [legitimate, necessary] and violence [fascism], between strength [legitimate, necessary] and cruelty [fascism], for that even finer distinction between the true and the false, between the man of the future and the cowardly gods you revere.[39]

Camus notably credits the longing for a homeland or *patrie* which fascism exploits. Our first attachments and loyalties are to those nearest to us, with whose lives we directly interact. But Nazism asks people to place love of the Fatherland and Führer above all other values. This is one-sided and excessive and a license for crime. "You are fighting against everything in man that does not belong to the mother country," Camus accuses his friend,[40] so "even the gods are mobilized in your country."[41]

Underlying this excessive devotion to the Fatherland that screens out all competing sources of loyalty and orientation, Camus also identifies a deeper despair—per the analysis later given in *The Rebel*. "For a long time, *we both thought* that this world had no ultimate meaning and that consequently we were cheated. *I still think so, in a way*," Camus concedes.[42] But referring to his basic philosophy of rebellion (Section 1.4), for which the human demand for dignity and meaning—unity, as against totality—is irremovable, Camus draws a limit:

> "What is truth?," you used to ask. To be sure, but at least we know what falsehood is: that is just what you have taught us. "What is spirit?" We know its contrary, which is murder. "What is man?" There I stop you. Man is that force which cancels all tyrants and gods. He is the force of evidence. Human evidence is what we must preserve.[43]

The psychologic of fascist nihilism is given its most complete portrait in *The Fall*, in the figure of "Jean-Baptiste Clamence": a man who eschews the "clemency" suggested by his surname, and whose ministry ("John the Baptist") in a seedy bar in Amsterdam is closed to all possibility of grace.[44] Jean-Baptiste had fancied himself a kind of Nietzschean Overman, but with a public-facing sense of morality: a high-flying lawyer and advocate for the downtrodden, the orphan and the widow. Today, he might be an online "thought leader." One night, walking home beside the Seine after one of his myriad trysts, he witnessed or half-witnessed, at least he heard, a woman commit suicide. With no one around, Jean-Baptiste did not leap in to the Seine to assist the suicide.[45] He came instead, reflecting on his failure to do anything, to see the falsity of his stance of public probity and *bienveillance*. Still lacking in fundamental modesty, Jean-Baptiste, however, did not conclude from this personal failure to the need to work harder, to more fully embody the ideals that he publically advertised. Instead, he inferred from his own case that all human nature is "fallen," hypocritical, and self-interested: its celebrated principles like justice and its other-directed affects like love, all a sham: "After prolonged research on myself, I brought out the fundamental duplicity of the human being."[46] From a hypocritical, imperfect idealism, Jean-Baptiste leaped to cynical nihilism. But he reasoned, if everyone was fallen, he at least had come to know and see clearly the reality of universal corruption: "I no longer have friends, only accomplices."⁴⁷ And this disillusioned cynicism gives him the advantage, the ability in his own eyes, once more, to triumphantly stand over others in Judgment and condemnation.

Many others in the twentieth and now our century, unlike Jean-Baptiste, have not only judged others. Proclaiming their higher strength, they have arrogated the right to enslave, deceive, and kill, since they have accepted the bitter supposed "truth" that life, without meaning beyond the play of forces, defaults to a violent struggle (*Kampf*) for the ego and its own (R, 184).

There is one line in *The Rebel*'s section on fascism (Section 5.3) which I believe portends and gives the key to Jean-Baptiste's hateful psychology in *The Fall*:

> The triumph of the man who kills or tortures is marred by only one shadow: he is unable to feel that he is innocent. Thus, he must create guilt in his victim so that, in a world that has no direction, universal guilt will authorize no other course of action than the use of force and give its blessing to nothing but success. When the concept of innocence disappears from the mind of the innocent victim himself, the value of power establishes a definitive rule over a world in despair. (R, 183–4)

The despair which Camus identifies at the heart of all forms of fascism, the despair of the kinds we opened this book by diagnosing in the world of 2025, readily gives way to a cynicism about all ideals. It is all a con, so why not choose con men who have no shame and exalt power and "owning" their foes, going along with the vicarious sense of empowerment? As Jean-Baptiste Clamence gloats: "when we are all guilty, there will be democracy … the others get theirs too, and at the same time as we—that's what counts. All together at last, but on our knees and with our heads bowed."⁴⁸ Since liberty is a sham, the liberty of billionaires and the top 10 percent at most; since equality before the law is mocked by money, power, and corruption, let alone material inequality: what this means is that fraternity can only be experienced in the "populist" forms of the mass rally, jingoism, the cult of a Great Man, the national emergency, the struggle against the common enemy, and the sports stadium. For the rest, there is the need to defend ourselves, by whatever means strength affords, against those whom the Leaders designate as the enemies of the hour: university professors, illegal immigrants, legal immigrants, student protestors, critical race theorists, trans-activists, liberal politicians, the mainstream media, the "lawfare" of the independent judiciary ...

Camus's identification of the fascist mechanism of creating universal guilt, and hence a moral equivalence licensing the craven assertion of power, seems especially prescient, considering the recent neofascist surge. If one wants to steal an election, one preemptively claims that the others have already done this, and doubles down; if one wants to normalize deceit and indifference to the truth, the way to do this is to claim that "the mainstream media" "fake news" has already done this; if one wants to politicize the judiciary and remove its independence from the Executive, the way to do that is to claim that it has already been "weaponized" against you; if one is up for criminal charges, one asserts that the entire system is "criminal" and needs to be purged. One is then only defending oneself, even "defending democracy" by undermining democratic precedents, the division of powers, and civic norms while openly expressing admiration for dictators. All these mechanisms, this infernal race to the ethical bottom where only brazen assertions and counter-assertions of power remain, we have been seeing play out over the last decade.

So, what does Camus' analysis of the psychological bases of people's embracing of forms of fascism suggest? "They thought they were free," leading Nazi Hans Frank declared of the German people at Nuremberg; "didn't they know that no one escapes from Hitlerism?" Camus replies:

> They did not know; nor did they know that the negation of everything is in itself a form of servitude, and that real freedom is an inner submission to a value which defies history and its successes. (R, 186)

Any revolt against the rising neofascism, as the political form of active nihilism, will involve reembracing the counterfactual ideals of modern democracy, led by freedom and justice. It will involve struggling against the forces of money and power to make these ideals real and active in people's lives. The critical "no" to the injustices and dishonesty of our imperfect democracies cannot become an absolute "no" to all democratic ideals. Only by removing the causes of popular despair and cynicism which level the ground for the messianic promises of "populist" Leaders, will their ability to seduce millions be dammed up. In place, we will need individually and collectively to affirm new forms of value, of happiness, creativity, beauty and friendship, new ways of life rooted in revived virtues beyond the sanctification of force and fact, egoism, "whataboutism," and the cult of success at any cost.

6

Nature, the Sacred, and Balance

6.1 Beyond Criticism or Negation: Camus's Philosophical Originality

We said in the Introduction that Camus matters today for two kinds of reasons. First, he addressed analogues of exactly the issues that we are facing today: alienation and nihilism, the polarization of public debate and preponderance of political lying and cynical exploitation, the divisions of the Left, and the rise of the Far Right. Secondly, we claimed, Camus is also an original, distinct thinker: someone whose views stand out, among much of twentieth-century philosophical thought. The preceding five chapters have tried to bear out the first claim. In examining Camus's diagnoses of, and responses to nihilism, to "post-truth," to political romanticism, and fascism, we have necessarily uncovered a good many of his affirmative positions. The rebel is someone whose critical "no" to injustice and senselessness is underlain by a "yes" to the "we are" of living human community (Section 2.3). Just so, Camus's opposition to nihilism is underwritten by his affirmation of limits surrounding human dignity, denying the legitimacy of systematic deceit, all forms of human enslavement, and murder (Chapter 2): and as such, the "state terrorism," either of authoritarian socialist states (Chapter 4) or of Far-Right regimes led by Nazism (Chapter 5). Camus argues for a balance of liberty and equality: the liberties to speak, protest, think, and cultivate leisure, with the kinds of basic, universal economic security without which poverty and the constant struggle against material necessity prevents people from being able to live except in anxiety and fear (Section 4.2). Camus appreciates the reasons why people are drawn to Far Right political movements and constructs a discerning psychology of fascism. Yet, he refuses to elevate love of one's own to "the one thing needful," or to see in "strong men" claiming civilizational renewal through hatred and revenge anything more than mediocrities and symptoms of nihilistic decline (Section 5.3). Everywhere, Camus opposes the mock wisdom of cynicism which denounces all ideals as illusions, and reduces life to a permanent struggle in which fact, force, and being a "winner" at any price are sanctified (Sections 2.2 and 5.4).

Nevertheless, as we said, Camus by the time of what became the last years of his life had tired of criticism, of saying "no." To address his uniqueness among so many twentieth-century thinkers, the second consideration about why Camus specifically matters today, is to uncover the positive visions of human nature, nature, and community that Camus charted. It is also to understand how his perspective, unlike almost all philosophers of the last century, was not primarily shaped by modern philosophy following Immanuel Kant, which has focused on the cultural, linguistic, or institutional shaping of who we are. As we glimpsed in the Introduction, Camus would always affirm that "my colleagues follow the path of German philosophers of the nineteenth century, but me, I was nourished by Greek philosophy ... I am the son of Greek philosophy."[1] Receiving the 1957 Nobel Prize for Literature in Sweden, Camus explained further:

> I have Christian preoccupations, but my nature is pagan. The sun ... I feel at ease amongst the Greeks ... the Pre-Socratics, Heraclitus, Empedocles, Parmenides ... I have faith in the ancient values, however much they have been badly represented since Hegel.[2]

What this means, in more concrete terms, is that Camus's thinking is oriented in fundamentally different directions than many of the more celebrated intellectuals of the last century. As we saw in Chapter 3, the post-structuralist (or "post-modernist") thinking which became so prominent in the 1970s through 1990s embraced the values of political romanticism, which by that time were going mainstream in marketing and even neoliberal managerial guides: valuing the exceptional, the singular, the excessive, the different, the heroic and the messianic. Camus's position is a form of classicism or romanticism restrained. His thought embraces limits, balance, measure, harmony and unity. Whereas critical theorizing in the Marxian tradition, and then in forms of post-structuralism, sought out the ways in which historical forces, forms of power, or linguistic or social structures, shape human experience, Camus challenges this exclusively cultural or historical focus. Increasingly after 1944, Camus counterposes what he terms "history" (human social and political life) to the beauty of nonhuman nature. Camus also aligns this beauty of nonhuman nature with a series of virtues (notably courage, intelligence, honesty, justice, friendship, forms of love, and generosity), and the capacities to doubt, dialogue, and produce enduring works of art which almost seem quaint for some forms of critical theorizing.[3] As Camus writes in the beautiful 1948 essay, "Helen's Exile," written at the height of his political activism (Chapter 4):

> We have exiled beauty; the Greeks took up arms for her. First difference, but one that has a history ... What imagination could we have left for that higher equilibrium in which nature balanced history, beauty, virtue, and which applied the music of numbers even to the blood of tragedy? We turn our backs on nature; we are ashamed of beauty ... This is why it is improper to proclaim today that we are the sons of Greece. Or else we are the renegade sons. Placing history on the throne of God, we are progressing toward theocracy like those whom the Greeks called Barbarians and whom

they fought to death in the waters of Salamis ... the world has been cut from everything that constitutes its permanence: nature, the sea, hilltops, evening meditation. Consciousness is to be found only in the streets, because history is to be found only in the streets—this is the edict.[4]

In order to draw out why Camus matters as more than a critic, someone who presents positive ways forwards for dark times, this chapter will start with what is arguably *the* crisis of our times, whose consequences we are bequeathing to future generations: that of climate change, mass extinctions, and resource exhaustion.

6.2 Ecological Crises and Our Discontents

Climate change has been described as a "wicked problem." Its consequences are potentially devastating, its causes many, its scale universal. Billions of people, in our times, are already affected. The consequences for future generations and global order are also enormous. However, so many people have so much invested, financially and therefore existentially, in continuing present modes of extraction, production, consumption, and pollution, that a practical solution seems impossible. It would require levels of good will between nations, and between the owners of the means of pollution and the rest of global populations, that at present seem utopian. Yet, outside of a small minority of scientists largely in the pay of the big extractors, the data is in. The IPCC released its first report on the projected severity of impacts of climate change in 1990. According to analyses by NASA (hardly a politically radical initiative) and other groups, the earth was about 2.65 degrees Fahrenheit (1.47 degrees Celsius) warmer in 2024 than at the end of the nineteenth century.[5] The decade of 2014–24 was the warmest in recorded history.[6] The ocean surface is as of 2025 warming four times faster than it was as recently as 1985, with the annual average sea surface temperature (SST) over the extra-polar ocean reaching a record 20.87°C in 2024.[7] Antarctica is melting on average about 150 billion tons per year, and Greenland is losing about 270 billion tons of ice per year,[8] contributing to rising sea levels.[9]

Climate change is only the most-heated, so to speak—that is, most politicized—sign that human beings, with the modern idea of infinite economic growth, are increasingly out of harmony with our ecological surrounds. According to leading authorities, the United States is set to run out of coal within two decades, and the world will have burned all of its oil by 2075. A third of the world's forests have been logged, with some ten million hectares being logged annually.[10] There is a global shortage of phosphorous needed for crop yields, human beings are running out of reserves of rare earth metals, soil violability is declining globally, zinc will soon begin to run out, around 40 percent of plants are at risk of extinction alongside about 25 percent of animal species, and there are real concerns about the future viability of the global fish supply by 2050.[11]

While climate denialism continues, insurance companies globally, whose bottom lines are affected, are struggling to cope with the emerging realities. The costs of natural catastrophes for the industry topped $100bn between 2021 and 2024, with thirty-seven $1 billion catastrophes in 2023–4 alone.[12] The World Economic Forum, as of 2019, calculated that global warming had cost the world economy some $1.5 trillion in the preceding ten years.[13] The current rise in temperatures of around 1.47°C above pre-industrial levels has already brought increased frequency and intensities of storms, fires, floods, heat waves, and famines. In 2023, the World Health Organization (WHO 2023) reported that climate change was currently responsible for at least 150,000 deaths per year.[14] They predict that this rate will double by 2030. In "The Mortality Cost of Carbon," R. Daniel Bressler estimates that below 2°C in excess of preindustrial temperatures, "projected yearly excess deaths from climate change are relatively constant at around 100,000 per year."[15] However, above 2°C, "projected yearly excess deaths from climate change increase at an increasing rate in global average temperatures, rising to over four million excess deaths at 4°C."[16] What this boils down to, so to speak, is that one person will effectively perish for every 4,434 metric tons of carbon humans add to the earth's atmosphere, beyond the 2020 rate of emissions. This is a trajectory tracking toward some eighty-three million excess, climate-related deaths by 2100, when the world will be some 4.4°C warmer, according to the UN in 2023.

However, instead of committing as one to reducing emissions, as of 2023, countries were "planning and projecting an average annual increase of 2 percent, which by 2030 would result in more than double the production consistent with the 1.5°C limit."[17] One of Mr. Trump's first executive orders was to withdraw the United States from the Paris Climate Accords, having campaigned on a slogan to "drill, baby, drill," which thrilled his base and leading American extractors. The world economy as of 2025 remains chronically addicted to endless economic (and population) growth, on a finite planet, although scientists warn that a 1 percent increase in global GDP equals a 0.5–0.7 percent increase in carbon emissions, with flow-on climate effects.[18] As we saw in Chapter 4, economistic abstractions about "growth" (which is always "good," presumptively for everyone) conceal the inequalities baked into the economic and political models which have become ascendent globally since 1975. Unsurprisingly, it is the "winners" in this scenario who have the resources and capabilities to have contributed most, as well as having the most to lose, when it comes to global warming. The richest 10 percent of the world's population, as of 2020, is estimated to have been responsible for almost half of carbon emissions since 1990. The top 1 percent, astonishingly, is responsible for more than twice the emissions as the poorest 50 percent of the global population.[19] There is gigantic money in fossil fuels, while these fuels remain to extract and for as long as political change can be prevented through the power of money, misinformation, and agnotology. Far from struggling under the weight of global criticism and calls to reign in emissions, the top five fossil fuel companies doubled their profits in 2022 to some $219 billion.[20] Far from being crippled by "woke" ideology and climate "extremists," the UN estimated that, in 2020 alone, G20 governments committed $233 billion to the fossil fuel industries, many of whom have dedicated sums of this money to artful marketing campaigns to signal their environmental virtues.

What can the philosophers of the twentieth century tell us about this crisis of humanity? On one hand, our ability to understand and chart the effects of climate change, as well as to devise alternative means of low emission energy, clearly depend upon the developments of the natural sciences. On the other hand, responding to the ecological crises that face humanity in the twenty-first century is going to depend upon the cultivation of changed conceptions of nonhuman nature, and a new humility about our dependence upon it. Nevertheless, with some notable exceptions, most of the prominent thinkers of the last century, certainly those honored in the critical humanities, arguably have little directly to contribute to these tasks.[21] Broadly, Anglo-American philosophers have taken the sciences as authoritative, when it comes to understanding the nonhuman world. Continental European philosophers have been more skeptical, if not directly of the sciences' claims to truth about nature, then about their potentials and roles within systems of administrative and political control. In some cases, forms of radical anti-realism have prevailed: positioning the sciences as one more "narrative" that particular social groups have constructed, to legitimate their claims to social power. In the neofascist age, the echo of such positions with the forms of "post-truth" which have licensed the wholesale spread of misinformation and conspiracy cultures has become clear. For MAGA followers in the United States and kindred spirits globally, the medical sciences, the WHO, as well as the humanities, let alone climate science, are all "elite" constructions with no especial epistemic legitimacy. They shape illegitimate claims to social power. To accept the validity of climate science and the urgency of acting in response to it, while holding radically skeptical stances toward the sciences, or to suspect the sciences of being wholly instruments of social control or avatars of modern nihilism, is to find oneself in a lamentable contradiction.

As for understandings of nature, philosophy in the age of the sciences has largely withdrawn from its former role of trying to give a reasoned account of "the whole." Instead, twentieth-century philosophy has focused on what the Greeks used to call "the human things": language, logic, "value theory," knowledge and skepticism, social and political questions. In his *Carnets*, Camus himself noted how for Hegel, "nature" is quickly "sublated" in his system, documenting the human Geist's (collective Spirit's) evolutionary search for self-consciousness.[22] In the tradition of Marxian ideology critique, then many forms of feminist and post-colonialist critique, any and all claims to "nature" tend to be deemed highly suspicious. This is, because of the way that—as we see in the return of evolutionary biology in someone like Jordan Peterson today[23]—they have been used to justify forms of inequality and oppression. Foucault tells us that the "human being" which forms of humanism invite us to free is the product of forms of power, not of any presocial "nature" that could be located.[24] Even Heidegger's philosophy of "Being" talks little about nonhuman nature, as against human categories for understanding it. Instead, he unfolds a "history of Being" in the form of a secularized eschatology of decline since the Greeks, and rebirth, through the agency of the German *Volk* and a new "thinking" of uncertain propositional content.[25] In large measure, that is, Camus's 1948 diagnosis of European thought remains discerning:

> "Only the modern city," Hegel dares write, "offers the mind a field in which it can become aware of itself." We are thus living in the period of big cities … Our most significant works show the same bias. Landscapes are not to be found in great European literature since Dostoevsky. History explains neither the natural universe that existed before it nor the beauty that exists above it. Hence it chose to be ignorant of them.[26]

Camus's thought hence stands out among the twentieth-century philosophers' in the age of climate change, as Diane Stuart has recently credited.[27] And this matters, insofar as this issue matters, and it is not difficult to see its challenge animating elements of big business in their shift toward supporting the new authoritarians. Firstly: because Camus's criticism of administrative abstraction never extended to a radical skepticism about the sciences. Secondly: insofar as his philosophy includes a form of contemplative naturalism, which seeks to reestablish limits to human power and a balanced sense of our belonging to nature.

6.3 Helen's Exile: Science, Nature, and *Mesure*

If we consider Camus's thinking, as people concerned with the fate of the planet and future generations, we do not need to do any fancy footwork around criticizing the sciences as producers/products of modern nihilism, and yet ... supporting climate science against its well-funded deniers. It is true that Camus was a critic of the form of "absolute rationality" claimed by Stalinists to license political terror (Chapter 4). It is true that Camus was a critic of forms of administrative abstraction and bureaucratese, which accompany societies (and private businesses) in which there are unaccountable asymmetries of power (Section 2.3). Invited to a forum on the future of civilization in Greece, Camus acknowledged the threats, as well as the opportunities, of technological development.[28] Yet, his criticism of modern technological *hybris*, and the dangers it presents to prospects of human freedom, equality, and fraternity, are framed against the background of his "Greek" conception of nature. And his criticisms of the illiberal applications of the sciences are framed within a fundamental appreciation of the cognitive achievement of the modern sciences and their epistemic preconditions.

If we look at how science figures in *The Myth of Sisyphus*, Camus's orientation is already clear. On the one hand, he expresses frustration at how, in his time, the physical models of the atom, and of subatomic elements, seemed to trade, inescapably, on metaphors of planetary systems: "You explain this world to me with an image. I realize then that you have been reduced to poetry: I shall never know. Have I the time to become indignant? You have already changed theories."[29] On the other hand, Camus's frustration is limited to the ability of the natural sciences to explain everything, with certainty. It is aligned, in this way, with his criticism of metaphysical and theological "theories of everything," all of which Camus believes involve "leaps" which lucidity cannot sanction—taking nothing for granted that cannot be demonstrated by reasoning and experience. But it is just this recourse to a notion of descriptive lucidity, eschewing total explanations, which aligns Camus with modern scientific rationality. Describing his own method in *Myth*, he directly identifies it with the scientific pursuit:

> if I become thoroughly imbued with that sentiment that seizes me in face of the world's scenes, with that lucidity imposed on me by the pursuit of a science, I must sacrifice everything to these certainties and I must see them squarely to be able to maintain them.[30]

As Sean B. Carroll documents in his moving work, *Brave Genius: A Scientist, A Philosopher, and Their Brave Adventures in the French Resistance*, Camus was a close friend with Jacques Monod, whose genetic researches would see him win the Nobel Prize in 1965.[31] It was via Monod that Camus was able to understand, then condemn, Lysenko's attempts in the USSR to challenge modern genetic research, in the name of a politicized "Soviet science."[32] But we must note the terms of Camus's criticisms of Lyskenkoism, which are levelled not against science as such, but in the very name of the sciences and their epistemic probity. Camus does not take Lysenko's "Soviet science," any more than the Nazis' "Aryan science," to show the falsity and inevitable political overdetermination (as "just another narrative,") of scientific pursuits as such. On the contrary, they show the need for Marxist social and political theory, to remain anything like scientific, to give up on the nineteenth-century paradigms of Marx's day:

> As it happens that all discoveries since the unexpected mutations established by De Vries have consisted in introducing, contrary to the doctrines of determinism, the idea of chance into biology, it has been necessary [in Soviet Russia] to entrust Lysenko with the task of disciplining chromosomes and of demonstrating once again the truth of the most elementary determinism. That is ridiculous: but put a police force under Flaubert's Monsieur Homais and he would no longer be ridiculous, and there we have the twentieth century … [T]he twentieth century has also witnessed the denial of the principle of indeterminism in science, of limited relativity, of the quantum theory, and, finally, of every general tendency of contemporary science. Marxism is only "scientific" today in defiance of Heisenberg, Bohr, Einstein, and all of the greatest minds of our time.[33]

Camus wants to preserve, in contrast to metaphysical and political totalizations, the descriptive power of the human intelligence. Knowing its own limits, such intelligence deigns to claim certainty, beyond the scope of what can be verified by experience, in accordance with our presently best theories. Instead, it proceeds hypothetically, tentatively, step-by-step. Camus aligns this tentative, fallible, limited sense of the power of the human intelligence in the modern sciences, increasingly after 1944, with the attitude of Socrates and what he finds most instructive in ancient Greek thought:

> A fragment attributed to … Heraclitus states simply: "Presumption, regression of progress." And centuries after the Ephesian, Socrates, threatened by the death penalty, granted himself no other superiority than this: he did not presume to know what he did not know. The most exemplary

life and thought of these centuries ends in a proud avowal of ignorance. In forgetting this, we have forgotten our virility.[34]

And here we come to what is arguably most philosophically profound in Camus's thinking. It involves a position whose singularity has been passed over or not widely understood. We saw in Chapter 2, Camus's notion that rebellion puts in place limits which surround the community ("we are") of living human beings, prohibiting systematic deceit, enslavement, and killing. By recourse to these limits, Camus opposes all forms of political messianism which promise some "we shall be," of a future community, whose achievement would license us to oppress contemporaries through revolutionary or counterrevolutionary violence and propaganda. Such limits, in Camus's philosophy, are rooted in the epistemic limits which Socrates recognized: human beings wish to know more than they can, whereas lucidity comes in knowing how much we do not know. Camus adds that, absent a totalizing theological or metaphysical explanation of the whole—which we all seek but cannot secure—we cannot claim to know enough to take others' lives (Section 2.3). Nor, as early modern thinkers from Montaigne to Bayle and Voltaire had argued,[35] can we deprive them of the opportunities to keep searching and striving to flourish:

> Politics is not religion, or if it is, then it is nothing but the Inquisition. How would society define an absolute? Perhaps everyone is looking for this absolute on behalf of all. But society and politics only have the responsibility of arranging everyone's affairs so that each will have the leisure and the freedom to pursue this common search. History can then no longer be presented as an object of worship. It is only an opportunity that must be rendered fruitful by a vigilant rebellion.[36]

For Camus, however, the same limit to human comprehension of the absolute does not lead to any kind of anti-realist denial of the order, structure, and the beauty of the nonhuman universe. On the contrary. When we acknowledge that there are elements of nature which elude our comprehension or our control, we are confronting the limits of legitimate human power over nature. We are "learning our place," to borrow a phrase we all probably hated from our schoolteachers. Actually, Camus argues, to recognize the beauty of nature, and its grandeur, is precisely to recognize how it is not made to our measure:

> At the heart of all beauty lies something inhuman, and these hills, the softness of the sky, the outline of these trees at this very minute lose the illusory meaning with which we had clothed them, henceforth more remote than a lost paradise. The primitive hostility of the world rises up to face us across millennia, for a second, we cease to understand it because for centuries we have understood in it solely the images and designs that we had attributed to it beforehand, because henceforth we lack the power to make use of that artifice. The world evades us because it becomes itself again.[37]

Camus's visceral sense of the extra-humanity of nature—up to and including nature's dark side, its ability to send plagues and natural catastrophes which can destroy entire cities—is one of the most unique aspects of his *oeuvre*. He aimed to put landscapes back into his literature, an ambition which we see especially clearly in the stories of *Exile and the Kingdom*, led by "The Adulteress" and "The Host/Guest," but even in the glimpses outside of the captured cities of Cadiz and Oran in *State of Siege* and *The Plague*. It is the way that nature exceeds the human scale, because it becomes itself again, which saw him at times resist another label so often assigned to him, that of being a "humanist." "I have nothing against humanism, of course. I find it inadequate, that is all," Camus would explain, "Greek thought for example was something other than a humanism. It was a thought that gave everything its place."[38] The key passage here, perhaps, is found in his early collection of lyrical essays, *Noces*, as he contemplates the Tuscan landscape, and measures what he sees against the aspiration to reduce everything, as people say, "to the human scale":

> The human scale? ... When a mind faces landscapes whose grandeur clutches him by the throat, each movement of his mind is a scratch on his perfection. And soon, crossed out, scarred and re-scarred by so many overwhelming certainties, man ceases to be anything at all but a formless stain knowing only passive truths, the world's colour or its sun. Landscapes as pure as this dry up the soul and their beauty is unbearable.[39]

There is therefore, for Camus, a larger natural order. Humans have a limited place within it. One register of that limitation is our inability to completely comprehend and control the natural world. At the same time, we have legitimate demands, set against the inhumanity both of nature itself, and of our fellow humans: for dignity, for a sense of meaning, and for belonging in community. Yet these demands are bound, appropriately, by a sense of *mesure* or moderation—the unfashionable, classical virtue that Camus sought to revive, despite the cultural climate of his times, and ours, which sees a mirage of the good (or even "Greatness") in everything exceptional or unbalanced, as well as in infinite growth:

> Whereas the Greeks used reason to restrain the will, we have come to put the will's impulse at the very heart of reason, and reason has therefore become deadly. For the Greeks, values pre-existed all action, of which they definitely set the limits. Modern philosophy places its values at the end of action. They are not but are becoming, and we shall know them fully only at the completion of history. With values, all limit disappears, and since conceptions differ as to what they will be, since all struggles, without the brake of those same values, spread indefinitely, today's messianisms confront one another and their clamours mingle in the clash of empires. Excess (*démesure*) is a fire, according to Heraclitus. The fire is gaining

ground. Nietzsche has been overtaken. It is no longer with hammer blows but with ammunitions that Europe philosophises.[40]

Today, the fire of the modern imaginary of infinite growth and dynamism is heating the earth. It is casting the balanced order of the ecosphere out of its bounds. Camus's "Helen Exile," again—this most beautiful of his essays, and arguably the most profound—speaks uncannily to us today. For the symptoms of Western *hybris* it diagnoses have remained unchallenged:

> The Greeks, who for centuries questioned themselves as to what is just, could understand nothing of our idea of justice. For them equity implied a limit ... At the dawn of Greek thought Heraclitus was already imagining that justice sets limits for the physical universe itself: "The sun will not overstep his measures; if he does, the Erinyes, the handmaids of justice, will find him out." We who have cast the universe and spirit out of our sphere laugh at that threat. In a drunken sky we light up the suns we want. But nonetheless the boundaries exist, and we know it.[41]

It is not then a question of "going back to nature"—whatever that could mean. Nor, for Camus, does our continuing interest in human justice, or our critical intelligence to uncover avoidable forms of inhumanity, in any way need to be cast aside. "Yes, there is beauty and there are the humiliated," Camus would explain his position. "Whatever may be the difficulties of the undertaking, I should like never to be unfaithful either to one or to the others."[42] There is however the possibility for those who do pursue justice and face the bitter elements of the human experience, that their outrage will devolve into an understandable cynicism—of the very kind which we saw in Chapter 5, and that perversely fuels fascism: the psychology of merciless judges and warriors who confuse pitiless despair and cruelty for strength or virtue. Even as ideals of justice and freedom are used cynically to engender their opposites, and bombs fall in the name of human rights, and so on, there is a need to hold onto these ideals and the forms of beauty and life-affirmation that can give strength and balance to political struggles.

Camus's other way of formulating his unique philosophy of *mesure* comes when he repeats that he wants to defend a philosophy, and a philosophical sense of existence, which "excludes nothing" of what presents itself to human experience. "Nothing is true which compels us to exclude," Camus maintains.[43] We saw that this thought, already, as it governed his recommendations against suicide in the face of the double-sidedness of the absurd in *The Myth of Sisyphus*. We saw that Camus's passion for equality and justice, in Chapter 4, was "balanced" against a need to recognize forms of political and social freedom, each limiting the other. Indeed, Camus argues that this philosophy of *mesure*, excluding nothing, applies to all of the famous "metaphysical" oppositions that have shaped Western thought:

> This law of *mesure* equally well extends to all the contradictions of rebellious thought. The real is not entirely rational, nor is the rational entirely real ... [T]he desire for unity not only demands that everything should be rational. It also wishes that the irrational should not be sacrificed. One cannot say that nothing has any meaning, because in doing so one affirms a value sanctified by this opinion; nor that everything has a meaning, because the word "everything" has no meaning for us. The irrational imposes limits on the rational, which, in its turn, gives it its *mesure* ... In the same way, ... [s]omething that is always in the process of development could not exist—... [at the same time as] being can only prove itself in development ... The historical dialectic, for example, is not in continuous pursuit of an unknown value. It revolves around the limit, which is its prime value.[44]

In the same Camusian way, we can say in the age of human-generated ecological imbalance, that there is an urgent need to rebalance the human interest in economic development and change, ascendant for two centuries, with a respect for the limits set by our own finite nature as human beings and that of the ecological world-system which is the precondition of our continual flourishing as a species. "Naturally, it is not a question of despising anything," Camus reflects in *The Rebel*, "but of simply saying that it [a philosophy which tries to balance political history against recognition of those parts of our nature, and of nature itself, which resist political totalization] is a thought which the world today cannot do without for very much longer."[45] That was 1951.

6.4 Jerusalem with Athens: From Exile Toward the Kingdom

Camus's philosophy of *mesure* is singular in twentieth-century philosophy, compared to the thinkers who have been canonized in humanities departments since the 1970s. Camus himself laughed in 1955, and his words would apply to many a "radical" seminar hall of the twenty-first century:

> If today, in a Parisian gathering, you were to evoke the notion of *mesure*, a thousand pairs of romantic arms would hit the roof. For them, *mesure* is nothing other than the diabolical moderation of the bourgeoisie.[46]

Yet, we have made the case that Camus's reappraisal of human *hybris*, and reestablishing of a sense of limits, speaks directly to the growing climate crisis, and the clear need for human beings, wisely using the sciences the modern era has bequeathed us, to become responsible stewards of the earth. For Camus as for the classical thinkers, choosing excess and the cult of the exceptional that our commercial culture extols is what is easy (Chapter 3). What is harder is the humility and self-limitation which will restore balance to the contemporary world, as it lurches further into disorder:

> Moderation, born of rebellion, can only live by rebellion. It is a perpetual conflict, continually created and mastered by the intelligence. It does not

triumph either in the impossible or in the abyss. It finds its equilibrium through them. Whatever we may do, excess will always keep its place in the heart of man, in the place where solitude is found. We all carry within us our places of exile, our crimes and our ravages. But our task is not to unleash them on the world; it is to fight them in ourselves and in others.[47]

Neither is such moderation a dour affair. By circumscribing a commitment to the living human community, for Camus, it involves a deeply life-affirmative position. In Camus's writing and his thought, as we have said, the sense of nature's beauty as a suprahuman whole in which we have a limited place is aligned with the value of liberty, as well as the human possibilities of creativity, art, love, and friendship. Rebellion, he claims in *The Rebel*, cannot exist without a strange form of love.[48] Indeed, the longing for justice and solidarity for the humiliated which is at issue in rebellion, Camus argues, cannot be lastingly sustained unless they are underwritten by "the two thirsts one cannot long neglect without drying up—I mean loving and admiring."[49] In "Return to Tipasa," alongside "Helen's Exile" the most philosophical of the mature lyrical essays, Camus reflects upon his own long experience as an "artist in the amphitheatre" in the decade following Hitler's invasion of France. He proposes that there is a need to balance the passion for justice with love, and political struggle with restorative leisure, to reconnect with the sources of what can give people joy:

> Violence and hatred dry up the heart itself; the long fight for justice exhausts the love that nevertheless gave birth to it. In the clamour in which we live, love is impossible, and justice does not suffice. This is why Europe hates daylight and is only able to set injustice up against injustice. But in order to keep justice from shrivelling up like a beautiful orange fruit containing nothing but a bitter, dry pulp, I discovered once more at Tipasa that one must keep intact in oneself a freshness, a cool wellspring of joy, love of the day that escapes injustice, and return to the combat having won that light.[50]

There is no question, as we have seen, that Camus's references and self-understanding, especially between 1944 and the early 1950s—his "rebellion" cycle of works, *The Plague, State of Siege* and *The Just*, and *The Rebel*—are principally drawn from classical philosophy and tragic literature. Against modern secularised messianisms, he pitches classical harmony and balance. Nevertheless, we saw above how Camus could acknowledge that many of his preoccupations, for all this Hellenism, were Christian: notably the problems of evil, suffering, and avoidable human injustice. In fact, if we look at the titles of the works of his final cycle, we see that they take up themes central to Christian theology and biblical thought—that is, *The Fall, Exile and the Kingdom*, and *The First Man*. What becomes clear is that, far from an anti-religious thinker, Camus's wrestling with the Christian and Jewish heritages only became more profound in the final, most difficult years of his life.

In the rebellion cycle of 1944–53, Christian thinking, with its linear account of history leading from creation, via incarnation, toward final judgment, are impugned for giving shape and precedent to the forms of secular messianism of the Far Right and Left. As Camus writes in *The Rebel*:

> In contrast to the ancient world, the unity of the Christian and Marxist world is astonishing. The two doctrines have in common a vision of the world which completely separates them from the Greek attitude. Jaspers defines this very well: "It is a Christian way of thinking to consider that the history of man is strictly unique." The Christians were the first to consider human life and the course of events as a history that is unfolding from a fixed beginning toward a definite end, in the course of which man achieves his salvation or earns his punishment. The philosophy of history springs from a Christian representation, which is surprising to a Greek mind. The Greek idea of evolution has nothing in common with our idea of historical evolution.[51]

Camus consistently challenged Augustinian Christianity for being, as he put it in 1944, "a doctrine of injustice."[52] On the one hand, he has in mind Christ's ultimate acceptance of his unjust execution at the hands of the Roman authorities. On the other hand, as we see dramatized in *The Plague*, it is medieval Christianity's acceptance of the idea that even children, inheritors of original sin, if they died unbaptized, would not deserve divine mercy.[53] In *The Plague*, Camus's rebellion against this notion is given powerful voice by Dr. Rieux, having witnessed the agonizing death of a child by plague. He has the Jesuit Father Paneloux at his side:

> Rieux was already going out of the ward, walking so quickly and with such a look on his face that when he overtook Paneloux, the priest held out his arm to restrain him. "Come now, doctor," he said. Without stopping as he swept along, Rieux turned round and spat out: "Ah, now that one, at least, was innocent, and you know it as well as I do!"[54]

The depraved figure of Jean-Baptiste Clamence who sets himself up in judgment of the entire fallen world in *The Fall* of 1956 (Section 5.4) has been interpreted as an even more bitter Camusian indictment of the Christian legacy, and affirmation of his neopaganism.[55] But there are reasons for caution about this assessment. It is clear from Camus's *Carnets* of the early 1940s, and a piece he wrote for *Combat*, that he was aware that his own concern for justice, and opposition to all forms of human degradation and enslavement, could find only partial support from the Greeks. The oligarchs of the Greek cities, he notes, used to swear an oath never to treat the ordinary people well.[56] Chattel slavery underlay the ancient economy of the Mediterranean world. Camus's instinctive and philosophical concern for justice, and his sense of the necessity for justice to be underlain by love for other human beings find easier precedents in the biblical heritage: iconically, Jerusalem more than Athens.

And so it is, in *The Fall*, that Jean-Baptiste Clamence—this man who judges everyone without anything like the clemency suggested by his surname—confesses to us along the way a number of telling curios. The first is that he is in possession of the missing panel of Jan Van Eyck's 1432 masterpiece, stolen from Saint Bavo's Cathedral in Ghent, entitled *The Just Judges*. This work (which forms the cover of this book) shows Christian judges on horseback, ascending to ask repentance or clemency from the lamb of God.[57] In the context of Clamence's confession of his profession as a judge-penitent who requires that there can be no forgiveness, misusing his own false penitence to condemn everyone, this forcible suppression of these penitent, "just judges" suggests strongly the inauthenticity of his position. He can only buy his mock-Augustinian (or Machiavellian) pessimism about the irredeemable evil of all human beings, at the price of artificially suppressing the impulses to justice and forgiveness found in human nature and at the heart of the Christian heritage.

Secondly, there is Jean-Baptiste's own remarkable Christology (his conception of Christ), which is characterized by a passionate identification with, if not the lamb of God, then the humanity of Jesus. The antihero has said earlier, epigrammatically, that he no longer has friends, only accomplices.[58] Yet, he addresses Jesus alone in the book as "my friend." And he protests, on Jesus's behalf, against what he perceives to be the historical misuse of his ministry, which aimed to cultivate fraternal love, to become a machinery of judgment:

> They have hoisted him onto a judge's bench, in the secret of their hearts, and they smite, they judge above all, they judge in his name. He spoke softly to the adulteress: "Neither do I condemn thee!" but that doesn't matter; they condemn without absolving anyone. In the name of the Lord, here is what you deserve. Lord? He, my friend, didn't expect so much. He simply wanted to be loved, nothing more. Of course, there are those who love him, even among Christians. But they are not numerous. He had foreseen that too; he had a sense of humour. Peter, you know, the coward, Peter denied him: "I know not the man … I know not what thou sayest … etc." Really, he went too far! And my friend makes a play on words: "Thou art Peter, and upon

this rock I will build my church." Irony could go no further, don't you think? But no, they still triumph! "You see, he had said it!" He had said it, indeed; he knew the question thoroughly. And then he left forever, leaving them to judge and condemn, with pardon on their lips and the sentence in their hearts.[59]

We saw in Chapter 1 how Camus denied that he was simply an atheist. He once described his aim as "imagining the sacred, without a sense of immortality."[60] In his early works, moved by his own youthful experiences in North Africa, Camus clearly located the Sacred in a kind of fugitive sense of oneness with nature. Its most exuberant, irreplaceable expression is in "Nuptials at Tipasa," describing his visit with a lover to Roman ruins on the Mediterranean coast:

Here, I understand what is meant by "glory": the right to love without limits. There is only one love in the world. To hold a woman's body is to hold in one's arms the strange joy that falls from the sky to the sea ... In a sense, it is truly my life that I'm playing here, a life that tastes of warm stone, full of the sighs of the sea and the cicadas who are starting to sing now. The breeze is cool and the sky blue. I love this life with abandon and want to speak of it with liberty: it makes me proud of my human condition. True, others have often told me there is nothing to be proud of. And yet, there is: this Sun, this sea, my heart leaping with youth, my body tasting of salt and the vast setting where tenderness and glory merge in the yellow and the blue.[61]

By the 1950s, after the experience of Nazism, the political struggles following the revelations concerning Stalin's crimes, his own exile from the *rive gauche* for his stance on this issue, as well as his failures as a husband, Camus's sense of where the Sacred could be located shifts. No longer only vertical, as it were, in the union of the individual with impersonal nature, Camus shifts to the biblical language of a "kingdom," *royaume*, which can be found in horizontal communion with other human beings. If we look at the stories Camus published in *Exile and the Kingdom*, we see characters haunted by loneliness, and their inability to establish such communion. There is a woman unhappy in a loveless marriage, a dysfunctional workplace where the manager and workers are each deaf to the other; a European in Algeria forced to play "host" to a silent Arab prisoner, who wrestles with delivering the man over to his persecutors or setting him free at personal risk; and finally, in the culminating story, "The Growing Stone," a somewhat jaded engineer, D'Arrast (who happens to be chauffeured by a character named Socrates), charged with constructing a sea-wall to protect the remote town of Iguape, in Brazil. D'Arrast ends by experiencing a kind of unlooked-for spiritual renewal through communion with the townspeople. This last story, particularly, is loaded with Christian symbolism, no less than *The Fall*. It culminates with the Frenchman, a secular Simon of Cyrene, taking up the burden of a heavy stone which a sailor, who had been miraculously saved at sea, was bearing up to the town church in gratitude to Jesus for his rescue. When the exhausted sailor doubles over under this weight, D'Arrast steps in to take up the load for the man, whom he has befriended the previous day. But he takes it not to the church. Rather, D'Arrast heaves it back to the man's own hut, where he sets it down. It is worth quoting the closing lines, with their poignant evocation of the sacred in community, at some length:

> When the inhabitants of the hut arrived, they found D'Arrast standing with his shoulders against the back wall and eyes closed. In the centre of the room, in the place of the hearth, the stone was half buried in ashes and earth. They stood in the doorway without advancing and looked at D'Arrast in silence as if questioning him. But he didn't speak … the brother led the cook up to the stone, where he dropped on the ground. The brother sat down too, beckoning to the others. The old woman joined him, then the girl of the night before, but no one looked at D'Arrast. They were squatting in a silent circle around the stone. No sound but the murmur of the river

reached them through the heavy air. Standing in the darkness, D'Arrast listened without seeing anything, and the sound of the waters filled him with a tumultuous happiness. With eyes closed, he joyfully acclaimed his own strength; he acclaimed, once again, a fresh beginning in life. At that moment, a firework went off that seemed very close. The brother moved a little away from the cook and, half turning toward D'Arrast but without looking at him, pointed to the empty place and said: "Sit down with us."[62]

To be sure, there is a criticism of the established churches here, as in the Christology Camus inserts so suggestively into *The Fall*. But this is hardly an anti-Christian position, in the lineage of a Nietzsche (Sections 1.3 and 3.4). Camus's is instead in these last works a critical stance which draws upon values at the heart of the Christian tradition. He seems to want to relocate these values in the hearths and struggles of ordinary men and women, rather than to denounce them as wholly misgiven, "resentful," "slavish," and so on.

Since Camus passed so suddenly in January 1960, with *The First Man* and any further philosophical statements as to his evolving perspective incomplete, it is impossible for any commentator to say with certainty what that perspective fully was or might have been. Two orientations however seem clear. Firstly, Camus became highly critical as his work developed of notions of "heroism," with the attendant longing for fame and desire to be exceptional.[63] We have seen his distance from political romanticism (Section 3.3), and Camus was aware of how the cult of the exception, the transgressive, and the singular hero informs fascism's Leader worship (Section 5.3). What was instead needed, Camus would propose in 1946, was what he called "an average universalism ... a universalism at the average level of man ... defending the values we need in daily life, in daily politics,"[64] rather than dreaming of "becoming great again" in whichever way different messianic ideologies might imagine.

Secondly, the last Camus opposes love, with forgiveness or even charity, to unrelenting justice, without mercy. If human beings are to require ethical or wider perfection of each other, Camus assesses, there will be no end of the recriminations. Human history as we know it, he agrees, has largely been that slaughter bench which Hegel thought to sanctify with his eschatology of *Geist*, in which the "greatness" of figures like Alexander which school children are taught to admire is largely an affair of force, "the power of the sword."[65] "Let's be fair," admits an old doctor of the French abuse of the Algerians in *The First Man*:

> we shut them up in caves with their whole brood, yes indeed, and they cut the balls off the first Berbers, who themselves … and so on all the way back to the first criminal—you know, his name was Cain—and since then it's been war; men are abominable, especially under a ferocious sun.[66]

What alone can break this cycle is fraternal understanding and a difficult, perhaps historically impossible, capacity for forgiveness. It is a matter of learning to live alongside others who, like us, are parochial and imperfect, vulnerable as we are to the passions and dreams of vindication that have given rise to endless cycles of violence leading back to the first man, who was also our brother. Unlike his Jean-Baptiste Clamence, that is, the last Camus seems to have been being drawn toward the notion that the precondition for anything like human communion, and an end to the infernal cycle of historical violence, was the willingness of people and peoples to step down from the judge's bench. The work of endlessly calling down vengeance for the evils of others can never finish. What was emerging as Sacred for this last Camus was the gift and endless burden of building postlapsarian communities of dialogue and solidarity:

> Even by his greatest effort man can only propose to diminish arithmetically the sufferings of the world. But the injustice and the suffering of the world will remain and, no matter how limited they are, they will not cease to be an outrage. Dimitri Karamazov's cry of 'Why?' will continue to resound; art and rebellion will die only with the last man.[67]

Conclusion

The work of this book is now complete. The twofold case for why Albert Camus matters today has been made: as a prescient responder to social, political, ethical, and philosophical problems which we have not resolved; and as the defender of a position, unique among twentieth-century philosophers, that extolled human limits, virtues, a moral universalism, as well as a call for reconsidering our modern disharmony with the natural world. It is difficult to know how to conclude, after the contents of this little book became so uncannily timely in the first year of the Trump administration. The nation that sent the marines to end fascism in Europe in 1944–5 had by February 2025 sent its glib young Vice President to lecture European nations on protecting "democracy," whilst brokering a deal with Russian dictator Vladimir Putin to divide democratic Ukraine, without any of the latter's representatives being present at the negotiating table. It seems clear, even to the disbelieving liberal commentariat, that the postwar international order, predicated on keeping the genii of fascism and the Far Right in their bottles, is ending. Meanwhile, the domestic ravages of the new US administration have continued to unfold, several per news cycle, amidst mass firings of American public servants, the defunding of the arts, rapid fire governance by executive order, the sackings of Inspector Generals charged with policing corruption, the vilification of media who refuse to agree that Trump has the unilateral right to rename the Gulf of Mexico, the reopening (and then, thankfully, closing) of Guantanamo for illegal immigrants, continuing mass deportations, an "alligator Alcatraz" with MAGA "merch" celebrating the cruelty, and Mr. Trump posting suggestively (and truly, after a July 2024 Supreme Court decision) on social media that, in acting to preserve the nation as he deems fit, he cannot be held accountable by law.

Camus's principled stance against the fascism of his time, predicated on directly confronting the despair and cynicism upon which it has again thrived, therefore seems to matter more and more, almost by the day. The first months of "Trump 2" also saw the tawdry spectacle of the world's richest man, a South African billionaire with direct access to the White House, hiring young men in their 20s to deleriously pull apart every progressive element of the modern American state they could, whilst Musk continued to draw down multimillion dollar federal contracts and set about reshaping the algorithms on his global social media platform (X, né Twitter) to boost Far Right parties. In such times as these, we need today to restore Camus's lucid awareness of how the concentration of economic power undermines democratic media, and sits all-too-comfortably with the rise of dictators who will keep the trains running on time and crush progressive dissent. The neoliberal story, the postmodernist story, as to how "totalitarianism" involves the hypertrophy of the administrative state, needs to be pulled down no less rapidly than DOGE has destroyed that state itself, with no democratic accountability. These intersecting Left- and Right-libertarian stories have enabled the hyper-accumulation of economic power in the US and elsewhere to present itself as a progress in "freedom," and as necessarily "anti-totalitarian." Yet, what is now clear is that they were creating the conditions for the openly authoritarian recasting of conservative politics, and shifting the political debate farther and farther to the Right in the world's leading democracies to a point where no return seems imaginable, certainly in the United States.

If Camus matters in 2025, it is to suggest that initiatives need to be begun, from the ground up, around the world, to combat the political-economic settings which have transferred unsustainable amounts of wealth into the hands of the very few. We can no longer afford to focus on culture alone, as if it floated free of material conditions, and on differences, as against what unites peoples against predatory forces looking to strip-mine the public weal, while praying to "patriotism" in the public square to command power. People globally need to undertake to rebuild solidary communities wherein human relationships are possible that are not mediated by money and anonymized algorithms which prey upon our worst natures. Dialogue must be promoted in place of polemic, civility instead of sensationalism and hyperbole, obligation and concern in place of "rights" alone and self-promotion, and the politics of fear and hatred combatted with affirmative initiatives to restore value to people's lives, foster real connections and shared stories, recreate the dignity and stability of labor, preserve the freedom for leisure afforded by basic economic securities for all, and create shared worlds wherein people can see that there really *are* alternatives to human beings experiencing their social existences as "dog eat dog" states of nature. The way that we think about social media and AI as "inevitabilities," like ancient fate, must also clearly be challenged, if we are not going to be made to collectively strike out our eyes. At best, these gadgets need to be refigured as instruments, serving human communities and their democratically agreed goals, not doomsday devices visited upon societies by the super-rich under the sign of "freedom," in such a way that they reshape the most basic human experiences, possibilities, and relationships. Like footloose international capital, footloose social media platforms must be reined in by domestic legislatures who serve their peoples, not the magnates who have profited from the collapse of democratic civilities and are now queuing up in the retinues of would-be tyrants. Humility needs to be reestablished as a public virtue, and its merits as a form of honesty and intersubjective respect counterposed to the crass bravado of politicians who have been rewarded for too long for behaving like King Kong, beating their chests and running rampant through norms and protections fought for by generations designed to hold shameless impunity in check. The modern social imaginaries of the unlimited and the excessive, the singular and the "genius," need to be challenged. For the exciting is not the true, nor is it the virtuous or the good. Genuine individual and social freedom, as Camus maintained, is not a festival or a sprint, a once-off Event, or the ability to cynically declaim about how "f**d things truly are," so you better learn to "deal" (click subscribe): "Oh, no! It's a chore, on the contrary, and a long-distance race, quite solitary and very exhausting."[1]

People must, at the limit, be ready to shed blood if genuine liberties, including freedoms from economic insecurity and to protest, are to be protected. This, Camus agrees with the American founders. Likewise for the other principal political virtue, justice. It too, like all of the ancient virtues, requires hard work, and may demand sacrifice: "justice must be achieved with the blood of men and women," for "the obstinacy of injustice can only be conquered by an obstinacy of justice." Indeed, "justice dies the moment when it becomes a comfort, when it ceases to be a burn, and an effort on oneself" This is a Camusian truth that our generations, raised in the peace, are now seemingly rediscovering.[2]

So, there is no easy take away the author can offer from this attempt to think through why Camus matters, as of early 2025. In a world of polemics, cynicism, and growing shamelessness, all I can say is that Camus's voice is one that we do well to hear. It can be refreshing for its disarming, earnest willingness to speak unironically a language of honor, truth, justice, freedom, and even of beauty and love—so far from the language of "hand to hand (*corps à corps*) combat" to "satisfy the thirst for strategy and heroism one finds in our literary society," and which today impresses so many callow youths online as realism itself.[3] Camus's literature and philosophy also speak to people today, even in our politically darkening times, of sources of joy and connection that we need to be able to return to, when things do get bad, and we are invited to accept that any hope for a better, saner world is a senseless naivety. In several places, Camus goes so far as to oppose to our modern world, in which everything—today, even the tunes of a songstress like Taylor Swift—is absurdly politicized, a "right to solitude":[4] a right to "disconnect," as we say today, and to reconnect with the orders of things outside of the angry political caves (aka. filter bubbles) which increasingly shut everything else out. "Totality is not unity," Camus is there to reassure us, when we are inclined to despair:

> The state of siege, even when it is extended to the very boundaries of the earth, is not reconciliation, ... [and] is supported ... only by rejecting two thirds of the world and by denying, to the advantages of history, both nature and beauty and by depriving man of the power of passion, doubt, happiness, and imaginative invention.[5]

Then there is always arguably the most profound of Camus's lines to keep close, when things seem hopeless, and with which we close:

> And it was in the midst of shouts rolling against the terrace wall in massive waves that waxed in volume and duration, while cataracts of coloured fire fell thicker through the darkness, that Dr. Rieux resolved to compile this chronicle, so that he should not be one of those who hold their peace but should bear witness in favour of those plague-stricken people; so that some memorial of the injustice and outrage done them might endure; and to state quite simply what we learn in a time of pestilence: that there are more things to admire in men than to despise.[6]

NOTES

Introduction

1 The first time a work by Camus is mentioned, as here, I will give the French original title in brackets. From that time onwards, I will use the recognized English titles.

2 My own take on Camus's conception of philosophy is found in the Introduction to *Camus, Philosophe: To Return to Our Beginnings* (Leiden: Brill, 2014).

3 The first time the title of a work by Albert Camus is used, I will add the French title in brackets, as here. This includes works still to be translated. Where Camus's work has been translated, I will cite the established published translations. Where small amendments are made, I will duly note this in the endnotes.

4 Albert Camus, *Christian Metaphysics and Neoplatonism*, translated with Introduction by Ronald Srigley (Columbia: University of Missouri Press, 2007).

5 See Albert Camus, "Create Dangerously," in *Resistance, Rebellion, Death*, translated by Justin O'Brien (Vintage, NY: 1960 [hereafter RRD]), pp. 249–72.

6 Matthew Sharpe, "Solitaire/Solidaire: Camus, Contemplation, and the *Vita Mixta*," *Telos* 196 (2021), pp. 31–53.

7 Albert Camus, "The Artist and His Age" (Lecture at Uppsala University, 1957), in *Speaking Out: Lectures and Speeches, 1937–1958*, translated by Quintin Hoare (London: Penguin, 2022 [hereafter SO]), p. 231.

8 Albert Camus, *The Myth of Sisyphus*, translated by Justin O'Brien (London: Penguin, 1978), 24–5, 26–7, 43–5.

9 Albert Camus, "Three Interviews" ("No, I Am Not an Existentialist"), *Albert Camus: Lyrical and Critical Essays*, edited by Phillip Thody, translated by Ellen Conroy Kennedy (New York: Vintage, 1987 [hereafter LCE]), p. 345.

10 Albert Camus, "The Enigma," *LCE*, p. 159.

11 Camus, cited at Olivier Todd, *Albert Camus: A Life* (New York: Alfred A. Knopf, 1997), p. 379.

12 Camus, *The Myth of Sisyphus*, pp. 39–40; "Interview for *Servir* (Entretien à *Servir*)" in *Albert Camus Oeuvres Completes II 1944–1948* (Paris: Gallimard Bibliothèque de la Pléiade: 2006), p. 659.

13 See Matthew Sharpe, "Camus and the Virtues," *Philosophy Today*, 61, no. 3 (2017): pp. 679–708.

14 Albert Camus, *The Rebel*, revised and complete translation by Anthony Bower, with a Foreword by Sir Herbert Read (New York: Vintage, 1956), p. 16.

15 Albert Camus, "Return to Tipasa," in *LCE*, pp. 159–60.

16 Sharpe, *Camus, Philosophe*.

17 As a starting sample, Alfred Cordes, *The Descent of the Doves: Camus' Journey of the Spirit* (Washington: University Press of America, 1980); John Cruickshank, *Albert Camus and the Literature of Revolt* (New York: Oxford University Press, 1959); Christine Margerrison, Mark Orme and Lissa Lincoln (eds.), *Albert Camus in the 21st Century: A Reassessment of His Thinking at the Dawn of the New Millennium* (Amsterdam, NY: Editions Rodopi B.V., 2008); Germaine Bree (ed.), *Camus: A Collection of Critical Essays* (Englewood Cliffs, NJ: Prentice-Hall, 1962); Roger Quilliot, *Sea and Prisons: A Commentary on the Life and Works of Albert Camus* (Alabama: University of Alabama Press, 1976); and Susan Tarrow, *Exile from the Kingdom* (Alabama: University of Alabama Press, 1985).

Chapter 1

1 Émile Durkheim, *Suicide: A Study in Sociology*, translated by John A. Spaulding (New York: Free Press, 1979).

2 Camus, *The Myth of Sisyphus*, p. 4. In this chapter as here, due to frequency of citation, references to this text will be abbreviated in brackets in the text, as MS.

3 Other suicides are principled deaths in the name of a larger cause, what Durkheim called "altruistic suicides" (cf. MS, 5).

4 Camus, "Enigma," p. 159; "Pessimism and Courage," in *Resistance, Rebellion, Death*, translated with Introduction by Justin O'Brien (New York: Vintage, 1960), p. 58; Jacqueline Levi-Valensi (ed.), *Camus at Combat: Writing 1944–1947*, trans. Arthur Goldhammer, with a Foreword by David Carroll (Princeton: Princeton University Press, 2006), p. 100.

5 The sense that the world lacked any larger, knowable order or meaning was almost ubiquitous: "with the exception of a professional rationalists, today people despair of true knowledge" (MS, 18).

6 Albert Camus, "Time of Murderers," SO, p. 87 (author's amended translation from *Oeuvres Complètes III*) (Paris: Gallimard Bibliothèque de la Pléiade: 2006, p. 353); see "Crisis of Man," SO, pp. 19–20.

7   Anne Case & Angus Deaton, "Mortality and Morbidity in the 21st century," Brookings Papers on Economic Activity, Spring 2017, pp. 397–476.

8   See Joint Economic Committee—Republicans, Chairman, Sen. Mike Lee, "Long-Term Trends in Deaths of Despair," *Social Capital Report*, no. 4-19, September 2019, p. 2. Although internationally, research is less well-developed, and initial results suggest that the numbers involved are not so dire, they are high enough in the land of the free.

9   Mahboubeh Shirzad, Gayane Yenokyan, Arik V. Marcell and Michelle R. Kaufman, "Deaths of Despair-Associated Mortality Rates Globally: A 2000–2019 Sex-Specific Disparities Analysis," (*Public Health*, 236, November 2024): pp. 35–42.

10 In the United States, over 49,000 by 2022, out of a staggering 1.6 million attempts, more than the number of homicides. National Council of Suicide Prevention, "USA Suicide Statistics for the Year 2022," published May 2024. Online at https://www.thencsp.org/_files/ugd/a0415f_1f03481ce0ea45d5af87930082c9c179.pdf.

11 Ruth Brauer et al., "Psychotropic Medicine Consumption in 65 Countries and Regions, 2008–19: A Longitudinal Study," *The Lancet Psychiatry*, 8, no. 12 (2021): pp. 1071–82. One needs to factor in here the greater availability of these medicines, and the growth of "big pharma" over the last decades which literally profits from selling more of these medications.

12 Albert Camus, *The Plague*, translated Stuart Gilbert (London: Penguin, 1971), pp. 139–41, 246.

13 Tyler F. Stillman et al., "Alone and Without Purpose: Life Loses Meaning Following Social Exclusion," *Journal of Experimental Social Psychology* 45, no. 4, July 2009, pp. 686–94. See "The Global Mental Health Crisis: 10 Numbers to Note," *Project HOPE*, online at https://www.projecthope.org/news-stories/story/the-global-mental-health-crisis-10-numbers-to-note/.

14 Esteban Ortiz-Ospina, "Loneliness and Social Connections—Our World in Data," February 2020, updated March 2024. online at https://ourworldindata.org/social-connections-and-loneliness.

15 Daniel L. Surkalim et al., "The Prevalence of Loneliness Across 113 Countries: Systematic Review and Meta-Analysis," | BMJ 2022 376, pp. 1–17. Online at https://www.bmj.com/content/376/bmj-2021-067068.

16 Lim M., Manera K., Owen K., Phongsavan P. and Smith B. "Chronic and Episodic Loneliness and Social Isolation: Prevalence and Sociodemographic Analyses from a Longitudinal Australian Survey." Published online 2022. doi:https://doi.org/10.21203/rs.3.rs-1607036/v1. Cf. The State of Loneliness and Social Isolation Research: Current Knowledge and Future Directions | BMC Public Health | Full Text. Also cf. Loneliness among Older Adults Before vs During COVID Pandemic U.S. 2020 | Statista.

17 "Public Trust in Government: 1958–2024," *Pew Research Centre* June 24, 2024. Online at https://www.pewresearch.org/politics/2024/06/24/public-trust-in-government-1958-2024/. "Trust in Government Worldwide 2023, by Country," *Statista Research Department*, Jul 4, 2024. Online at https://www.statista.com/statistics/1362804/trust-government-world/#:~:text=The%20level%20of%20trust%20in%20governments%20around%20the,years%20and%20a%20lack%20of%20a%20critical%20press.

18 UN/DESA Policy Brief #108, "Trust in Public Institutions: Trends and Implications for Economic Security," Department of Economic and Social Affairs. Online at https://desapublications.un.org/policy-briefs/undesa-policy-brief-108-trust-public-institutions-trends-and-implications-economic.

19 Lucas Walsh et al., "Youth Barometer Paints Bleak Picture of Young Australians in 2024," Monash Lens. Online at https://lens.monash.edu/@education/2024/08/01/1386898/youth-barometer-paints-a-bleak-picture-of-young-australians-in-2024.

20 Max Roser and Hannah Ritchie, "Optimism and Pessimism," Our World in Data. Online at https://ourworldindata.org/optimism-and-pessimism.

21 Albert Camus, *The Stranger*, translated by Stuart Gilbert (New York: Vintage, 1946).

22 Jon Stewart, *A History of Nihilism in the Nineteenth Century: Confrontations with Nothingness* (Cambridge: Cambridge University Press, 2024), p. 2.

23 Alan Woolfolk, "Toward a Theory of Nihilism," *Sociological Analysis* 51, no. 1 (1990), Spring, p. 105.

24 Camus, *The Rebel*, pp. 37–46.

25 See Losurdo, *Nietzsche*, p. 496.

26 Obereit, at Stephen Wagner Cho, "Nihilism Before Nietzsche," Graduate Faculty Philosophy Journal, 18, no. 1 1995, p. 207.

27 Losurdo, *Nietzsche*, p. 494.

28 Losurdo, *Nietzsche*, pp. 493–4.

29 See Camus, *The Rebel*, pp. 62–5.

30 Camus, *The Rebel*, pp. 55–61.

31 Camus, *The Rebel*, p. 68.

32 Camus, *The Rebel*, pp. 66–7.

33 Friedrich Nietzsche, *Will to Power*, in Oscar Levy (ed.), *The Complete Works of Nietzsche*, translated by Anthony M. Ludovici (Edinburgh & London: T.N. Foulis, 1914), I, 3.

34 See Friedrich Nietzsche, *Beyond Good and Evil: Preface to a Philosophy of the Future*, translated by Judith Norman edited by Rolf-Peter Horstmann

(Cambridge: Cambridge University Press, 2002); *The Antichrist*, in *The Antichrist, Ecce Homo, Twilight of the Idols and Other Writings*, translated by Judith Norman, edited by Judith Norman & Aaron Ridley (Cambridge: Cambridge University Press, 2005); *Twilight of the Idols*, in *The Antichrist, Ecce Homo, Twilight of the Idols and Other Writings*

35 Nietzsche, *Will to Power*, I, "A Plan," 1

36 Camus, *The Rebel*, pp. 67–8.

37 Losurdo, *Nietzsche*, p. 491; Camus, *The Rebel*, 62–5.

38 Camus, *The Rebel*, pp. 67–8.

39 That is to say, the ambivalence of the term "nihilism" extends further, even beyond the total opposition of Christian and Nietzschean uses of the term, and the four uses we have now seen. "Nihilism," notably in Christian thinkers, is a pejorative term. The belief in nothing lasting being the final, most openly futile result of revolt against God (as Turgenev's Bazarov says, aiming "to smash things" (at Domenico Losurdo, *Nietzsche, The Aristocratic Rebel* (Leiden: Brill, 2020), pp. 495–6)), the urgent task is to oppose and overcome it. Yet, other thinkers have proudly claimed the label as describing an affirmative intellectual, or even (ironically) an ethical or political program. This is the case of the Russian nihilists like Nechaev whose thought and careers Camus examines in *The Rebel*, pp. 153–76. When Stirner announces at the end of his 1845 work *Der Einziger und sein Eigentum (The Unique and Its Characteristics)* that he has "constructed my case on nothing," he is associating nihilism with a lucid, principled, and wholly disillusioned attitude to reality (*The Rebel*, pp. 62–4). Nietzsche in his later thought, similarly, counterposes against the complacent, almost bovine, "passive" or "incomplete" nihilism of the vast majority of moderns—those "last men" scathingly denounced by his Zarathustra, longing for nothing more noble than the material comforts afforded by modern societies—what he calls "active nihilism." The point is not to exit from nihilism as such, for Nietzsche. For this nihilism, in modern skepticism about revealed religion, is predicated for him as for Stirner on a courageous stance of seeing the world as it is, shorn of all comforting fables concerning a God of justice or love, and any afterlife. See Losurdo, *Nietzsche*, pp. 592–6.

40 Friedrich Nietzsche, KSA XII, p. 350, cited at Losurdo, *Nietzsche*, p. 506. The notes now collected chronologically in the complete works in German [KSA] were those previously compiled thematically as *Will to Power*. On the history of the texts, see Thomas H. Brobjer, "Nietzsche's *Magnum Opus*," *History of European Ideas*, 32, no. 3 (2006), pp. 278–94.

41 Friedrich Nietzsche, KSA, XII, p. 354, cited at Losurdo, *Nietzsche*, 595.

42 Albert Camus, "Three Interviews," p. 345.

43 Camus, LCE, p. 169.

44 Already in *The Myth of Sisyphus*, we see why Camus's position might better be approached by the epistemic term, "agnostic," that is, someone who does not know whether God exists, rather than someone who categorically denies that He does. In fact, much of his work is suffused with a sense of the sacred, and he once described his philosophical aim, in strikingly non-nihilistic terms, as "imagining the sacred without a belief in immortality." (Albert Camus, *Carnets 1942–1951*, translated with Introduction & notes by Philip Thody (London: Hamish Hamilton, 1966), p. 7) See Chapter 6.

45 See Matthew Sharpe, "On a Neglected Argument in French Philosophy: Sceptical Humanism in Montaigne, Voltaire and Camus," *Critical Horizons* 16, no. 1 (2015), pp. 1–26.

46 Camus, LCE, p. 286.

47 Camus, LCE, p. 160.

48 Camus talks of three cycles of his works, the first on the absurds (from c. 1938–43), the second on revolt or rebellion (c. 1944–53), and an incomplete "cycle" on love and nemesis. Each phase contained philosophical essays as well as a novel and one or more plays.

49 Albert Camus, "Letter to Roland Barthes on *The Plague*," LCE 253–5.

50 Although people continue to make this mistake, he would also stress the great distances between himself and Meursault, the nihilistic, murdering antihero of *The Stranger*. Camus undoubtedly condensed something of his own earlier sensibilities into his most famous literary character, as he did with every literary creation—but to identify him with Meursault, or Doctor Rieux from *The Plague*, not to mention Jean-Baptiste Clamence from *The Fall* is to make an error.

51 Camus, *The Rebel*, pp. 178–87.

52 Camus, *The Rebel*, p. 178.

53 Camus, "Crisis of Man," SO, p. 22.

54 Camus, SO, p. 77.

55 Camus, SO, p. 85.

56 Camus, SO, p. 85.

57 Camus, *The Rebel*, p. 3.

58 Camus, *The Plague*, p. 152.

59 Matthew Sharpe, "On a Neglected Argument in French Philosophy: Sceptical Humanism in Montaigne, Voltaire and Camus," *Critical Horizons* 16, no. 1 (2015), pp. 1–26; *The Other Enlightenment: Self-Othering, Race and Gender* (USA: Lexington, 2023).

60 Camus, SO, p. 44.

61 Francois Jeanson, "Soul in Revolt," in David A. Sprintzen & Adrian van den Hoven eds. and trans. *Camus and Sartre: A Historic Confrontation* (Humanity Books: New York 2004), p. 93.

62 Albert Camus, *Camus at Combat,* 41, 65. Yet, if the heart has its reasons, they are often partial, and not altogether discerning. Camus himself, in *The Myth of Sisyphus*, stresses that he wishes to ground his philosophical assessment of suicide in logic and lucidity, although absurdity presents itself firstly as a sentiment. (MS, 6 ff.)

63 Camus, *The Rebel*, p. 10.

64 Camus, *The Rebel*, p. 10.

65 Camus, *The Rebel*, p. 6.

66 Camus, *The Rebel*, p. 22.

Chapter 2

1 See James Ball, *Post-Truth: How Bullshit Conquered the World* (USA: Biteback Books, 2018); Yael Brahms, "Philosophy of Post-Truth," *Institute for National Security Studies* 2020, pp. 1–20.

2 71 "Trump's False or Misleading Claims Total 30,573 over 4 years," *Washington Post*, January 24, 2021. Online at https://www.washingtonpost.com/politics/2021/01/24/trumps-false-or-misleading-claims-total-30573-over-four-years/.

3 See Mike Rothschild, *The Storm Is Upon Us: How QAnon Became a Movement, Cult, and Conspiracy Theory of Everything* (USA: Melville House, 2021).

4 Hannah Arendt, "Truth and Politics," in Peter Baehr (ed.), *The Portable Hannah Arendt* (London: Penguin, 2000). See Matthew Sharpe, "A Question of Two Truths? Remarks on *Parrhesia* and the 'Political-Philosophical' Difference," *Parrhesia: A Journal of Critical Philosophy* (2007): 89–108.

5 Joshua Norman, "Post-truth" Named Word of the Year for 2016 by Oxford Dictionaries," CBS News, November 17, 2016. Online at https://www.cbsnews.com/news/post-truth-word-of-the-year-2016-oxford-dictionaries/.

6 See Sharpe, *Other Enlightenment*, Chapter 1.

7 See Kevin James Shay, *Operation Chaos: The Capitol Attack and the Campaign to Erode Democracy* (USA: Random House, 2021).

8 Donie O'Sullivan, "'2000 Mules' Creator Admits Some of Film's Claims Are Flawed," CNN Politics, December 2, 2024. Online at https://edition.cnn.com/2024/12/02/politics/2000-mules-creator-admits-some-of-films-claims-are-flawed/index.html.

9   Katelyn Caralle, "New RNC Hires Are Asked If They Believe the 2020 Election Was Stolen: Lara Trump and New Leadership Team's Recruitment Policy Is Revealed After Ronna McDaniel's Spectacular Ouster," *Daily Mail*, April 2024. Online at https://www.msn.com/en-us/news/politics/new-rnc-hires-are-asked-if-they-believe-the-2020-election-was-stolen-lara-trump-and-new-leadership-team-s-recruitment-policy-is-revealed-after-ronna-mcdaniel-s-spectacular-ouster/ar-BB1kDYA3#image=3.

10 Lee Macintyre, *On Disinformation: How to Fight for Truth and Protect Democracy* (Cambridge, MA: MIT Press, 2023); Robert N. Proctor and Londa Schiebinger (eds.), *Agnotology, the Making and Unmaking of Ignorance* (Stanford: Stanford University Press, 2017). See Georgina Kenyon, "The Man Who Studies the Spread of Ignorance," BBC, January 6, 2016. Online at https://www.bbc.com/future/article/20160105-the-man-who-studies-the-spread-of-ignorance.

11 In fact, the political Right's acceptance since the 1990s that they are engaged in a life-or-death cultural struggle or "culture war" has always arguably been its own, more bitter version of the postmodernism it reviles. For in a war, one has enemies. Enemies are those people whom "we" must defeat, even at the price of a willingness to lie—indeed, with the full license of our "being at war" to say anything necessary to win. It is their narrative against ours, their interests versus ours, "Us" versus "Them."

12 Shoshana Zuboff, *The Age of Surveillance Capitalism: The Fight for a Human Future at the New Frontier of Power* (London: Profile Books, 2019); Max Fisher, The Chaos Machine: The Inside Story of How Social Media Rewired Our Minds and Our World (London: Littlebrown and Company, 2022).

13 See Andrew Marantz, *Antisocial: Online Extremists, Techno-Utopians, and the Hijacking of the American Conversation* (London: Penguin, 2020); Fisher, Chaos Machine.

14 For examples pf families estranged over QAnon, see Rothschild, The Storm Is Upon Us.

15 There is Left social media, and there is Right social media. As of 2024, following Trump's creation of the Orwellian-named "Truth Social," Right-wing billionaire Elon Musk's takeover of Twitter (now X), and then the creation of "Bluesky" as a liberal social media platform, we have arrived at the advent of alternative informational universes which online citizens choose between. The prospects for democracy of such a scenario seem grim.

16 "Language: A Key Mechanism of Control: Newt Gingrich's 1990 GOPAC memo." Online at https://www.transcend.org/tms/wp-content/uploads/2019/11/Newt-Gingrich-Language-A-Key-Mechanism-of-Control-1990.pdf.

17 As such, many of our fellow citizens adhere to such unlikely, "hyper-true" propositions (as we might dub them) as that a convicted felon and adjudicated sex offender facing dozens of indictments, including for defrauding the American people and stoking a insurrection, is a God-sent, Christ-like saviour sent to save "Western

civilization" from the infamies of "wokeism," "antifa," "trans-activists," "globalism," "the lamestream media," "George Soros," "BLM," and so on.

18 Albert Camus, "Une des plus belles professions que je connais …," *Oeuvres Complètes III, 1949-1956*, pp. 879–81.

19 Albert Camus, *The Misunderstanding*, in *Caligula and Three Other Plays*, a new translation by Ryan Bloom (New York: Vintage, 2023).

20 Camus, "The Crisis of Man," in SO, p. 21.

21 Camus, "Crisis of Man," p. 29.

22 Camus, "Crisis of Man," p. 29.

23 Camus, "Crisis of Man," p. 22.

24 Instead, as we signaled above, different online subgroups, insulated behind algorithmic walls from the arguments of others, and behind screens and anonymity online from seeing others' faces, develop in-groups jargons, slanderous terms for their real and imagined enemies, and opinions which impugn others as not simply mistaken, but evil.

25 Camus, SO, p. 84.

26 Albert Camus, "Bread and Freedom," in SO, p. 138.

27 Camus, "Crisis of Man," p. 23.

28 André Spicer, *Business Bullshit* (London: Routledge, 2017).

29 Albert Camus, "State of Siege," in *Caligula & Three Other Plays* (USA: Knopf, 1958), p. 170.

30 Cited at Donald Lazere, "Camus on Doublespeak," *The English Journal*, 66, no. 7 (1977), p. 24.

31 Camus, "Crisis of Man," p. 23.

32 Camus, "Crisis of Man," p. 31.

33 Camus, "Are We Pessimists?," SO, p. 37.

34 Timothy Snyder, "The American Abyss," *The New York Times*, January 9, 2021. Online at https://www.nytimes.com/2021/01/09/magazine/trump-coup.html.

35 Camus, *The Plague*, p. 110.

36 Camus, *The Rebel*, p. 22.

37 Camus, *The Rebel*, p. 14.

38 Camus, *The Rebel*, p. 22, pp. 15–16.

39 Camus, *The Rebel*, p. 101, p. 102.

40 Camus, *The Rebel*, pp. 21–2.

41 Camus, *The Rebel*, p. 293.

42 Camus, *The Rebel*, p. 284.

43 Albert Camus, "Reflections on the Guillotine," in RRD, p. 223.

44 Camus, "Reflections on the Guillotine."

45 Camus, *The Rebel*, p. 289.

46 Albert Camus, "Interventions à la table ronde," *Oeuvres Complètes*, II, p. 681. We will return in Section 4.2 to Camus' position on socialism, and his opposition of all forms of servitude, whether to forms of public or private governments, forms of political or economic domination. Camus, *The Rebel*, p. 283.

47 Camus, *The Rebel*, p. 283.

48 *Camus at Combat*, p. 56.

49 Camus, "Crisis of Man," p. 30.

50 Camus, "Time of Murderers," p. 98.

51 Camus, "Time of Murderers," SO, p. 98; *The Rebel*, p. 283.

52 Camus, "Time of Murderers," p. 104. After 1945, it is notable that Camus begins to celebrate Socrates, and his commitment to dialogue, over his earlier admiration for Nietzsche, the philosopher of the will to power. "Plato is right and not Moses and Nietzsche," he writes in *The Rebel*, pp. 283–4: "Dialogue on the level of mankind is less costly than the gospel preached by totalitarian regimes in the form of a monologue dictated from the top of a lonely mountain. On the stage as in reality, the monologue precedes death …" See Section 3.4.

53 Albert Camus, "Misery in Kabylia," *Algerian Chronicles*, pp. 37–84.

54 Camus, *The Plague*, p. 3.

55 *Camus at Combat*, p. 24.

56 *Camus at Combat*, p. 24.

57 *Camus at Combat*, p. 25.

58 *Camus at Combat*, p. 33.

59 *Camus at Combat*, p. 33.

60 *Camus at Combat*, p. 34.

61 *Camus at Combat*, p. 34.

62 Albert Camus, "Le dialogue et le Vocabulaire (decembre 1952-navier 1953)," *Oeuvres Complètes* III, pp. 1105–8.

63 Camus, "Crisis of Man," p. 20.

64 *Camus at Combat*, p. 22.

65 *Camus at Combat*, p. 170.

66 *Camus at Combat*, p. 85.

67 *Camus at Combat*, p. 85.

Chapter 3

1 Camus, *The Rebel*.

2 Thomas Frank, *The Conquest of Cool: Business Culture, Counterculture, and the Rise of Hip Consumerism* (Chicago: University of Chicago Press, 1997), p. 26.

3 Frank, *Conquest of Cool*, pp. 65–6.

4 Jerry Delia Femina, *From Those Wonderful Folks Who Gave You Pearl Harbor* (London: Sir Isaac Pittman and Sons, 1971), p. 24.

5 Luc Boltanski and Eve Chiapello, *The New Spirit of Capitalism* translated by Gregory Elliot (London: Verso, 2007); Michel Clouscard, *Néo-fascisme et idéologie du désir* (Paris: Le Castor Astral, 1999).

6 Frank, *Conquest of Cool*, p. 89.

7 Frank, *Conquest of Cool*, p. 89.

8 Matthew Sharpe, "The 'Revolution' in Advertising and University Discourse," in Justin Clemens and Rusell Grigg (eds.) Jacques Lacan and the Other Side of Psychoanalysis (USA: Duke University Press, 2006), pp. 301–2.

9 Cited in Frank, *The Conquest of Cool*, p. 90.

10 Cited in Frank, *The Conquest of Cool*, p. 90.

11 Fredric Jameson, *The Cultural Turn: Selected Writings on the Postmodern, 1983-1998* (London: Verso), p. 19.

12 Boltanski & Chiapello, *The New Spirit of Capitalism*, pp. 36ff., 167 ff., 198, 326, 441 ff.

13 Thomas Frank, *One Market Under God: Extreme Capitalism, Market Populism, and the End of Economic Democracy* (USA: Doubleday, 2000), p. 179.

14 Frank, *One Market Under God*, p. 195.

15 Frank, *One Market Under God*, p. 190.

16 Frank, *One Market Under God*, p. 173.

17 Frank, *One Market Under God*, p. 186.

18 At Frank, *One Market Under God*, p. 205.

19 At Frank, *One Market Under God*, p. 202.

20 See David A. Sprintzen (ed.), *Sartre and Camus: An Historic Confrontation* (New York: Humanity books, 2004).

21 Jean-Paul Sartre, "Jean-Paul Sartre répond" (interview)," L'Arc 40 (October 1966), p. 89.

22 See for Foucault's criticisms of French academic Marxism, Michel Foucault, *Power/Knowledge: Selected Interviews and Writings*, edited by Colin Gordon, translated by Colin Gordon et al (New York: Pantheon Books, 1977), pp. 52–3, 57–9, 65, 75–6, 110–11.

23 Jean-Francois Lyotard, *The Postmodern Condition: A Report on Knowledge* (USA: University of Minnesota Press, 1984), pp. xxiv, 11–13, 36–7.

24 Jacques Derrida, *Spectres of Marx*, translated by Peggy Kamuf (New York: Routledge 1994).

25 See on Peterson, Ben Burgis et al, *Myth and Mahem: A Leftist Critique of Jordan Peterson* (USA: ZERO Books, 2020), pp. 14, 19, 220; Matthew Sharpe, "After Trickle Down, Kicking Down: On Jordan Peterson, Naturalizing Inequality, and Neofascist Indirect Apologetics," *Critical Sociology* 2024, pp. 1–19.

26 See Gary Gutting, *Thinking the Impossible: French Philosophy since 1960* (Oxford: Oxford University Press, 2011; Luc Ferry and Alain Renaut, *French Philosophy of the Sixties: An Essay on Anti-Humanism* (Amherst: University of Massachusetts Press, 1990).

27 See Losurdo, *Nietzsche: Aristocratic Rebel*; Hugo Ott, *Martin Heidegger: A Political Life* trans. by Allan Blunden (New York: Basic, 1993); Emmanuel Faye, *Martin Heidegger, The Introduction of Nazism into Philosophy in Light of the Unpublished Seminars of 1933–1935*, translated by Michael B. Smith (Yale University Press, 2009); and Richard Wolin, *The Heidegger Controversy* (USA: MIT Press, 1993); Charles R. Heidegger's *Roots: Nietzsche, National Socialism, and the Greeks* (Cornell University Press, 2003); Richard Wolin, *Heidegger in Ruins: Between Philosophy and Ideology* (Yale University Press, 2023).

28 Gyorgy Lukacs, *History and Class Consciousness*, translated by R. Livingstone (Cambridge, MA: MIT Press, 1971).

29 There is a massive wealth of secondary material on the post-structuralist thinkers. For some of the best critical treatments, see Gary Gutting, *Thinking the Impossible: French Philosophy since 1960* (Oxford and New York: Oxford University Press, 2011); Juergen Habermas, *The Philosophical Discourse of Modernity: Twelve Lectures*, translated by T. McCarthy (Massachusetts: MIT Press, 1990); Alex Callinicos, *Against*

Postmodernism: A Marxist Critique (London: Polity Press, 1990); Terry Eagleton, *The Illusions of Postmodernism* (London: Wiley-Blackwell, 1996); Thomas McCarthy, "The Critique of Impure Reason: Foucault and the Frankfurt School," *Political Theory* Vol. 18, No. 3 (Aug. 1990): 437–69; Thomas McCarthy, "The Politics of the Ineffable: Derrida's Deconstructionism in Hermeneutics in Ethics and Social Theory," *Philosophical Forum* 21 (1–2) (1989): 146–68; Nancy Fraser, "Foucault on Modern Power: Empirical Insights and Normative Confusions," *Praxis International* 1 (1981): 272–87.

30 See Ian Hunter, "The History of Theory," *Critical Inquiry* 33, no. 1 (Autumn 2006): 78–112.

31 Gilles Deleuze, "Postscript on Societies of Control" (1990), *The Deleuze Seminars* May 1, 1990. Online at https://deleuze.cla.purdue.edu/resource/gilles-deleuze-postscript-on-societies-of-control/.

32 See Thomas McCarthy, "The Politics of the Ineffable: Derrida's Deconstructionism in Hermeneutics in Ethics and Social Theory," *Philosophical Forum* 21, nos. 1–2, 1989: 146–68.

33 See Matthew Sharpe, *Camus, Philosophe*, pp. 288–92.

34 See Dominique Janicaud (ed.), *Phenomenology and the "Theological Turn": The French Debate* (New York: Fordham University Press, 2000).

35 Giorgio Agamben, *The Time That Remains. A Commentary on the Letter to the Romans*, translated by Patricia Dailey (Stanford: Stanford University Press, 2005); Alain Badiou, *Saint Paul: The Foundation of Universalism*, translated by Ray Brassier (Stanford: Stanford University Press, 2003).

36 See Gabriel Rockhill, "The Myth of 1968 Thought and the French Intelligentsia: Historical Commodity Fetishism and Ideological Rollback," *Monthly Review* June 1, 2023. Online at https://monthlyreview.org/2023/06/01/the-myth-of-1968-thought-and-the-french-intelligentsia-historical-commodity-fetishism-and-ideological-rollback/.

37 Rockhill, "The Myth of 1968 Thought and the French Intelligentsia."

38 Joel Bakan, *The New Corporation: How "Good" Corporations Are Bad for Democracy* (London: Random House, 2020).

39 I have made these comparisons in *Camus, Philosophe*, pp. 61–95, 153–64; and Matthew Sharpe, "The Plague and the Panopticon: Camus, With and Against the Total Critiques of Modernity," *Thesis Eleven* 133, no. 1, 2016: 59–79.

40 Camus, "Create Dangerously," RRD, pp. 249–72.

41 Camus, *The Rebel*, pp. 36–54, 81–100. [From here on in this chapter, due to frequency of citation, *The Rebel* will be abbreviated in text as R, with page number].

42 Modris Eksteins, *The Rites of Spring: The Great War and the Birth of the Modern Age* (New York: Anchor Press/Doubleday, 1990).

43 Like a Nick Land today who has moved to well-ordered China, having extolled the "appetite for annihilation" as a younger theoretical firebrand, and continuing to call down accelerationist collapse to bring on the advent of super-AI, a high-tech version of Nietzsche's overman he imagined we should want to welcome.

44 See Jennifer Ratner-Rosenhagen, *American Nietzsche: A History of an Icon and His Ideas* (Chicago: University of Chicago Press, 2012); Aymeric Monville, *Misère du nietzschéisme de gauche* (Paris: Les Éditions Delga, 2007); Jan Rehmann, *Deconstructing Postmodern Nietzscheanism: Deleuze and Foucault* (Leiden: Brill, 2021).

45 Losurdo, *Nietzsche*, pp. 723–45.

46 Monville, *Misère du nietzschéisme de gauche*.

47 It is also true that this chapter of *The Rebel* is dedicated to a reading of *The Will to Power* specifically (R, 66, note). This was not only a central text in the Nazi appropriations of the philosopher. Based on the philosopher's notes, it is the text which contains many of Nietzsche's most openly exterminist passages: texts to which we might well have expected Camus to pay especial attention, yet which he largely passes over.

48 See Rehmann, *Deconstructing Postmodern Nietzscheanism*.

49 See for instance Nietzsche, *Genealogy of Morals* III, 15: "'I suffer: someone or other must be guilty'—and every sick sheep thinks the same. But his shepherd, the ascetic priest, says to him, 'Quite right, my sheep! Somebody must be to blame: but you yourself are this somebody, you yourself alone are to blame for it, you yourself alone are to blame for yourself'. … That is bold enough, wrong enough: but at least one thing has been achieved by it, the direction of *ressentiment* is, as I said—*changed*." See Losurdo, *Nietzsche*, pp. 448–52.

50 Nietzsche, *Will to Power*, 868.

Chapter 4

1 Camus, *The Plague*, p. 115.

2 Dianna Chang et al., "The Determinants Of COVID-19 Morbidity and Mortality Across Countries." Scientific Reports" 12, article no. 5888, 2022 Online at https://www.nature.com/articles/s41598-022-09783-9#Sec32; Arielle Mitropolous, "For Red and Blue America, a Glaring Divide in COVID-19 Death Rates Persists 2 Years Later. Post-Vaccine, Death Rates in Red States Were 38% Higher Than in Blue States." *ABC News* March 28, 2022. Online at https://abcnews.go.com/Health/red-blue-america-glaring-divide-covid-19-death/story?id=83649085.

3 Emily Stewart, "Why the Stock Market Went Up During the Covid-19 Pandemic and High Unemployment," *Vox* May 10, 2021. Online at https://www.vox.com/business-and-finance/22421417/stock-market-pandemic-economy.

4   Beyond cognitive dissonance, there is surely something profoundly inhumane about the spectacle of soaring stocks and bullish investors, as hundreds of millions of people were rendered unemployed globally, and a pandemic that would kill seven million human beings by January 2025 was running through the American, Italian, Brazilian and other populations.

5   Loukas Karabarbounis and Brent Neiman, "The Global Decline of the Labor Share," *The Quarterly Journal of Economics* 129, no, 1, February 2014, pp.61–103; Walter Paternesi Meloni, Antonella Stira, "The Decoupling Between Labour Compensation and Productivity in High-Income Countries: Why is the Nexus Broken?" British Journal of Industrial Relations 61, 2023, pp. 425–63.

6   Soriano Mena | The Extent and Causes Of the Declining Labour Share Of Income Across the Globe | Essex Student Journal

7   Les Leopold, *Runaway Inequality: An Activist's Guide to Economic Justice* (New York: Labor Institute Press, 2015), pp. 13–14.

8   Guy Standing, "Economic Insecurity and Global Casualisation: Threat or Promise?," *Social Indicators Research* 88, pages 15–30. See also "Statistics on Unemployment and Labour Underutilization," *International Labor Organisation*, January 17, 2025. Online at https://ilostat.ilo.org/topics/unemployment-and-labour-underutilization/. In almost all countries, the percentages of fixed term contract, temporary workers and involuntary temporary workers (who want more work) have grown over the last decades. They presently amount to around 11 percent of the global workforce, yet account for as much as around 70 percent of the workforce in countries like Pakistan and Cambodia. (Around one in four Australians works "casual"). Australian Council of Trade Unions Media release, Casual workers earn $11.59 less per hour than permanent employees - Australian Council of Trade Unions, May 22, 2023. Online at https://www.actu.org.au/media-release/casual-workers-earn-11-59-less-per-hour-than-permanent-employees/s.

9   [US] Congressional Research Services, "Real Wage Trends, 1979 to 2018." Online at https://crsreports.congress.gov/product/pdf/R/R45090/12.

10 Nick Hanauer, "America's 1% Has Taken $50 Trillion From the Bottom 90%," *Time*, September 14, 2021. Online at https://time.com/5888024/50-trillion-income-inequality-america/.

11 Carter C. Price and Kathryn A. Edwards, "Trends in Income From 1975 to 2018," Rand, September 14, 2020. Online at https://www.rand.org/pubs/working_papers/WRA516-1.html.

12 Oxfam, "Richest 1% Bag Nearly Twice As Much Wealth As the Rest Of the World Put Together Over the Past Two Years," January 16, 2023, reports that the number of billionaires globally has doubled over the last ten years and the richest 1 percent accumulated nearly two-thirds of all new wealth since 2020. In addition, since 2020, 63 percent of all new wealth went to the richest 1 percent of the global population and for every $1 of new global wealth earned by someone in the bottom 90 percent

a billionaire accumulated approximately $1.7 million. Online at https://www.oxfam.org/en/press-releases/richest-1-bag-nearly-twice-much-wealth-rest-world-put-together-over-past-two-years. See "Survival Of the Richest: How Billionaires Are Amassing Eye-Watering Wealth Amid Crisis," Oxfam Australia, January 16, 2023. Online at https://www.oxfam.org.au/2023/01/survival-of-the-richest-how-billionaires-are-amassing-eye-watering-wealth-amid-crisis/.

13. Leopold, *Runaway Inequality*, p. 102.

14. Leopold, *Runaway Inequality*, pp. 102–3.

15. Yenni Kwok, "Global Super-Rich Hide $21 Trillion in Tax Havens," CNN Business, July 25, 2012. Online at https://edition.cnn.com/2012/07/23/business/super-rich-hidden-wealth-offshore/index.html.

16. Leopold, *Runaway Inequality*, pp. 40–1.

17. David Richardson, "The Rise and Rise Of the Big Banks: Concentration of Ownership," Australia Institute Technical Brief No. 15, December 2012. Online at TB-15-The-rise-and-rise-of-the-big-banks_4.pdf.

18. Malcolm Sawyer, "Monopoly Capitalism in the Past Four Decades," Cambridge Journal of Economics, 46, no. 2, 2022: 1225–41.

19. Malcolm Sawyer, "Secular Stagnation and Monopoly Capitalism," *Journal of Post Keynesian Economics*, 46, no. 4, 2023: 545–65.

20. Sawyer, "Secular Stagnation and Monopoly Capitalism," p. 552.

21. Simcha Barkai and Seth G. Benzell, "70 Years of US Corporate Profits," *Promarket* May 30, 2018. Online at https://www.promarket.org/2018/05/30/70-years-us-corporate-profits/; Catherine Rampell, "Real Corporate Profits," *New York Times* (graph). Online at https://archive.nytimes.com/economix.blogs.nytimes.com/2012/11/29/record-corporate-profits/.

22. Cited at Leopold, *Runaway Inequality*, p. 219.

23. Leopold, *Runaway Inequality*, p. 186.

24. CEIC Date, "US Private Debt: % of Nominal GDP, 1951–2024." Online AT https://www.ceicdata.com/en/indicator/united-states/private-debt–of-nominal-gdp.

25. For example: Peter Abelson et al., "Housing Prices and Rents in Australia 1980-2023: Facts, Explanations and Outcomes." Online at https://esacentral.org.au/365/images/PeterAbelsonHousingpricesandreturnsinAustralia1980-2023.pdf.

26. For readers unfamiliar with the situation "down under," the ratio of Australian house prices to annual median income has bounced from under 5:1 as recently as 1970 to over 12:1 in a city like Sydney. To ever purchase such a house on the back of their own enterprise, let alone pay down the mortgage, is increasingly beyond the imaginings of many younger Australians. Even amongst those with higher education, outside of

the wealthiest families. The national "dream" of a "quarter acre block" in the inner suburban rings of Sydney, Melbourne, or even Adelaide is now an historical taunt for upcoming generations, where a single square metre in desirable suburbs can cost over $10,000. See Domain, "The Melbourne Suburbs Where Buyers Pay a Premium For Space." Online at https://www.domain.com.au/news/the-melbourne-suburbs-where-buyers-pay-a-premium-for-space-2-1270471/?msockid=09a3015b36696b0f24da13873 7f96a48.

27 Camus, "Misery in Kabylia."

28 See Les Leopold, *Wall Street's War on Workers: How Mass Layoffs and Greed Are Destroying the Working Class and What to Do about It* (New York: Chelsea Green, 2024).

29 Michael Thompson, "Introduction," in Gregory Smulewicz-Zucker and Michael J. Thompson *(eds.) Radical Intellectuals and the Subversion of Progressive Politics: The Betrayal of Politics* (London: Palgrave Macmillan, 2015), pp. 1–2.

30 Nancy Fraser, "The End of Progressive Neoliberalism," January 2, 2017. Online at https://www.dissentmagazine.org/online_articles/progressive-neoliberalism-reactionary-populism-nancy-fraser/.

31 By the later twenty-teens, it became possible to see paid representatives of Corporate Banks in some nations carrying multi-colored progressive banners at ostensibly counter-cultural protests to defend minority rights. Such spectacles have enraged sensitive culture warriors who see it as proof positive of the "woke" takeover of the professional-managerial heights of society, and even corporate power. What their criticism misses is how the banks' PR reps were there not to change fundamental economic settings. It is a matter of cynically green- or rainbow-washing their central roles in the economic realities which were already by 2010 seeding angry Right-wing movements, on- and offline, presenting themselves as "populist" voices of the "silent majority." Profitability for the big banks in countries like Australia has continued to rise, independently of these exercises of praying in the marketplace in order to be seen. Sue Lannin, "Bank Profits Jump But Rising Interest Rates Are a Double-Edged Sword," *ABC News*, November 12, 2022. Online at https://www.abc.net.au/news/2022-11-12/bank-profits-jump-but-rising-interest-rates-a-double-edged-sword/101640472.

32 For example: Albert Camus, "[Knowledge is Universal] Message Read Out Be Jean Amrouche At the Maison de la Chimie, 1946," SO, pp. 51–52; "The Unbeliever and Christians," SO, p. 66; "Time of Murderers," SO, p. 97.

33 Albert Camus, "The Europe of Loyalty," SO, p. 103.

34 Camus's increasingly radical break with Sartre and the French communists after 1946 led voices in his own time, and today, to mistake him as a "reactionary"—or even, in one ridiculous polemic, a "fascist." Camus, "Le dialogue et le Vocabulaire.") In our time, some elements on the political Right have tried to claim him, in ways he'd also arguably profoundly disagree with.

35 The following paragraphs draw on Emmett Parker, *Albert Camus, The Artist in the Arena* (Madison: University of Wisconsin Press, 1966), and Herbert R. Lottmann, *Albert Camus: A Biography* (Core Madera, California: Gingko Press, 1997).

36 Some comments suggest he did so as early as May 1935, after Pierre Laval's visit to the USSR made it clear that the Algerian Communist Party would soften its hostility toward French colonial power in Africa, to focus on combating the rising threat of the Right (see Section 4.5). He was in any case removed from the Party, for supporting Messal Hadj's claim that the Communists had been responsible for repressing the *Etoile Nord-Africaine*, an Algerian independence movement allied at that time with the PCF (*Parti communiste Francaise*). Parker, *Camus, Artist in the Arena*, p. 6.

37 October 7, 1944, *Camus at Combat*, pp. 62–4.

38 Parker, *Camus, Artist in the Arena*, pp. 55–9.

39 Parker, *Camus, Artist in the Arena*, pp. 60–1.

40 *Camus at Combat*, p. 13.

41 October 1, 1944, *Camus at Combat*, p. 55.

42 *Camus at Combat*, p. 170: "We have always said that liberation was not liberty and that the fight against the Nazi enemy was for us identical with the fight against the power of money."

43 *Camus at Combat*, pp. 23–48, 47–8, 51–2, 68–9, 83–5, 110, 114, 130–1, 143.

44 October 1, 1944, *Camus at Combat*, p. 55

45 *Camus at Combat*, p. 31.

46 Albert Camus, "Neither Victims nor Executioners. November 9, 1946: A New Social Contract," *Camus at Combat*, 272, n. 74.

47 Parker, *Camus, Artist in the Arena*, p. 15.

48 Camus, *The Rebel*, p. 283.

49 Camus, "Bread and Freedom," SO, p. 134.

50 *Camus at Combat*, pp. 277–93.

51 Lottmann, *Camus*, pp. 426–65.

52 Lou Marin, "The Unknown Camus: Albert Camus and the Impact of His Contributions As a Journalist to the Pacifist, Anarchist and Syndicalist Press," in Camus and Gandhi—Essays on Political Philosophy in Hammarskjöld's Times (Seden: Dag Hammarskjöld Foundation, 2024), pp. 9–21.

53 *Camus at Combat*, p. 85. For Camus's condemnation of the concentration of wealth, and its impact on justice as well as the prospects of a genuinely free and responsible press, see *Camus at Combat*, pp. 83, 110, 114, 130–1, 143, 170, 175, 177.

54 Jacques Derrida, *Spectres of Marx*, translated by Peggy Kamuf (NY: Routledge 1994).

55 See Gary Gutting, *Thinking the Impossible: French Philosophy Since 1960* (Oxford and New York: Oxford University Press, 2011); Matthew Sharpe & Geoffrey Boucher, *Zizek and Politics* (Edinburgh: Edinburgh University Press, 2010).

56 Camus, *The Rebel*, p. 209. See p. 201.

57 Camus, *The Rebel*, p. 188.

58 Camus, *The Rebel*, pp. 210–26.

59 Camus, *The Rebel*, pp. 189–97.

60 Camus, *The Rebel*, pp. 133–48.

61 Camus, *The Rebel*, p. 205.

62 Camus, *The Rebel*, pp. 69–70.

63 Camus, *The Rebel*, p. 208.

64 Nietzsche, *Beyond Good and Evil*, §203.

65 Camus, *The Rebel*, pp. 218–19.

66 Camus, SO, p. 70.

67 Parker, *Camus, the Artist in the Arena*, p. 11.

68 *Camus at Combat*, p. 62.

69 *Camus at Combat*, p. 121.

70 *Camus at Combat*, p. 63.

71 *Camus at Combat*, p. 122.

72 Camus, "Bread and Freedom," p. 132.

73 Camus, "Bread and Freedom," pp. 132–3.

74 Albert Camus, "The Wager of our Generation," RRD, p. 248.

75 Camus, *The Rebel*, p. 291. As we will see in chapter 6, Camus also associates freedom with the pursuits of leisure which give life its beauty and savor: notably, the joys of love, desire, creation, beauty, and friendship.

76 Camus, *The Rebel*, p. 284.

77 Camus, *The Rebel*, p. 71.

78 *Camus at Combat*, pp. 109–11.

79 *Camus at Combat*, 47, 48, 52–3, 110, 114.

80 Camus, *The Rebel*, pp. 287–8. See *The Rebel*, p. 71.

81 Camus, SO, p. 136.

82 Albert Camus, *Algerian Chronicles* translated by Arthur Goldhammer with an Introduction by Alice Kaplan (Cambridge, Massachusetts: Belknap Press, 2013), pp.114, 123; cf. pp. 153–4.

83 Camus, *Algerian Chronicles*, p. 114.

84 Camus, *Algerian Chronicles*, p. 126.

85 On this famous incident, and the debates about it, see James Le Sueur, *Uncivil War: Intellectuals and Identity Politics During the Decolonization* (US: University of Pennsylvania Press, 2001), pp. 123–31; Michael Walzer, "Commitment and Social Criticism: Camus' Algerian war," *Dissent* Fall 1984, pp. 424–32; & Robert Zaretsky, "Silence Follows: Albert Camus in Algeria," in Stephen G. Kellman (ed.) *Critical Insights: Albert Camus* (Pasadena, California: Salem Press, 2012), p. 130.

86 Camus, "Misery in Kabylia," *Algerian Chronicles*, pp. 37–84.

87 Albert Camus, "Mediterranean Humanism," in Neil Foxlee (ed.), *Albert Camus' "The New Mediterranean Culture": A Text and Its Contexts* (Bern: Peter Lang, 2010), pp. 88–9.

88 May 13–15, 1945, "Crisis in Algeria," "Algeria asks for Ships and Justice," in *Camus at Combat*, pp. 198–205.

89 Camus, *Algerian Chronicles*, pp. 179–81.

90 Camus, *Algerian Chronicles*, pp. 179–81.

91 Camus, *Algerian Chronicles*, p. 180.

92 Camus, *Algerian Chronicles*, p. 31.

93 Camus, "Neither Victims nor Executioners," p. 269.

94 *Camus at Combat*, pp. 291–2.

95 May 21, 1945 "It is Justice that will save Algeria from hatred," *Camus at Combat*, p. 216.

96 *Camus at Combat*, p. 216.

97 Camus, *Algerian Chronicles*, p. 153.

Chapter 5

1 See Roger Griffin, *The Nature of Fascism* (Pinters Publisher, 1991).

2 Whereas in the interwar years, there was a somewhat coordinated global Left, moreover, we've seen how the Left has been divided and largely conquered in the

Neoliberal years, remaining sinister and powerful only in the heated rhetoric of the New Right's monetized "thought leaders" (Sections 3.2 and 4.2). The advent of international, placeless social media platforms owned by Far-Right billionaires (Musk – X), or morally challenged, opportunistic "tech bros" (Zuckerberg – Meta) makes the kinds of concerted popular fronts between conservatives, liberals, and socialists necessary to oppose Far Right regimes even harder to presently imagine (Section 2.1).

3   This field, in a way which is contestably, seeks after an essentialist definition of "fascism" in ways which have made it largely a specialist field. The orientations considered here are those of thinkers from the fields of social theory and philosophy, whose works also have had wider impacts within neoliberal, Marxist, and political debates. It is beyond the scope of this book to adjudicate more fine-grained definitional debates in fascism studies, although we invoke Roger Griffin's notion of "ultranationalist palingenesis" in the preceding section.

4   Camus, *The Rebel*, p. 181.

5   Camus, *The Plague*, pp. 222–3.

6   Friederich Hayek, *The Road to Serfdom* (London: Routledge, 1944).

7   See Andrew Gamble, *Hayek: The Iron Cage of Liberty* (Boulder, CO: Westview Press, 1996); Matthew Sharpe, "Is Neoliberalism a Liberalism, or a Stranger Kind of Bird?," *Critical Horizons: A Journal of Philosophy and Social Theory* 10, no. 1 2009, pp. 76–98.

8   Theodor Adorno & Max Horkheimer, *The Dialectic of Enlightenment*, translated by John Cumming (New York: Continuum, 1989).

9   Adorno & Horkheimer, *Dialectic of Enlightenment*, p. 1.

10 Adorno & Horkheimer, *Dialectic of Enlightenment*, pp. 1–12.

11 See Hugo Ott, *Martin Heidegger: A Political Life* trans. Allan Blunden (New York: Basic, 1993); Emmanuel Faye, *Martin Heidegger, The Introduction of Nazism into Philosophy in Light of the Unpublished Seminars of 1933–1935*, translated by Michael B. Smith (Yale: Yale University Press, 2009); and Richard Wolin, *The Heidegger Controversy* (USA: MIT Press, 1993); Charles R. Heidegger's *Roots: Nietzsche, National Socialism, and the Greeks*. Cornell University Press, 2003; Richard Wolin, *Heidegger in Ruins: Between Philosophy and Ideology* (Yale: Yale University Press, 2023).

12 Martin Heidegger, "The Question Concerning Technology," in David Farrell Krell (ed.), *Basic Writings* (USA: HarperCollins, 1993).

13 See Donatella Di Cesare, "Heidegger and the Jews: The Black Notebooks" (New York: Policy, 2018).

14 Martin Heidegger, *Bremen und Freiburger Vorträge*, GA 79, ed. Paetra Jaegar (Francfort-am-Main, 1994), p. 27, 56.

15 See Matthew Sharpe and MattKing, "Reclaiming the Differences: Three Neglected Marxian Theories of Fascism in Lukács, Marcuse, and Bloch, Socialism and Democracy," *Socialism and Democracy* 2023; Aurel Kolnai, *The War Against the West* (London: Viking Press, 1938).

16 Gyorgy Lukacs, *Destruction of Reason*, translated by Peter Palmer (London: Merlin Press, 1980).

17 For this idea of "ethnocide" committed by multi-cultural, liberal societies, and its use to create equivalence licensing openly fascistic violence or genocide in Aleksandr Dugin, see Matthew Sharpe, "Old Wine in a Postmodern Bottle: Aleksandr Dugin's "Fourth Political Theory" and Aurel Kolnai's War Against the West," *Studies in Eastern European Thought*, [Special edition - Russian conservatism, ed. G. Love] (in press, 2024–5).

18 Lukacs, *Destruction of Reason*, p. 85.

19 Jeffrey C. Isaac, *Arendt, Camus, and Modern Rebellion* (Yale: Yale University Press, 1994).

20 See Dana Vila, "Totalitarianism, Tradition, and The Human Condition," *Arendt Studies* 2, 2018, pp. 61–72. Hannah Arendt, *Origins of Totalitarianism* (New York: Harvest Books, 2007), pp. 392–418.

21 Arendt, *Origins of Totalitarianism*, p. 459, pp. 474–6. See Peter Baehr, "The 'Masses' in Hannah Arendt's Theory of Totalitarianism," *The Good Society* 2007; Margaret Canovan, "The Leader and the Masses: Hannah Arendt on Totalitarianism and Dictatorship," in Peter Baehr and Melvin Richter (eds.), *Dictatorship in History and Theory: Bonapartism, Caesarism, and Totalitarianism* (Cambridge: Cambridge University Press, 2013), pp. 241–60.

22 Cf. Camus, *The Plague*, p. 148.

23 Arendt, *Origins of Totalitarianism*, pp. 392–418. See Raymond Aron, "The Essence of Totalitarianism according to Hannah Arendt," in G. Williams (ed.) *Hannah Arendt: Critical Assessments of Leading Political Philosophers. Volume I: Arendt and Political Events* (Oxford: Routledge, 2006), pp. 145–56. See Matthew Sharpe, "When the Logics of the World Collapse – Žižek with and Against Arendt on 'Totalitarianism,'" Subjectivity 3, no, 1, 2010, pp. 54–55. Online at https://www.researchgate.net/publication/248877025_When_the_logics_of_the_world_collapse_-_Zizek_with_and_against_Arendt_on_%27totalitarianism%27.

24 Arendt, *Origins of Totalitarianism*, pp. 458–471.

25 Emmanuel Faye, *Arendt et Heidegger: Extermination nazie et destruction de la pensée* (Albin Michel, 2016), 333–46.

26 Hannah Arendt, *Eichmann in Jerusalem* (London: Penguin, 2006). See Hannah Arendt, *Life of the Mind* (New York: Harcourt Brace Jovanovich, 1969), pp. 1–3, p. 212.

27 Albert Camus, "Socialism of the Gallows," RRD, p. 171.

28 *Camus at Combat*, pp. 37–43.

29 *Camus at Combat*, p. 37.

30 *Camus at Combat*, pp. 37–38.

31 Infamously, Nazi after Nazi passed blame onto the deceased Leader and his inner circle, protesting that they were only doing their duty, even as they lied, tortured, killed, and deceived millions to their deaths.

32 Camus pays particular attention to the ways the Nazis forced victims to participate in their own self-destruction, as in the camp system in which Jewish *sonderkommandos* and *kapos* were forced to do much of the SS's dirty work, to save their own skins. The aim, one of consummate cynicism, is to create a world in which "only the rocks are innocent." Then, since everybody is guilty, "universal guilt licenses no other course of action than the use of force and gives its blessing to –nothing but success." Camus, *The Rebel*, p. 184; cf. Section 5.4

33 Herbert Marcuse, "The Struggle Against Liberalism in the Totalitarian View of the State." In *Negations* translated by James Shapiro (London: Penguin Allen Lane, 1968).

34 See Matthew Sharpe, "Letter to a Germanist Friend: On Camus and Heidegger," *Camus Studies* 8, 2016, pp. 221–50.

35 See Kurt Anderson, *Evil Geniuses: The Unmaking of America. A Recent History* (London: Penguin, Random House, 2020); Thom Hartmann, *The Hidden History of American Oligarchy: Reclaiming Our Democracy from the Ruling Class* (USA: Berrett-Koehler, 2021).

36 Matthew Sharpe, *Camus, Philosophe: To Return to Our Beginnings* (Leiden: Brill, 2014), "Appendix Three: Philosophy United to Rhetoric: The 'Master Argument' in 'Letters to a German Friend'," pp. 406–11.

37 Albert Camus, "Letters to a German Friend," in *RRD*, p. 7.

38 *Camus at Combat*, p. 37.

39 Camus, "Letters to a German Friend," pp. 9–10.

40 Camus, "Letters to a German Friend," p. 14.

41 Camus, "Letters to a German Friend," p. 18.

42 Camus, "Letters to a German Friend," p. 27.

43 Camus, "Letters to a German Friend," p. 14.

44 Albert Camus, *The Fall* translated by Justin O'Brien (New York: Vintage, 1956).

45 Camus, *The Fall*, pp. 69–70.

46 Camus, *The Fall*, p, 84.

47 Camus, *The Fall*, p. 73.

48 Camus, *The Fall*, p. 136.

Chapter 6

1 Albert Camus, "Albert Camus à Athènes, *To Vina*, Athenes: 29 April 1955," at Barbara Papastavrou, "Albert Camus: De l'Amour Platon à son Engagement envers les Grecs," in A. Fosty (ed.), *Albert Camus et la Grèce* (Aix-en-Provence: Ecritures du Sud, 2007), p. 107.

2 Camus at Francois Bousquet, *Camus L'Ancien, Camus Le Mediterraneen* (Sherbrooke, Quebec, Canada: Editions Naaman, 1977), p. 101. See Henri Peyre, "Camus the Pagan," in *Camus, A Collection of Critical Essays*, pp. 65–70; Matthew Sharpe, "Camus' Hellenic Heart, Between Augustine and Hegel," in Adam Goldwyn et al. (ed.), *The Brill Companion to Classical Reception* (Leiden: Brill, 2016).

3 I make this argument in more detail in *Camus, Philosophe*, pp. 256–62.

4 Albert Camus, "Helen's Exile," in LCE, pp. 148–9.

5 NASA, "Temperatures Rising: NASA Confirms 2024 Warmest Year on Record," January 10, 2025. Online at https://www.nasa.gov/news-release/temperatures-rising-nasa-confirms-2024-warmest-year-on-record/#:~:text=Earth%E2%80%99s%20average%20surface%20temperature%20in%202024%20was%20the,%281951-1980%29%2C%20which%20tops%20the%20record%20set%20in%202023.

6 NASA, "Global Temperature | Vital Signs – Climate Change: Vital Signs of the Planet," 2024. Online at https://climate.nasa.gov/vital-signs/global-temperature/?intent=121.

7 James Ashworth, "Climate Change Set to Breach 1.5°C Limit for First Time by 2027," Natural History Museum, May 17, 2023. Online at https://www.nhm.ac.uk/discover/news/2023/may/climate-change-set-breach-limit-for-first-time-by-2027.html.

8 NASA, "Ice Sheets | Vital Signs – Climate Change: Vital Signs of the Planet," 2024. Online at https://science.nasa.gov/earth/explore/earth-indicators/ice-sheets/.

9 NASA, "Tracking 30 Years of Sea Level Rise." Online at https://earthobservatory.nasa.gov/images/150192/tracking-30-years-of-sea-level-rise; Copernicus. Europe's Eyes on Earth, "Global Climate Highlights 2024." Online at https://climate.copernicus.eu/global-climate-highlights-2024.

10 Hannah Richie, "Deforestation and Forest Loss," Our World in Data. Online at https://ourworldindata.org/deforestation.

11 Renee Piccard, "11 Examples of Depletion of Natural Resources," Green Coast, March 20, 2023. Online at https://greencoast.org/depletion-of-natural-resources/#:~:text=This%20article%20explains%20why%20and%20how%20natural%20resources,we%20tell%20which%20natural%20resources%20are%20being%20depleted%3F.

12 Financial times Series, "The Uninsurable World: How the Insurance Industry Fell Behind on Climate Change." Online at https://www.ft.com/content/11ef0 21c-d95b-44d4-b8f8-e9b2624d3ff7.

13 Emma Charlton, "This is What Climate Change Costs Economies Around the World," World Economic Forum, November 29, 2023. Online at https://www.weforum.org/stories/2023/11/climate-crisis-cost-global-economies/.

14 Dinah V. Parums, "A Review of the Increasing Global Impact of Climate Change on Human Health and Approaches to Medical Preparedness," Pub Med Cental. Online at https://pmc.ncbi.nlm.nih.gov/articles/PMC11302257/.

15 R. Daniel Bresser, "The Mortality Cost of Carbon," *Nature Communications*, 12, 2021, Article number: 4467. Online at https://www.nature.com/articles/s41 467-021-24487-w.

16 Bresser, "The Mortality Cost of Carbon."

17 UN Environment Report, "Governments Plan to Produce Double the Fossil Fuels in 2030 Than the 1.5°C Warming Limit Allows," November 2023. Online at https://www.unep.org/news-and-stories/press-release/governments-plan-produce-double-fossil-fuels-2030-15degc-warming.

18 Diane Stuart, "The Human Crisis Revisited: Albert Camus and Climate Rebellion," *Critical Horizons*, 25, no. 4, 2024, pp. 111–28. See Paul J. Burke et al., "Carbon Dioxide Emissions in the Short Run: The Rate and Sources of Economic Growth Matter." Global Environmental Change 33, 2015, pp. 109–21; Steffen et al. 2018; Hao Chen et al., "Does Energy Consumption, Economic Growth, Urbanization, and Population Growth Influence Carbon Emissions in the BRICS? Evidence from Panel Models Robust to Cross-Sectional Dependence and Slope Heterogeneity." Environmental Science and Pollution Research, 29, no. 25, 2022, pp. 37598–616; Will Stefan et al. "Trajectories of the Earth System in the Anthropocene." Proceedings of the National Academy of Sciences, 115, no. 33, 2018, pp. 8252–9.

19 Sivan Kartha et al.., "The Carbon Inequality Era: An Assessment of the Global Distribution of Consumption Emissions Among Individuals from 1990 to 2015 and Beyond." 2020. https://oxfamilibrary.openrepository.com/handle/10546/621049.

20 Ron Bousso, "Big Oil Doubles Profits in Blockbuster 2022," *Reuters*, February 8, 2023.

21 Evidently, we cannot undertake a full analysis of these philosophies here. The argument here is developed in more detail in Sharpe, *Camus, Philosophe*, pp. 258–65.

22 Camus, *Carnets II*, p. 103.

23 Sharpe, "After Trickle Down, Kicking Down."

24 Michel Foucault, *Discipline and Punish*, translated by Alan Sheridan (New York: Vintage, 1977), 30.

25 See Heidegger, *Basic Writings*.

26 Camus, "Helen's Exile," pp. 150–1.

27 Stuart, "The Human Crisis Revisited: Albert Camus and Climate Rebellion."

28 Camus, "The Future of Civilization."

29 Camus, *The Myth of Sisyphus*, p. 20.

30 Camus, *The Myth of Sisyphus*, p. 21.

31 Sean B. Carroll, *Brave Genius: A Scientist, a Philosopher, and Their Daring Adventures from the French Resistance to the Nobel Prize* (USA: Crown Press, 2013).

32 Carroll, *Brave Genius*, pp. 302–19.

33 Camus, *The Rebel*, pp. 221–2.

34 Camus, "Helen's Exile," pp. 159–60.

35 Sharpe, "On a Neglected Argument in French Philosophy."

36 Camus, *The Rebel*, p. 302.

37 Camus, *The Myth of Sisyphus*, p. 30.

38 Albert Camus, *Carnets 1942–1951*, translated with Introduction & notes by Philip Thody (London: Hamish Hamilton, 1966), p. 88.

39 Albert Camus, "The Desert," in LCE, p. 102, see p. 101.

40 Camus, "Helen's Exile," p. 151.

41 Camus, "Helen's Exile," p. 149.

42 Albert Camus, "Return to Tipasa," pp. 169–70.

43 Camus, "Return to Tipasa," p. 169.

44 Camus, *The Rebel*, p. 296.

45 Camus, *The Rebel*, p. 300.

46 Albert Camus, "The Future of Civilization," in SO, p. 148.

47 Camus, *The Rebel*, p. 301.

48 Camus, *The Rebel*, p. 304.

49 Camus, "Return to Tipasa," p. 168.

50 Camus, "Return to Tipasa," p. 168.

51 Camus, *The Rebel*, p. 190.

52 September 8, 1944, "Justice and Freedom," in *Camus at Combat*, p. 32; *Carnets II*, p. 112.

53 Camus, "Unbeliever and Christians," RRD 72–3. In a note in his *Carnets* at the time of this 1946 speech, Camus comments: "The only great Christian mind to

look at the problem of evil in the face was Saint Augustine. His conclusion was the terrifying '*nemo bonus*'. Since then, Christianity has spent its time giving the problem temporary solutions. The result is there for everyone to see. It took time, but men are today poisoned by an intoxication that dates back two thousand years. They have had enough of evil, or they are resigned to it, which amounts to pretty much the same thing. But at least they can no longer put up with deception (*le mensonge*) on that subject." C II 179; C II Eng 92.

54 Camus, *The Plague*, p. 177.

55 See for example, Ronald Srigley, *Albert Camus' Critique of Modernity* (Missouri: Missouri University Press, 2011).

56 *Camus at Combat*, p. 145; *Carnets II*, p. 211.

57 Camus, *The Fall*, pp. 128–9. See Burton W. Wheeler, "Beyond Despair: Camus' The Fall and Van Eyck's 'Adoration of the Lamb'," *Contemporary Literature* 23, no. 3, Summer 1982, pp. 343–64.

58 Camus, *The Fall*, p. 73.

59 Camus, *The Fall*, p. 115. For an excellent exploration of the Christian symbolism in *The Fall*, see especially Cortes, *The Descent of the Doves*.

60 Camus, *Carnets 1942–1951*, p. 7.

61 Camus, "Nuptials at Tipasa," LCE, pp. 68–9.

62 Albert Camus, "The Growing Stone," in *Exile and the Kingdom*, translated by Justin O'Brien (USA: Viking, 1958), pp. 212–13.

63 See Camus, *Carnets II*, p. 62; Albert Camus, "Defence de *L'Homme Révolté*," *Oeuvres Complètes III*, p. 374; "Entretien sur la révolte," *Oeuvres Complètes III*, p. 401; Matthew Sharpe, *Camus, Philosophe*, pp. 364–5.

64 Albert Camus, "The Unbeliever and Christians," SO, p. 66.

65 Camus, "[The Artist and his Age] Lecture at Uppsala University [1957]," SO, p. 234.

66 Albert Camus, *The First Man*, translated by David Hapgood (London: Penguin, 1996), p. 137.

67 Camus, *The Rebel*, p. 303.

Conclusion

1 Camus, *The Fall*, p. 132–3.

2 The preceding Camus quotes come from Marcel J. Melancon, *Albert Camus. Analyse de sa pensée* (Suisse: Les Editions universitaire Fribourg, 1976). p. 167, p. 171.

3 Camus, "Defence de *L'Homme Révolté*," *Oeuvres Complètes* III, p. 374.

4 Camus, *Oeuvres complètes II*, p. 494. See Sharpe, "Solitaire/Solidaire: Camus, Contemplation, and the *Vita Mixta*."

5 Camus, *The Rebel*, p. 240.

6 Camus, *The Plague*, p. 251.

BIBLIOGRAPHY

Texts by Albert Camus

Camus, Albert. *The Stranger*, translated by Stuart Gilbert (New York: Vintage, 1946).
Camus, Albert. *The Rebel*, revised and complete translation by Anthony Bower, with a Foreword by Sir Herbert Read (New York: Vintage, 1956).
Camus, Albert. *The Fall* translated by Justin O'Brien (New York: Vintage, 1956).
Camus, Albert. "The Growing Stone," in *Exile and the Kingdom*, translated by Justin O'Brien (USA: Viking, 1958), pp. 81–108.
Camus, Albert. "Letters to a German Friend," in *Resistance, Rebellion, and Death*, translated with Introduction by Justin O'Brien (New York: Vintage, 1960), pp. 1–32.
Camus, Albert. "Pessimism and Courage," in *Resistance, Rebellion, Death*, pp. 57–60.
Camus, Albert. "The Unbeliever and Christians," in *Resistance, Rebellion, and Death*, pp. 67–74.
Camus, Albert. "Socialism of the Gallows," in *Resistance, Rebellion, and Death*, pp. 165–72.
Camus, Albert. "Reflections on the Guillotine," in *Resistance, Rebellion, and Death*, 173–233.
Camus, Albert. "The Wager of our Generation," in *Resistance, Rebellion, Death*, pp. 237–48.
Camus, Albert. "Create Dangerously," in *Resistance, Rebellion, Death*, pp. 249–72.
Camus, Albert. *Carnets 1942-1951*, translated with Introduction & notes by Philip Thody (London: Hamish Hamilton, 1966).
Camus, Albert. *The Plague*, translated Stuart Gilbert (London: Penguin, 1971).
Camus, Albert. *The Myth of Sisyphus*, translated by Justin O'Brien (London: Penguin, 1978).
Camus, Albert. *Lyrical and Critical Essays*, edited by Phillip Thody, translated by Ellen Conroy Kennedy (Vintage: New York, 1987).
Camus, Albert. "Nuptials at Tipasa," in *Lyrical and Critical Essays*, pp. 65–72.
Camus, Albert. "The Desert," in *Lyrical and Critical Essays*, pp. 93–105.
Camus, Albert. "Helen's Exile" (from *Summer*) in *Lyrical and Critical Essays*, pp. 148–53.
Camus, Albert. "The Enigma." "The Enigma," *Lyrical and Critical Essays*, pp. 154–61.
Camus, Albert. "Three Interviews," in *Lyrical and Critical Essays*, pp. 345–65.
Camus, Albert. "Letter to Roland Barthes on *The Plague*," in *Lyrical and Critical Essays*, 338–41.
Camus, Albert. *The First Man*, translated by David Hapgood (London: Penguin, 1996).

Camus, Albert. *Camus at Combat: Writing 1944-1947*, edited by Jacqueline Levi-Valensi, translated by Arthur Goldhammer, with a Foreword by David Carroll (Princeton: Princeton University Press, 2006).

Camus, Albert. "Neither Victims nor Executioners. November 9, 1946: A New Social Contract," *Camus at Combat*, pp. 254-76.

Camus, Albert. "Interview for *Servir* (Entretien à *Servir*)" in *Albert Camus Oeuvres Completes II 1944-1948* (Paris: Gallimard Bibliothèque de la Pléiade: 2006), pp. 659-61.

Camus, Albert. "Interventions à la table ronde," *Oeuvres Complètes*, II, pp. 681-4.

Camus, Albert. "Misery in Kabylia," *Algerian Chronicles*, pp. 37-84.

Camus, Albert. "Le dialogue et le Vocabulaire (decembre 1952-navier 1953)," *Oeuvres Complètes* III, pp. 1105-8.

Camus, Albert. *Christian Metaphysics and Neoplatonism*, translated with Introduction by Ronald Srigley (Columbia & London: University of Missouri Press, 2007).

Camus, Albert. "Albert Camus à Athènes, *To Vina*, Athènes: 29 April 1955," at Barbara Papastavrou, "Albert Camus: De l'Amour Platon à son Engagement envers les Grecs," in A. Fosty (ed.), *Albert Camus et la Grèce* (Aix-en-Provence: Ecritures du Sud, 2007).

Camus, Albert. "Défence de *L'Homme Révolté*," in *Oeuvres Complètes III* (Paris: Gallimard, 2008), pp. 366-79.

Camus, Albert. "Entretien sur la révolte," *Oeuvres Complètes III*, pp. 397-403.

Camus, Albert. "Une des plus belles professions que je connais ...," *Oeuvres Complètes III* (Paris: Gallimard, 2008), *1949-1956*, pp. 879-81.

Camus, Albert. "Mediterranean Humanism," in Neil Foxlee (ed.), *Albert Camus' "The New Mediterranean Culture": A Text and Its Contexts* (Bern: Peter Lang, 2010), pp. 88-9**

Camus, Albert. *Algerian Chronicles* translated Arthur Goldhammer with an Introduction by Alice Kaplan (Cambridge, Massachusetts: Belknap Press, 2013).

Camus, Albert."Crisis of Man," in *Speaking Out: Lectures and Speeches, 1957-58* (London: Penguin, 2022), pp. 17-33.

Camus, Albert. "Are We Pessimists?," in *Speaking Out*, pp. 34-38.

Camus, Albert. "[Knowledge is Universal] Message Read Out By Jean Amrouche At the Maison de la Chimie, 1946," in *Speaking Out*, pp. 51-2.

Camus, Albert. "Time of Murderers," in *Speaking Out*, pp. 83-100.

Camus, Albert. "The Europe of Loyalty," in *Speaking out*, pp. 101-7.

Camus, Albert. "Bread and Freedom," in *Speaking Out*, pp. 130-7.

Camus, Albert. "[Knowledge is Universal] Message Read Out By Jean Amrouche At the Maison de la Chimie, 1946," in *Speaking Out*, pp. 49-51.

Camus, Albert. "[The Artist and his Age] Lecture at Uppsala University [1957]," in *Speaking Out*, pp. 229-46.

Camus, Albert. "The Future of European Civilization," in *Speaking Out*, pp. 143-64.

Camus, Albert. "The Artist and His Age" (Lecture at Uppsala University, 1957), in *Speaking Out*, pp. 229-46.

Camus, Albert. *The Misunderstanding*, in *Caligula and Three Other Plays*, a new translation by Ryan Bloom (New York: Vintage, 2023).

Texts by other authors

"Language: A Key Mechanism of Control: Newt Gingrich's 1990 GOPAC memo." Online at https://www.transcend.org/tms/wp-content/uploads/2019/11/Newt-Gingrich-Language-A-Key-Mechanism-of-Control-1990.pdf.

"Statistics on Unemployment and Labour Underutilization," *International Labor Organisation*, January 17, 2025. Online at https://ilostat.ilo.org/topics/unemployment-and-labour-underutilization/.

"Trump's False or Misleading Claims Total 30,573 over 4 years," *Washington Post*, January 24, 2021. Online at https://www.washingtonpost.com/politics/2021/01/24/trumps-false-or-misleading-claims-total-30573-over-four-years/.

Abelson, Peter et al., "Housing Prices and Rents in Australia 1980-2023: Facts, Explanations and Outcomes." Online at https://esacentral.org.au/365/images/PeterAbelsonHousingpricesandreturnsinAustralia1980-2023.pdf.

Adorno, Theodor & Max Horkheimer, *The Dialectic of Enlightenment*, translated by John Cumming (New York: Continuum, 1989).

Agamben, Giorgio. *The Time That Remains. A Commentary on the Letter to the Romans*, translated by Patricia Dailey (Stanford: Stanford University Press, 2005).

Anderson, Kurt. *Evil Geniuses: The Unmaking of America. A Recent History* (London: Penguin, Random House, 2020).

Arendt, Hannah. *Life of the Mind* (New York: Harcourt Brace Jovanovich, 1969).

Arendt, Hannah. "Truth and Politics," in Peter Baehr (ed.), *The Portable Hannah Arendt* (London: Penguin, 2000), pp. 545–75.

Arendt, Hannah. *Eichmann in Jerusalem* (London: Penguin, 2006).

Arendt, Hannah. *Origins of Totalitarianism* (New York: Harvest Books, 2007).

Aron, Raymond. "The Essence of Totalitarianism according to Hannah Arendt," in G. Williams (ed.) *Hannah Arendt: Critical Assessments of Leading Political Philosophers. Volume I: Arendt and Political Events* (Oxford: Routledge, 2006), pp. 145–56.

Ashworth, James. "Climate Change Set to Breach 1.5°C Limit for First Time by 2027," Natural History Museum, May 17, 2023. Online at https://www.nhm.ac.uk/discover/news/2023/may/climate-change-set-breach-limit-for-first-time-by-2027.html.

Australian Council of Trade Unions Media release. "Casual workers earn $11.59 less per hour than permanent employees." *Australian Council of Trade Unions*, May 22, 2023. Online at https://www.actu.org.au/media-release/casual-workers-earn-11-59-less-per-hour-than-permanent-employees/s.

Badiou, Alain. *Saint Paul: The Foundation of Universalism*, translated by Ray Brassier (Stanford: Stanford University Press, 2003).

Baehr, Peter. "The 'Masses' in Hannah Arendt's Theory of Totalitarianism," *The Good Society* 2007.

Bakan, Joel. *The New Corporation: How "Good" Corporations Are Bad for Democracy* (London: Random House, 2020).

Ball, James. *Post-Truth: How Bullshit Conquered the World* (USA: Biteback Books, 2018).

Bambach, Charles R. *Heidegger's Roots: Nietzsche, National Socialism, and the Greeks* (Cornell University Press, 2003).
Barkai, Simcha & Seth G. Benzell, "70 Years of US Corporate Profits," *Promarket* May 30, 2018. Online at https://www.promarket.org/2018/05/30/70-years-us-corporate-profits/.
BMC Public Health, "The State of Loneliness and Social Isolation Research: Current Knowledge and Future Directions."
Boltanski, Luc and Eve Chiapello, *The New Spirit of Capitalism* translated by Gregory Elliot (London: Verso, 2007).
Bousquet, Francois. *Camus L'Ancien, Camus Le Mediterraneen* (Sherbrooke, Quebec, Canada: Editions Naaman, 1977).
Bousso, Ron. "Big Oil Doubles Profits in Blockbuster 2022," *Reuters*, February 8, 2023.
Brahms, Yael. "Philosophy of Post-Truth," *Institute for National Security Studies* 2020, pp. 1–20.
Brauer, Ruth et al., "Psychotropic Medicine Consumption in 65 Countries and Regions, 2008–19: A Longitudinal Study," *The Lancet Psychiatry*, 8, no. 12 (2021): pp. 1071–82.
Brée, Germaine (ed.), *Camus: A Collection of Critical Essays* (Englewood Cliffs, NJ: Prentice-Hall, 1962).
Bresser, R. Daniel. "The Mortality Cost of Carbon," *Nature Communications*, 12, 2021, Article number: 4467. Online at https://www.nature.com/articles/s41467-021-24487-w.
Brobjer, Thomas H. "Nietzsche's *Magnum Opus*," *History of European Ideas*, 32, no. 3 (2006), pp. 278–94.
Burgis, Ben and Matt Mcmanus, *Myth and Mahem: A Leftist Critique of Jordan Peterson* (USA: ZERO Books, 2020).
Burke, Paul J. et al., "Carbon Dioxide Emissions in the Short Run: The Rate and Sources of Economic Growth Matter." *Global Environmental Change* 33, 2015, pp. 109–21.
Callinicos, Alex. *Against Postmodernism: A Marxist Critique* (London: Polity Press, 1990).
Canovan, Margoret. "The Leader and the Masses: Hannah Arendt on Totalitarianism and Dictatorship," in Peter Baehr and Melvin Richter (eds.), *Dictatorship in History and Theory: Bonapartism, Caesarism, and Totalitarianism* (Cambridge: Cambridge University Press, 2013), pp. 241–60.
Caralle, Katelyn. "New RNC Hires Are Asked If They Believe the 2020 Election Was Stolen: Lara Trump and New Leadership Team's Recruitment Policy Is Revealed After Ronna McDaniel's Spectacular Ouster," *Daily Mail*, April 2024. Online at https://www.msn.com/en-us/news/politics/new-rnc-hires-are-asked-if-they-believe-the-2020-election-was-stolen-lara-trump-and-new-leadership-team-s-recruitment-policy-is-revealed-after-ronna-mcdaniel-s-spectacular-ouster/ar-BB1kDYA3#image=3.
Carroll, Sean B. *Brave Genius: A Scientist, a Philosopher, and Their Daring Adventures from the French Resistance to the Nobel Prize* (USA: Crown Press, 2013).
Case, Anne & Angus Deaton, "Mortality and Morbidity in the 21st century," Brookings Papers on Economic Activity, Spring 2017, pp. 397–476.
CEIC. "US Private Debt: % of Nominal GDP, 1951–2024." Online at https://www.ceicdata.com/en/indicator/united-states/private-debt–of-nominal-gdp.
Chang, Dianna et al. "The Determinants Of COVID-19 Morbidity and Mortality Across Countries." Scientific Reports" 12, article no. 5888, 2022. Online at https://www.nature.com/articles/s41598-022-09783-9#Sec32.

Charlton, Emma. "This Is What Climate Change Costs Economies Around the World," World Economic Forum, November 29, 2023. Online at https://www.weforum.org/stories/2023/11/climate-crisis-cost-global-economies/.

Chen, Hao et al. "Does Energy Consumption, Economic Growth, Urbanization, and Population Growth Influence Carbon Emissions in the BRICS? Evidence from Panel Models Robust to Cross-Sectional Dependence and Slope Heterogeneity." *Environmental Science and Pollution Research*, 29, no. 25, 2022, pp. 37598–616.

Clouscard, Michel. *Néo-fascisme et idéologie du désir* (Paris: Le Castor Astral, 1999).

[US] Congressional Research Services, "Real Wage Trends, 1979 to 2018." Online at https://crsreports.congress.gov/product/pdf/R/R45090/12.

Cordes, Alfred. *The Descent of the Doves: Camus' Journey of the Spirit* (Washington: University Press of America, 1980).

Cruickshank, Joanna. *Albert Camus and the Literature of Revolt* (New York: Oxford University Press, 1959).

Della Femina, Jerry. *From Those Wonderful Folks Who Gave You Pearl Harbor* (London: Sir Isaac Pittman and Sons, 1971).

Deleuze, Gilles. "Postscript on Societies of Control" (1990), *The Deleuze Seminars* May 1, 1990. Online at https://deleuze.cla.purdue.edu/resource/gilles-deleuze-postscript-on-societies-of-control/.

Derrida, Jacques. *Spectres of Marx*, translated by Peggy Kamuf (New York: Routledge 1994).

Di Cesare, Donatella. "Heidegger and the Jews: The Black Notebooks" (New York: Policy, 2018).

Domain. "The Melbourne Suburbs Where Buyers Pay a Premium For Space." Online at https://www.domain.com.au/news/the-melbourne-suburbs-where-buyers-pay-a-premium-for-space-2-1270471/?msockid=09a3015b36696b0f24da138737f96a48.

Durkheim, Émile. *Suicide: A Study in Sociology*, translated by John A. Spaulding (New York: Free Press, 1979).

Eagleton, Terry. *The Illusions of Postmodernism* (London: Wiley-Blackwell, 1996).

Eksteins, Modris. *The Rites of Spring: The Great War and the Birth of the Modern Age* (New York: Anchor Press/Doubleday, 1990).

Faye, Emmanuel. *Martin Heidegger, The Introduction of Nazism into Philosophy in Light of the Unpublished Seminars of 1933–1935*, translated by Michael B. Smith (Yale University Press, 2009).

Faye, Emmanuel. *Arendt et Heidegger: Extermination nazie et destruction de la pensée* (Albin Michel, 2016).

Ferry, Luc & Alain Renaut, *French Philosophy of the Sixties: An Essay on Anti-Humanism* (Amherst: University of Massachusetts Press, 1990).

Financial times Series. "The Uninsurable World: How the Insurance Industry Fell Behind on Climate Change." Online at https://www.ft.com/content/11ef021c-d95b-44d4-b8f8-e9b2624d3ff7.

Fisher, Max. *The Chaos Machine: The Inside Story of How Social Media Rewired Our Minds and Our World* (London: Littlebrown and Company, 2022).

Foucault, Michel. *Power/Knowledge: Selected Interviews and Writings*, edited by Colin Gordon, translated by Colin Gordon et al (New York: Pantheon Books, 1977).

Foucault, Michel. *Discipline and Punish*, translated by Alan Sheridan (New York: Vintage, 1977).
Frank, Thomas. *The Conquest of Cool: Business Culture, Counterculture, and the Rise of Hip Consumerism* (Chicago: University of Chicago Press, 1997).
Frank, Thomas. *One Market Under God: Extreme Capitalism, Market Populism, and the End of Economic Democracy* (USA: Doubleday, 2000).
Fraser, Nancy. "Foucault on Modern Power: Empirical Insights and Normative Confusions," *Praxis International* 1 (1981): 272–87.
Fraser, Nancy. "The End of Progressive Neoliberalism," January 2, 2017. Online at https://www.dissentmagazine.org/online_articles/progressive-neoliberalism-reactionary-populism-nancy-fraser/.
Gamble, Andrew. *Hayek: The Iron Cage of Liberty* (Boulder, CO: Westview Press, 1996).
Griffin, Roger. *The Nature of Fascism* (Pinters Publisher, 1991).
Gutting, Gary. *Thinking the Impossible: French Philosophy since 1960* (Oxford: Oxford University Press, 2011).
Habermas, Jürgen. *The Philosophical Discourse of Modernity: Twelve Lectures*, translated by T. McCarthy (Massachusetts: MIT Press, 1990).
Hanauer, Nick. "America's 1% Has Taken $50 Trillion From the Bottom 90%," *Time*, September 14, 2021. Online at https://time.com/5888024/50-trillion-income-inequality-america/.
Hartmann, Thom. *The Hidden History of American Oligarchy: Reclaiming Our Democracy from the Ruling Class* (USA: Berrett-Koehler, 2021).
Hayek, Friedrich. *The Road to Serfdom* (London: Routledge, 1944).
Heidegger, Martin. "The Question Concerning Technology," in David Farrell Krell (ed.), *Basic Writings* (USA: HarperCollins, 1993).
Heidegger, Martin. *Bremen und Freiburger Vorträge*, GA 79, ed. Paetra Jaegar (Francfort-am-Main, 1994).
Hunter, Ian. "The History of Theory," *Critical Inquiry* 33, no. 1, Autumn 2006: 78–112.
Isaac, Jeffrey C. *Arendt, Camus, and Modern Rebellion* (Yale: Yale University Press, 1994).
Jameson, Frederic. *The Cultural Turn: Selected Writings on the Postmodern, 1983-1998* (London: Verso, 20**).
Janicaud, Dominique (ed.), *Phenomenology and the "Theological Turn": The French Debate* (New York: Fordham University Press, 2000).
Jeanson, Francois. "Soul in Revolt," in David A. Sprintzen & Adrian van den Hoven eds. and trans. *Camus and Sartre: A Historic Confrontation* (Humanity Books: New York 2004), pp. 79–106.
Joint Economic Committee—Republicans, Chairman, Sen. Mike Lee. "Long-Term Trends in Deaths of Despair," *Social Capital Report*, no. 4–19, September 2019.
Karabarbounis, Loukas & Brent Neiman, "The Global Decline of the Labor Share," *The Quarterly Journal of Economics* 129, no, 1, February 2014, pp. 61–103.
Kartha, Sivan et al., "The Carbon Inequality Era: An Assessment of the Global Distribution of Consumption Emissions Among Individuals from 1990 to 2015 and Beyond." 2020. https://oxfamilibrary.openrepository.com/handle/10546/621049.

Kenyon, Georgina. "The Man Who Studies the Spread of Ignorance," BBC, January 6, 2016. Online at https://www.bbc.com/future/article/20160105-the-man-who-studies-the-spread-of-ignorance.

Kwok, Yenni. "Global Super-Rich Hide $21 Trillion in Tax Havens," CNN Business, July 25, 2012. Online at https://edition.cnn.com/2012/07/23/business/super-rich-hidden-wealth-offshore/index.html.

Lannin, Sue. "Bank Profits Jump But Rising Interest Rates Are a Double-Edged Sword," *ABC News*, November 12, 2022. Online at https://www.abc.net.au/news/2022-11-12/bank-profits-jump-but-rising-interest-rates-a-double-edged-sword/101640472.

Lazere, Donald. "Camus on Doublespeak," *The English Journal*, 66, no. 7 (1977), p. 24**.

Leopold, Les. *Runaway Inequality: An Activist's Guide to Economic Justice* (New York: Labor Institute Press, 2015).

Leopold, Les. *Wall Street's War on Workers: How Mass Layoffs and Greed Are Destroying the Working Class and What to Do about It* (New York: Chelsea Green, 2024).

Le Sueur, James. *Uncivil War: Intellectuals and Identity Politics During the Decolonization* (US: University of Pennsylvania Press, 2001).

Lim, M., Manera K., Owen K., Phongsavan P. and Smith B. "Chronic and Episodic Loneliness and Social Isolation: Prevalence and Sociodemographic Analyses from a Longitudinal Australian Survey." Published online 2022. doi:https://doi.org/10.21203/rs.3.rs-1607036/v1.

Losurdo, Domenico. *Nietzsche: Aristocratic Rebel*, translated by G. Benson (Leiden: Brill, 2020).

Lottmann, Herbert R. *Albert Camus: A Biography* (Core Madera, California: Gingko Press, 1997).

Lukács, György. *History and Class Consciousness*, translated by R. Livingstone (Cambridge, MA: MIT Press, 1971).

Lukács, György. *Destruction of Reason*, translated by Peter Palmer (London: Merlin Press, 1980).

Lyotard, Jean-Francois. *The Postmodern Condition: A Report on Knowledge* (USA: University of Minnesota Press, 1984).

Macintyre, Lee. *On Disinformation: How to Fight for Truth and Protect Democracy* (Cambridge, MA: MIT Press, 2023).

Marantz, Andrew. *Antisocial: Online Extremists, Techno-Utopians, and the Hijacking of the American Conversation* (London: Penguin, 2020).

Marcuse, Herbert. "The Struggle Against Liberalism in the Totalitarian View of the State." In *Negations*, translated by James Shapiro (London: Penguin Allen Lane, 1968).

Margerrison, Christine, Mark Orme and Lissa Lincoln (eds.), *Albert Camus in the 21st Century: A Reassessment of His Thinking at the Dawn of the New Millennium* (Amsterdam, NY: Editions Rodopi B.V., 2008).

Marin, Lou. "The Unknown Camus: Albert Camus and the Impact of His Contributions As a Journalist to the Pacifist, Anarchist and Syndicalist Press," in *Camus and Gandhi— Essays on Political Philosophy in Hammarskjöld's Times* (Seden: Dag Hammarskjöld Foundation, 2024), pp. 9–21.

McCarthy, Thomas. "The Critique of Impure Reason: Foucault and the Frankfurt School," *Political Theory* 18, No. 3 (Aug. 1990): 437–69.

McCarthy, Thomas. "The Politics of the Ineffable: Derrida's Deconstructionism in Hermeneutics in Ethics and Social Theory," *Philosophical Forum* 21 (1–2) (1989): 146–68.

Melancon, Marcel J. *Albert Camus. Analyse de sa pensée* (Suisse: Les Editions universitaire Fribourg, 1976).

Mena, Soriano. "The Extent and Causes Of the Declining Labour Share Of Income Across the Globe," *Essex Student Journal* **

Mitropolous, Arielle. "For Red and Blue America, a Glaring Divide in COVID-19 Death Rates Persists 2 Years Later. Post-Vaccine, Death Rates in Red States Were 38% Higher Than in Blue States." *ABC News* March 28, 2022. Online at https://abcnews.go.com/Health/red-blue-america-glaring-divide-covid-19-death/story?id=83649085.

Monville, Aymeric. *Misère du nietzschéisme de gauche* (Paris: Les Éditions Delga, 2007).

NASA. "Ice Sheets | Vital Signs—Climate Change: Vital Signs of the Planet," 2024. Online at Ice Sheets | Vital Signs—Climate Change: Vital Signs of the Planet

NASA. "Tracking 30 Years of Sea Level Rise." Online at https://earthobservatory.nasa.gov/images/150192/tracking-30-years-of-sea-level-rise; Copernicus. Europe's Eyes on Earth, "Global Climate Highlights 2024." Online at https://climate.copernicus.eu/global-climate-highlights-2024.

National Council of Suicide Prevention. "USA Suicide Statistics for the Year 2022," published May 2024. Online at https://www.thencsp.org/_files/ugd/a0415f_1f03481ce0ea45d5af87930082c9c179.pdf.

NASA. "Global Temperature | Vital Signs—Climate Change: Vital Signs of the Planet," 2024. Online at https://climate.nasa.gov/vital-signs/global-temperature/?intent=121.

NASA. "Temperatures Rising: NASA Confirms 2024 Warmest Year on Record," January 10, 2025. Online at https://www.nasa.gov/news-release/temperatures-rising-nasa-confirms-2024-warmest-year-on-record/#:~:text=Earth%E2%80%99s%20average%20surface%20temperature%20in%202024%20was%20the,%281951-1980%29%2C%20which%20tops%20the%20record%20set%20in%202023.

Nietzsche, Friedrich. *Will to Power*, in Oscar Levy (ed.), *The Complete Works of Nietzsche*, translated by Anthony M. Ludovici (Edinburgh & London: T.N. Foulis, 1914), I, 3.

Nietzsche, Friedrich. *Beyond Good and Evil: Preface to a Philosophy of the Future*, translated by Judith Norman edited by Rolf-Peter Horstmann (Cambridge: Cambridge University Press, 2002).

Nietzsche, Friedrich. *The Antichrist*, in *The Antichrist, Ecce Homo, Twilight of the Idols and Other Writings*, translated by Judith Norman, edited by Judith Norman & Aaron Ridley (Cambridge: Cambridge University Press, 2005).

Nietzsche, Friedrich. *Twilight of the Idols*, in *The Antichrist, Ecce Homo, Twilight of the Idols and Other Writings* (Cambridge: Cambridge University Press, 2005).

Norman, Joshua. "'Post-truth' Named Word of the Year for 2016 by Oxford Dictionaries," *CBS News*, November 17, 2016. Online at https://www.cbsnews.com/news/post-truth-word-of-the-year-2016-oxford-dictionaries/.

Ortiz-Ospina, Esteban. "Loneliness and Social Connections—Our World in Data," February 2020, updated March 2024. online at https://ourworldindata.org/social-connections-and-loneliness.

O'Sullivan, Donie. "'2000 Mules' Creator Admits Some of Film's Claims Are Flawed," *CNN Politics*, December 2, 2024. Online at https://edition.cnn.com/2024/12/02/politics/2000-mules-creator-admits-some-of-films-claims-are-flawed/index.html.

Oxfam. "Richest 1% Bag Nearly Twice as Much Wealth as the Rest of the World Put Together over the Past Two Years," January 16, 2023. Online at https://www.oxfam.org/en/press-releases/richest-1-bag-nearly-twice-much-wealth-rest-world-put-together-over-past-two-years.

Oxfam. "Survival of the Richest: How Billionaires Are Amassing Eye-Watering Wealth Amid Crisis." *Oxfam Australia*, January 16, 2023. Online at https://www.oxfam.org.au/2023/01/survival-of-the-richest-how-billionaires-are-amassing-eye-watering-wealth-amid-crisis/.

Parums, Dinah. "A Review of the Increasing Global Impact of Climate Change on Human Health and Approaches to Medical Preparedness," Pub Med Cental. Online at https://pmc.ncbi.nlm.nih.gov/articles/PMC11302257/.

Parker, Emmett. *Albert Camus, The Artist in the Arena* (Madison: University of Wisconsin Press, 1966).

Paternesi, Meloni, Walter & Antonella Stira, "The Decoupling Between Labour Compensation and Productivity in High-Income Countries: Why Is the Nexus Broken?" *British Journal of Industrial Relations* 61, 2023, pp. 425–63.

Pew Research Centre. "Public Trust in Government: 1958–2024," *Pew Research Centre*, June 24, 2024. Online at https://www.pewresearch.org/politics/2024/06/24/public-trust-in-government-1958-2024/.

Peyre, Henri. "Camus the Pagan," in *Camus, A Collection of Critical Essays*, pp. 65–70.

Piccard, Renee. "11 Examples of Depletion of Natural Resources," Green Coast, March 20, 2023. Online at https://greencoast.org/depletion-of-natural-resources/#:~:text=This%20article%20explains%20why%20and%20how%20natural%20resources,we%20tell%20which%20natural%20resources%20are%20being%20depleted%3F.

Price, Carter C. and Kathryn A. Edwards, "Trends in Income From 1975 to 2018," Rand, September 14, 2020. Online at https://www.rand.org/pubs/working_papers/WRA516-1.html.

Proctor, Robert N. and Londa Schiebinger (eds.), *Agnotology, the Making and Unmaking of Ignorance* (Stanford: Stanford University Press, 2017).

Project Hope. "The Global Mental Health Crisis: 10 Numbers to Note." Online at https://www.projecthope.org/news-stories/story/the-global-mental-health-crisis-10-numbers-to-note/.

Quilliot, Roger. *Sea and Prisons: A Commentary on the Life and Works of Albert Camus* (Alabama: University of Alabama Press, 1976).

Rampell, Catherine. "Real Corporate Profits," *New York Times* (graph). Online at https://archive.nytimes.com/economix.blogs.nytimes.com/2012/11/29/record-corporate-profits/.

Ratner-Rosenhagen, Jennifer. *American Nietzsche: A History of an Icon and His Ideas* (Chicago: University of Chicago Press, 2012).

Rehmann, Jan. *Deconstructing Postmodern Nietzscheanism: Deleuze and Foucault* (Leiden: Brill, 2021).

Richardson, David. "The Rise and Rise Of the Big Banks: Concentration of Ownership," Australia Institute Technical Brief No. 15, December 2012. Online at TB-15-The-rise-and-rise-of-the-big-banks_4.pdf.

Richie, Hannah. "Deforestation and Forest Loss," Our World in Data. Online at https://ourworldindata.org/deforestation.

Rockhill, Gabriel. "The Myth of 1968 Thought and the French Intelligentsia: Historical Commodity Fetishism and Ideological Rollback," *Monthly Review* June 1, 2023. Online at https://monthlyreview.org/2023/06/01/the-myth-of-1968-thought-and-the-french-intelligentsia-historical-commodity-fetishism-and-ideological-rollback/.

Roser, Max and Hannah Ritchie, "Optimism and Pessimism," Our World in Data. Online at https://ourworldindata.org/optimism-and-pessimism.

Rothschild, Mike. *The Storm Is Upon Us: How QAnon Became a Movement, Cult, and Conspiracy Theory of Everything* (USA: Melville House, 2021).

Sartre, Jean-Paul. "Jean-Paul Sartre répond" (interview)," *L'Arc* 40 (October 1966), p. 89.

Sawyer, Malcolm. "Monopoly Capitalism in the Past Four Decades," *Cambridge Journal of Economics*, 46, no, 2 (2022).

Sawyer, Malcolm. "Secular Stagnation and Monopoly Capitalism," *Journal of Post Keynesian Economics*, 46, no. 4 (2023).

Sharpe, Matthew. "The 'Revolution' in Advertising and University Discourse," in Justin Clemens and Rusell Grigg (eds.), *Jacques Lacan and the Other Side of Psychoanalysis* (USA: Duke University Press, 2006), pp. 301–2**.

Sharpe, Matthew. "A Question of Two Truths? Remarks on *Parrhesia* and the 'Political-Philosophical' Difference," *Parrhesia: A Journal of Critical Philosophy* (2007): 89–108.

Sharpe, Matthew. "Is Neoliberalism a Liberalism, or a Stranger Kind of Bird?," *Critical Horizons: A Journal of Philosophy and Social Theory* 10, no. 1 (2009), pp. 76–98.

Sharpe, Matthew. "When the Logics of the World Collapse—Žižek with and Against Arendt on 'Totalitarianism,'" *Subjectivity* 3, no. 1 (2010), pp. 54–55. Online at https://www.researchgate.net/publication/248877025_When_the_logics_of_the_world_collapse_-_Zizek_with_and_against_Arendt_on_%27totalitarianism%27.

Sharpe, Matthew. *Camus, Philosophe: To Return to Our Beginnings* (Leiden: Brill, 2014).

Sharpe, Matthew. "On a Neglected Argument in French Philosophy: Sceptical Humanism in Montaigne, Voltaire and Camus," *Critical Horizons* 16, no. 1 (2015), pp. 1–26.

Sharpe, Matthew. "The Plague and the Panopticon: Camus, With and Against the Total Critiques of Modernity," *Thesis Eleven* 133, no. 1 (2016), pp. 59–79.

Sharpe, Matthew. "Letter to a Germanist Friend: On Camus and Heidegger," *Camus Studies* 8, 2016, pp. 221–50.

Sharpe, Matthew. "Camus' Hellenic Heart, Between Augustine and Hegel," in Adam Goldwyn et al. (ed.), *The Brill Companion to Classical Reception* (Leiden: Brill, 2016).

Sharpe, Matthew. "Camus and the Virtues," *Philosophy Today*, 61, no. 3 (2017), pp. 679–708.

Sharpe, Matthew. "Solitaire/Solidaire: Camus, Contemplation, and the *Vita Mixta*," *Telos* 196 (2021), pp. 31-53.
Sharpe, Matthew. *The Other Enlightenment: Race, Gender, and Self-estrangement* (London: Bloomsbury, 2024).
Sharpe, Matthew. "After Trickle Down, Kicking Down: On Jordan Peterson, Naturalizing Inequality, and Neofascist Indirect Apologetics," *Critical Sociology* 2024, pp. 1–19.
Sharpe, Matthew. "Old Wine in a Postmodern Bottle: Aleksandr Dugin's "Fourth Political Theory" and Aurel Kolnai's War Against the West," *Studies in Eastern European Thought* [Special edition—Russian conservatism, ed. G. Love] (2025): 1-20.
Sharpe, Matthew & Geoffrey Boucher, *Zizek and Politics* (Edinburgh: Edinburgh University Press, 2010).
Sharpe, Matthew and MattKing, "Reclaiming the Differences: Three Neglected Marxian Theories of Fascism in Lukács, Marcuse, and Bloch, Socialism and Democracy," *Socialism and Democracy* 2023; Aurel Kolnai, *The War Against the West* (London: Viking Press, 1938).
Shay, James and Kevin James. *Operation Chaos: The Capitol Attack and the Campaign to Erode Democracy* (USA: Random House, 2021).
Shirzad, Mahboubeh Shirzad, Gayane Yenokyan, Arik V. Marcell and Michelle R. Kaufman, "Deaths of Despair-Associated Mortality Rates Globally: A 2000–2019 Sex-Specific Disparities Analysis," (*Public Health*, 236, November 2024).
Snyder, Timothy. "The American Abyss," *The New York Times*, January 9, 2021. Online at https://www.nytimes.com/2021/01/09/magazine/trump-coup.htm
Spicer, André. *Business Bullshit* (London: Routledge, 2017).
Sprintzen, David A. (ed.), *Sartre and Camus: An Historic Confrontation* (New York: Humanity books, 2004).
Srigley, Ronald. *Albert Camus' Critique of Modernity* (Missouri: Missouri University Press, 2011).
Standing, Guy. "Economic Insecurity and Global Casualisation: Threat or Promise?," *Social Indicators Research* 88, pp. 15–30.
Statistica. "Loneliness among Older Adults Before vs During COVID Pandemic U.S. 2020."
Statista Research Development. "Trust in Government Worldwide 2023, by Country," *Statista Research Department*, Jul 4, 2024. Online at https://www.statista.com/statistics/1362804/trust-government-world/#:~:text=The%20level%20of%20trust%20in%20governments%20around%20the,years%20and%20a%20lack%20of%20a%20critical%20press.
Stefan, Will et al. "Trajectories of the Earth System in the Anthropocene." *Proceedings of the National Academy of Sciences*, 115, no. 33, 2018, pp. 8252–9.
Stewart, Emily. "Why the Stock Market Went Up During the Covid-19 Pandemic and High Unemployment," *Vox* May 10, 2021. Online at https://www.vox.com/business-and-finance/22421417/stock-market-pandemic-economy.
Stewart, Jon. *A History of Nihilism in the Nineteenth Century: Confrontations with Nothingness* (Cambridge: Cambridge University Press, 2024).
Stillman, Tyler F. et al., "Alone and Without Purpose: Life Loses Meaning Following Social Exclusion," *Journal of Experimental Social Psychology* 45, no. 4 (July 2009), pp. 686–94.

Stuart, Diane. "The Human Crisis Revisited: Albert Camus and Climate Rebellion," *Critical Horizons*, 25, no. 4 (2024), pp. 111–28.

Surkalim, Daniel L. et al., "The Prevalence of Loneliness Across 113 Countries: Systematic Review and Meta-Analysis," | BMJ 2022 376, pp. 1–17. Online at https://www.bmj.com/content/376/bmj-2021-067068.

Tarrow, Susan. *Exile from the Kingdom* (Alabama: University of Alabama Press, 1985).

Thompson, Michael. "Introduction," in Gregory Smulewicz-Zucker and Michael J. Thompson (eds.) *Radical Intellectuals and the Subversion of Progressive Politics: The Betrayal of Politics* (London: Palgrave Macmillan, 2015).

Todd, Olivier. *Albert Camus: A Life* (New York: Alfred A. Knopf, 1997).

UN Environment Report, "Governments Plan to Produce Double the Fossil Fuels in 2030 Than the 1.5°C Warming Limit Allows," November 2023. Online at https://www.unep.org/news-and-stories/press-release/governments-plan-produce-double-fossil-fuels-2030-15degc-warming.

UN/DESA Policy Brief #108. "Trust in Public Institutions: Trends and Implications for Economic Security," *Department of Economic and Social Affairs*. Online at https://desapublications.un.org/policy-briefs/undesa-policy-brief-108-trust-public-institutions-trends-and-implications-economic.

Vila, Dana. "Totalitarianism, Tradition, and The Human Condition," *Arendt Studies* 2, 2018, pp. 61–72.

Wagner Cho, Stephen. "Nihilism Before Nietzsche," *Graduate Faculty Philosophy Journal*, 18, no. 1 1995, pp. **.

Walsh, Lucas et al. "Youth Barometer Paints Bleak Picture of Young Australians in 2024," Monash Lens. Online at https://lens.monash.edu/@education/2024/08/01/1386898/youth-barometer-paints-a-bleak-picture-of-young-australians-in-2024.

Walzer, Michael. "Commitment and Social Criticism: Camus' Algerian war," *Dissent* Fall 1984, pp. 424–32.

Wheeler, Burton W. "Beyond Despair: Camus' The Fall and Van Eyck's 'Adoration of the Lamb'," *Contemporary Literature* 23, no. 3 (Summer 1982), pp. 343–64.

Wolin, Richard (ed.) *The Heidegger Controversy* (USA: MIT Press, 1993).

Wolin, Richard. *Heidegger in Ruins: Between Philosophy and Ideology* (Yale University Press, 2023).

Woolfolk, Alan. "Toward a Theory of Nihilism," *Sociological Analysis* 51, no. 1 (1990), Spring, pp. 105–107.

Zaretsky, Robert. "Silence Follows: Albert Camus in Algeria," in Stephen G. Kellman (ed.) *Critical Insights: Albert Camus* (Pasadena, California: Salem Press, 2012).

Zuboff, Shoshana. *The Age of Surveillance Capitalism: The Fight for a Human Future at the New Frontier of Power* (London: Profile Books, 2019).

INDEX

absurd, the 2, 6, 10, 14, 16, 22, 24, 26–31, 32, 36, 37, 47, 48, 55–7, 60, 77, 162, 184 n.48
Adorno, Theodor 128, 130, 132, 140
advertising/marketing 44, 66–70, 71, 72, 77, 99, 189 n. 8
Algeria, Algerian 1, 3, 48, 60, 101, 109, 115–18, 133, 141, 169, 171
anomie 13, 16, 35, 97
anxiety 4, 16–17, 30, 98, 148
Arab population in Algeria 18, 44, 115–18, 169
artist, life or personae of 1–4, 33, 68, 69, 78, 80, 81, 82, 83, 84, 87, 98, 100, 164
Augustine, Augustinian Christianity 166, 167, 204–5 n. 53
avant gardes, avant gardism in arts and theory 68, 69, 77–8, 82–3, 84, 87, 98, 100

Badiou, Alain 75, 77, 81, 105
baptism, unbaptised children deemed sinful 166
Baudelaire, Charles 78, 80, 82
balance, especially of freedom and justice (political ideal) and with nature 5, 7, 10, 97, 100, 110–15, 117, 148, 149–50, 155, 161, 162, 162, 164, 165
beyond nihilism (Camus's stated goal) 8, 19, 37, 139–40
Breton, André 78, 82

Christianity 3, 9, 10–11, 14, 20, 21, 23–4, 25, 32, 74, 86–88, 102, 107, 135, 148, 165–167, 169, 170

Clamence, Jean-Baptiste (antihero in *The Fall*) 7, 48, 143, 144, 166–7, 171
classicism, style and sensibility 149
communion, *royaume*, as ideal, "kingdom" 56, 168–9, 171
courage (virtue) 2, 6, 8, 149
culture wars 5, 43, 47, 50, 64, 73, 98, 101, 109, 122, 186 n. 11, 195 n. 31
cynicism (scorn) 7, 9, 10, 11, 35, 41, 42–4, 46, 47, 48, 50, 53, 58, 59, 87, 89, 100, 101, 134, 136, 139, 143–144, 146, 147, 148, 161, 171, 176, 195 n. 31, 201 n. 32

deception, lying 7, 53, 54, 57, 58, 60, 61, 62, 103, 108, 110, 134, 145, 147, 158, 205 n. 53
Deleuze, Gilles 43, 75, 77, 84
Derrida, Jacques 43, 73, 74, 75, 77, 78, 105
dialogue 50, 54, 59, 62, 100, 103, 115, 140, 149, 171, 175, 188 n. 52, 195 n, 34

efficiency, as pseudo-value 35, 53, 142
equality (as normative) 24, 32, 69, 87, 99, 110, 114, 116, 131, 132, 144, 148, 155, 162
evil 26, 32, 35, 46, 47, 55, 79, 80, 88, 108, 120, 124, 126, 132, 135, 141, 165, 167, 171, 187 n. 24, 204–205 n. 53
exile 128, 149, 164, 168
excluding nothing (in Camus) 162
eugenics 22

fascism, Nazism 5, 6, 7, 9, 12, 14, 32, 33, 53, 84–90, 102, 108, 123, 125–127, 130–146, 147, 148, 161, 170, 173–174, 199 n. 3
Foucault, Michel 43, 72–3, 75, 77, 78, 81, 84, 154

Frank, Thomas
    Conquest of Cool 66–69
    One Market Under God 70–72

God, death of 14, 22, 24
Greece, thought of Greeks (influence on Camus) 2, 3, 12, 20, 54, 74, 113, 139, 148, 149, 154, 155, 157, 159, 160, 161, 165, 166

Hegel, W. G. F. 29, 79, 107, 134, 140, 148, 154, 171
Hellenism, philhellenism (Camus's) 165
Horkheimer, Max 128, 129, 130, 132, 140

Inequality 5, 6, 12, 15, 91–4, 99, 105, 139, 144, 154
intelligence, clear-sightedness (wisdom, Camusian virtue) 2, 8, 60, 142, 149, 157, 161, 163

Jesus, Camus's views on, as "friend" to Clamence 167, 169
justice (virtue, political ideal) 2, 7, 8, 22, 28, 35, 51, 53, 58, 63, 79, 80, 85, 97, 100, 102, 103, 108, 110, 111–13, 114, 115, 116, 117, 134, 136, 143, 146, 145, 149, 161, 162, 164, 165, 166, 167, 170, 171, 176, 177, 183 n. 39, 196 n. 3

labor, work, dignity of 92, 93, 98, 100, 104, 106, 107, 175
Leninism, Marxism-Leninism, Lenin (Vladimir) 7, 74, 106, 107, 109, 109, 111, 120, 134
loneliness, isolation, separation 16–17, 169
Lyotard, Jean-Francois 43, 73, 75, 77, 81

MAGA ("Make America Great Again" movement) 47, 120–4, 126, 153, 174
managerial theory 66, 69–72, 77, 93, 98, 149, 169
Marx, Marxism 7, 69, 71–4, 77, 79, 82, 98, 101, 104–11, 113, 123, 126, 129, 134, 149, 154, 157, 165

mesure or moderation (Camusian virtue) 8, 9, 113, 155, 160, 162, 163
messianism 76, 78, 104, 105–7, 146, 149, 158, 160, 165, 170
murder, premeditated and mass- (genocide) 7, 18, 31, 33–7, 48, 51, 53, 55, 57–8, 60, 84, 85, 88–89, 100, 103, 108–110, 134, 143, 147, 184 n. 50

neofascism 90, 110, 119, 122, 125, 166
Nietzsche, Friedrich
    project and thought 7, 18, 19, 22–24, 25, 30, 32, 56, 59, 71, 73–74, 78, 83, 84–90, 104, 107–108, 130, 131, 134, 138, 140, 143, 161, 170, 183 n. 39, 188 n. 52
    Camus's critique of (as implicated in Nazism) 84–90
nihilism 4, 5, 6, 7, 8, 9, 12, 18–24, 25, 28, 30, 31–35, 37, 40, 49, 55, 57, 86, 88, 90, 100, 133, 134 (moral nihilism), 137, 140, 143, 146, 147, 154, 155, 18–24
    preCamusian meanings 18–24
    active nihilism (Nietzschean) 23–24, 30

Plague, pandemics, COVID-19 32, 52, 55, 60, 78, 91–2, 127, 159, 166, 177
politicisation (of everything) 49, 53
postmodernism (post-structuralism) 9, 20, 24, 42, 69, 72–7, 78, 93, 98, 99
post-truth 4, 6, 25, 39–47, 49, 50, 53, 57, 59, 60, 97, 147, 153
Presocratics (philosophers) 148

rebellion 6, 7, 10, 20, 30, 36–7, 54–7, 60, 65–8, 70, 74, 77–82, 90, 112–113, 136, 143, 158, 163–6, 171
rebellion, metaphysical 20, 78–9, 82
rebellion, of poets 78–82
Rieux, Dr (narrator in *The Plague*) 55, 60, 127, 166, 177, 184 n. 50
Rimbaud 78, 80, 83
romanticism 4, 6, 7, 26, 78–84, 86, 88, 100, 130, 131, 147, 149, 163, 170

Sade, Marquis de 20, 79, 129, 141
secularisation (of Christian ideas esp. of history) 107, 154, 165
Snyder, Timothy 53
Socrates 24, 54, 59, 74, 86, 157, 158, 169, 188, n. 52
Stalin 2, 3, 7, 14, 33, 35, 44, 58, 72, 100, 104, 106, 113, 126, 128, 132, 135, 136, 137, 141, 168
style, Camus's (romanticism restrained) 149

surrealism 68. 78, 82

theory, "radical theory", "French theory", "theory of the sixties" 66, 72–7
trade unions 77, 98, 103, 106, 193 n. 8
tragedy, Greek tragedy, tragedians 12, 48, 149, 165

woke, wokeness (derogatory) 99, 114, 124, 153, 187 n. 17, 195 n. 31

REFERENCES TO CAMUS'S WORK BY TITLE

"Bread and Freedom" 51

Caligula 112, 133
Carnets 1942–1951 154, 166
Christian Metaphysics and Neoplatonism (Camus' thesis) 3
"Crisis of Man" 34, 49, 126, 134, 152

The Fall 1, 7, 11, 48, 126, 141–3, 144, 165, 166, 169, 170
The First Man 165, 170, 171
"The Future of European Civilization" 155

"The Growing Stone," in *Exile and the Kingdom* 169–70

"Helen's Exile" 149, 155, 164

"Letters to a German Friend" 102, 141
"Letter to Roland Barthes on *The Plague*" 32

"Misery in Kabylia" (early journalistic article in Algeria) 60, 97, 116
The Misunderstanding 11, 48
The Myth of Sisyphus 2, 6, 7, 13, 14, 15, 17–18, 19, 24, 26, 30–4, 36, 37, 101, 156, 162, 184 n. 44

"Nuptials at Tipasa" 168

The Outsider / Stranger 1, 2, 18, 184 n. 50

The Plague 1, 2, 16, 32, 55. 60, 78, 91, 126, 127, 159, 165, 166

The Rebel 2, 6, 7, 20, 32, 34. 36, 37, 55–7, 70, 78–80, 84, 85, 101, 103, 113, 126, 134, 142, 144, 147, 163–5
"Reflections on the Guillotine" 57

"Time of Murderers" 15, 33, 126

"Une des plus belles professions que je connais ..." 48